the encyclopedia of
Vegetable Gardening

the encyclopedia of
Vegetable Gardening

Brenda Little

SILVERLEAF
PRESS

Silverleaf Press Books are available exclusively
through Independent Publishers Group.

For details write or telephone
Independent Publishers Group, 814 North Franklin St.
Chicago, IL 60610, (312) 337-0747

Silverleaf Press
8160 South Highland Drive
Sandy, Utah 84093

Contents

Introduction

Although most gardeners don't initially conceive it, many gardens have space that could be easily converted into a vegetable garden. Possibly there is more lawn than is needed and an area of the turf could be removed to make an attractive and productive garden—a simple but brilliant scheme.

If appearance bothers you, why not enclose the vegetable area with a small neat hedge of herbs? Rosemary, thyme, sage, and marjoram would be particularly appealing and appropriate. Some gardens surround the vegetable plot with low-growing annuals; the petite marigold is not only decorative but also useful—it repels nematodes (the root-damaging eelworms).

Vegetables are not only healthy and edible, but also decoratively appealing. Many vegetables have attractive leaves and clumps of carrots, parsley, beets, lettuce, artichokes, peppers, eggplant and dwarf tomatoes can look quite at home among your flowers.

Vegetable gardening is easier than you think. A family of four can maintain a continual supply of fresh vegetables from a small "conventional" garden plot. Imagine your area sub-divided into 6 beds, plus one larger bed for "special" growings. The border of the plot can be retained by brick or timber to prevent the intrusion of grass and provide for access paths between the beds. Line these quaint and convenient pathways with all-weather materials such as wood chips or pebbles. These small vegetable plots are versatile as they can occupy the corner of a large suburban garden or a small city garden, provided it has essential sunshine.

This encyclopedia will help you after you've made the first big step: deciding to become a genuine vegetable gardener.

Vegetables

Artichoke, Globe

Common names: artichoke, globe
artichoke

Botanic name: *Cynara scolymus*

Origin: Southern Europe, North
America

The artichoke is a thistle-like,
tender perennial that grows
3–4 feet (1–1.25m) tall and
wide. It is grown for its flower buds,
which are eaten before they begin
to open. The elegant, architectural
leaves make the artichoke very
decorative, but because it is tender
and hates cold weather, it's not for
all gardens.

PLANTING

Artichokes have a definite prefer-
ence for a long, frost-free season
with damp weather. They cannot

handle heavy frost or snow, and in areas where the temperature goes below freezing need special care and mulching. Temperature should not be over 70°F (21°C) by day, or under 55°F (13°C) at night. S.T. Sow in spring (February–March). T-late winter. C-mid-winter.

HOW TO PLANT

Artichokes are grown from offshoots, suckers, or seed. For best results, start with offshoots or suckers from a reputable nursery or garden center; artichoke plants grown from seed vary tremendously in quality. Artichokes need rich, well-drained soil that will hold moisture, and a position in full sunlight. When preparing the soil for planting, work in a low-nitrogen (5-10-10) fertilizer at the rate of 1lb per 95sq feet (450g per 9sq m). Too much nitrogen will keep the plant from flowering. Space plants 3 feet (1m) apart in rows 3 feet (1m) apart.

FERTILIZING AND WATERING

Fertilize before planting and again at midseason, at the same rate as the rest of the garden.
Keep the soil evenly moist.

SPECIAL HANDLING

For the roots to survive the winter in cooler areas, cut the plant back to about 10 inches (25cm), cover with a basket and then mulch with about 24 inches (60cm) of leaves to help maintain an even soil temperature. Artichokes bear best the second year and should be started from new plants every three to four years.

PESTS

Aphids can be controlled chemically by spraying the foliage with Malathion or Diazinon or non-chemically by handpicking or hosing them off the plants.

DISEASES

Crown rot may occur where drainage is poor or where the plants have to be covered in winter. To avoid this problem, don't mulch until the soil temperature drops to 41°F (5°C) and don't leave the mulch in place longer than necessary.

Cut down on the incidence of disease by planting disease-resistant varieties, maintaining the general health of your garden, and avoiding handling the plants when they're wet. If a plant does become infected, remove and destroy it so it cannot spread disease to healthy plants.

HARVESTING

Time from planting to harvest is 50–100 days for artichokes grown from suckers; at least a year until the first bud forms when grown from seed. To harvest, cut off the globe artichoke bud with 1–1½ inches (2.5–3.5cm) of stem before the bud begins to open.

VARIETIES

Imperial Star, Violetto, Grande Beurre.

STORING AND PRESERVING

Artichokes can be stored in the refrigerator for up to two weeks, or in a cold, moist place up to one month. Artichoke hearts can also be frozen, canned or pickled.

Freezing

1. Choose artichokes that are uniformly green, with a compact globe shape and tightly adhering leaves. Size doesn't affect quality or flavor, but do handle artichokes of similar size together.
2. Remove the outer leaves until you come to light yellow or white leaves or bracts. Cut off the tops of the buds and trim the heart and stem to a cone shape. Wash each heart in cold water just as soon as you've finished trimming it. Drain.
3. Blanch 7 minutes. Cool; drain well.
4. Pack into containers.
5. Seal, label and freeze.
6. Cook frozen artichokes about 5 to 10 minutes or until tender.

Jerusalem Artichoke:
1. Choose fresh, firm roots with no bad spots.
2. Scrub well; if necessary, cut into chunks.
3. Blanch 3 to 5 minutes, depending on size. Cook, drain well.
4. Pack in containers. Seal, label and freeze.
5. Cook frozen Jerusalem artichokes just until tender.

SERVING SUGGESTIONS

Cook artichokes in salted water with a squeeze of lemon juice to help retain their color. With hot artichokes serve a Hollandaise sauce; a vinaigrette is delicious when they're cold. They're not as messy to eat as you may imagine—anyway, it's quite legitimate to use your fingers. Stuff artichokes with seafood or a meat mixture and bake them. To stuff, spread open the leaves and remove some of the center leaves; cut off some of the hard tips of the outer leaves. An interesting Italian-style stuffing mix is seasoned breadcrumbs with anchovies, topped with a tomato sauce. For an Armenian-style dish, try ground lamb and bulgur (cracked wheat). Baby artichokes are delicious in stews, or marinated in olive oil, vinegar and garlic as part of an antipasto. The Romans used to bottle artichokes in vinegar and brine.

Asparagus

Common name: asparagus

Botanic name: *Asparagus officinalis*

Origin: Mediterranean

Asparagus is a long-lived hardy perennial with fleshy roots and fernlike, feathery foliage. The plant grows about 3 feet (1m) tall, and the part you eat is the tender young stem. It takes patience to establish an asparagus bed, but it's worth it; once established, it's there for the duration. Fresh asparagus is a delicacy that commands a devoted following—the first asparagus is as welcome to the gourmet as the first crocus is to the gardener.

PLANTING

Asparagus likes a climate where the winters are cold enough to freeze the top few centimeters of soil and provide it with the necessary period of dormancy. Advance planning is essential when you're starting an asparagus bed, because it's virtually impossible to move the bed once it's established. Sow—seed—in spring in all climates. Plant 2-year crowns—winter and spring in all climates.

HOW TO PLANT

Asparagus needs well-drained soil, with a pH over 6. Full sun is best, but asparagus will tolerate a little shade. When you're preparing the soil, spade down 8–12 inches (20–30cm) and dig in 1lb per 95 sq feet (0.5 kg per 9 sq m) of a complete, well-balanced fertilizer. Asparagus is usually grown from crowns; look for well-grown, well-rooted specimens, and be sure they don't dry out. To plant asparagus crowns dig out a trench or furrow 9 inches (25cm) wide and 8–12 inches (25–30cm) deep, and put in 2–4 inches (5–10cm) of loose soil. Space the crowns in the prepared bed in rows 18 inches (45cm) apart, leaving 12–18 inches (30–45cm) between plants. Place the crowns on the soil, with the roots well spread out, and cover with 2 inches (5cm) more of soil. As the spears grow, gradually fill in the trench to the top.

FERTILIZING AND WATERING

Apply a high-nitrogen (15-10-10) fertilizer after harvesting the spears, at the rate of 1lb per 95sq feet (450g per 9sq m).

It is important to give asparagus enough water when the spears are forming. The plant is hardy and will survive without extra watering, but the stalks may be stringy and woody if you don't keep the soil moist.

SPECIAL HANDLING

Do not handle the plants when they are wet. Asparagus does not relish competition, especially from grass plants. Weed thoroughly by hand; control weeds conscientiously, or they will lower your yield considerably.

PESTS

The asparagus beetle may attack your plants, but should not be a problem except in commercial asparagus-growing areas. If you do encounter this pest, pick it off, or spray with Carbaryl.

DISEASES

Fusarium wilt or crown rot may be a problem. Use disease-free crowns or seed. If you are starting with seedlings, do not overharvest. Rogue plants that are severely diseased. Remove and discard or destroy entire infested plant along with immediately surrounding soil and soil clinging to roots. Asparagus can also develop rust; you can lessen the incidence of disease by opting for a rust-resistant variety. Generally, asparagus is a problem-free crop and suitable for the organic gardener.

HARVESTING

Asparagus should not be harvested until it's three years old; the crowns need time to develop fully. During the third season, cut off the spears at or slightly below soil level. Move a little soil gently aside as you cut the spears so you can see what you're doing—if you cut blind you may damage young spears that have not yet pushed through the surface. Harvest asparagus when the spears are 8–12 inches (20–30cm) tall; if the stalks have started to feather out, it's too late to eat them. Stop harvesting when the stalks start coming up pencil-thin; if you harvest them all, you'll kill the plants.

VARIETIES

Mary Washington, Martha Washington, Early California 500, Hybrid Waltham, Jersey Centennial, Jersey Knight, Jersey Prince, Jersey Giant, Jersey King, Brock Imperial, Princeville, Viking KB3.

STORING AND PRESERVING

The Romans began to dry their asparagus for out-of-season dining as early as 200 B.C. These days, you can store it up to one week in the refrigerator—keep it upright in 1 inch (2.5cm) or so of water. You can also freeze or bottle it, but it's best eaten fresh.

Freezing

1. Choose very fresh stalks that are brittle and beautifully green. The tips should be compact and tightly closed.
2. Wash well and sort by size. Remove scales with a sharp knife.
3. Break off the tough ends. Leave the stalks whole or cut into 1–2 inch (2.5–5cm) lengths.
4. Blanch small stalks for 1½ to 2 minutes; medium stalks 2 to 3 minutes; large stalks 3 to 4 minutes. Cool; drain well.
5. Tray freeze or pack into containers, alternating tip and stem ends.
6. Seal, label and freeze.
7. Cook frozen asparagus 5 to 10 minutes.

SERVING SUGGESTIONS

In the first century the Emperor Augustus told his minions to carry out executions "quicker than you can cook asparagus", and they knew they'd better get the job done fast. One of the earliest records of asparagus being eaten recommends it with "oyl and vinegar," which is still one of the best ways. Steam asparagus quickly, or cook it upright in a pan, so the stems cook faster than the tender tips. Fresh asparagus adorned with nothing but a little melted butter is superb—or try it with creamed chicken on toast or laid on toast and topped with a thin slice of prosciutto and cream sauce. Chive mayonnaise, mustard butter, or a caper butter sauce are all splendid alternative dressings for asparagus.

Bean, Broad

Common names: bean, broad bean, horse bean, fava bean

Botanic name: *Vicia faba*

Origin: Central Asia

The broad bean is a bushy, hardy annual that grows 3–5 feet (1–1.5m) tall; it has square stems with leaves divided into leaflets. The white flowers are splotched with brown. The pods are 6–8 inches (15–20cm) long and when mature contain four to six or more light-brown seeds. The broad bean has quite a history. Upper class Greeks and Romans thought that eating "horse beans" would cloud their vision, but the species became a dietary staple of the Roman legionnaires (who knew them as fava beans) and later of the poor people in England. In fact, they're not true beans at all but are related to the vetch, another legume.

PLANTING

Broad beans will grow in cool weather that would be unsuitable for French beans. They like full sun but need cool weather to set their pods. They prefer temperatures below 68°F (20°C) and will not produce in summer heat. Sow — S.T.-early autumn. T & C-autumn and winter.

HOW TO PLANT

Choose a location in full sunlight with soil that is fertile, high in organic matter, and well drained. Broad beans prefer an alkaline soil. When preparing the soil for planting, work in a complete, well-balanced fertilizer at the rate of 1lb per 95sq feet (450g per 9sq m).

Plant broad bean seeds 1–2 inches (2.5–5cm) deep in rows 4 feet (1.25m) apart. When the seedlings are growing strongly, thin them to 8–12 inches (20–30cm) apart.

FERTILIZING AND WATERING

Beans set up a mutual exchange with soil microorganisms called nitrogen-fixing bacteria, which help them produce their own fertilizer. Some gardeners recommend that if you haven't grown beans in the plot the previous season, you should treat the bean seeds before planting with a nitrogen-fixing bacteria inoculant to help them convert organic nitrogen compounds into usable organic compounds. This is a perfectly acceptable practice but it isn't really necessary; the bacteria in the soil will multiply quickly enough once they've got a growing bean plant to work with.

Fertilize before planting and again at midseason, at the same rate as the rest of the garden. Water broad beans before the soil dries out, but don't overwater—wet soil conditions combined with high temperatures are an invitation to root diseases.

PESTS

Beans are attacked by aphids, bean beetles, leafhoppers and mites. Aphids, leafhoppers and mites can be controlled chemically by spraying with Malathion or Diazinon. Bean beetles can be controlled chemically by spraying with Carbaryl. Beans are almost always attacked by large numbers of pests that cannot be controlled by organic methods; this doesn't mean they can't be grown organically, but it does mean that yields may be lower if only organic controls are used.

DISEASES

Beans are susceptible to blight, mosaic, and anthracnose. You can cut down on the incidence of disease by planting disease-resistant varieties, maintaining the general health of your garden and avoiding handling the plants when they're wet. If a plant does become infected, remove it and destroy it so it can't spread disease to healthy plants.

HARVESTING

Broad beans can be harvested when the beans are still the size of a pea and used like French beans. It's more usual, however, to let them reach maturity and eat only the shelled beans. Time from planting to harvest is about 4½ –5 months.

VARIETIES

Aquadulce, Bell, Bonnie Lad, Broad Windsor, Colossal, Express, Hava, Masterpiece, Minica, Primo, Toto.

STORING AND PRESERVING

Unshelled beans can be kept up to one week in the refrigerator. You can freeze, bottle or dry the shelled beans. Dried shelled broad beans can be stored in a cool, dry place for 10–12 months.

Freezing

Young:
1. Choose wide, flat beans that are tender, meaty and stringless.
2. Wash well, snip off the ends, and cut or break them into 1½ inch (3.5cm) pieces.
3. Blanch 3 minutes. Cool; drain well.
4. Tray freeze or pack into containers. Seal, label and freeze.
5. Cook frozen beans about 10 minutes.

Shelled:
1. Choose well-filled pods of young, green, tender beans.
2. Wash, shell and wash again. Sort by size.
3. Blanch small beans 1 minute; medium beans 2 minutes; large beans 3 minutes. Cool; drain well.

4. Tray freeze or pack into containers. Seal, label and freeze.
5. Cook large beans 15 to 20 minutes; small beans 6 to 10 minutes.

Drying

1. Choose fresh, just-mature beans.
2. Shell the beans; then wash and drain.
3. Blanch in boiling water 15 minutes. Drain well, chill and pat dry with paper towels.
4. Arrange the beans in a single, even layer on baking sheets or racks.
5. Dry until brittle, 4 to 12 hours.
6. Put the dried vegetables into a deep container, cover lightly with cheesecloth and condition, stirring once a day for a week to 10 days.
7. Pack into vapor/moistureproof, airtight containers or double plastic bags and store in a cool, dark, dry place for up to 12 months.
8. Rehydrate in 2½ cups of boiling water for each cup of beans, about 1½ hours.

SERVING SUGGESTIONS

Broad beans are good steamed and served with a light white or cheese sauce. Or top steamed broad beans with a little sautéed parsley, garlic, and onion. Use them in a casserole with onions, tomatoes and cheese, or add them to a hearty vegetable soup along with any other vegetables you've got on hand.

Bean, Dry

Common names: pinto beans, navy beans, horticultural beans, flageolet

Botanic name: *Phaseolus* species

Origin: South Mexico, Central America

Dry beans are tender annuals. Their leaves are usually composed of three leaflets, and the small flowers are pale yellow or white. Dry beans are seldom planted in the home vegetable garden because it's so easy and inexpensive to buy them. They're fairly easy to grow, however, and give good yields, so if you have space in your garden you may want to try them.

You can grow either dwarf or climbing varieties of beans. Dwarf beans are generally easier to handle; they grow only 12–24 inches (30–60cm) tall, and mature earlier. Climbing beans require a trellis for support; they grow more slowly, but produce more beans per plant.

PLANTING

Beans require warm soil to germinate. You can start the seed indoors in peat pots and transplant the seedlings when the soil has warmed up. Time your planting

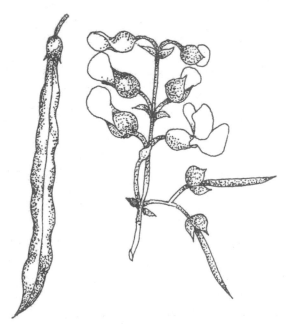

so that the beans will mature before very hot weather; they will not set pods at temperatures over 82°F (28°C).

You can plant dwarf beans every two weeks to extend the harvest, or start with them and follow up with climbing beans.

HOW TO PLANT

Choose a bed in full sunlight; beans tolerate partial shade, but partial shade tends to mean a partial yield. When preparing the soil, mix in 1lb (450g) of low-nitrogen (5-10-10) fertilizer—don't use a high-nitrogen fertilizer; too much nitrogen will promote growth of foliage but not of the beans. Bean seeds may crack and germinate poorly when the moisture content of the soil is too high. Don't soak the seeds before planting and don't over-water immediately afterwards.

Plant the bean seeds 1 inch (2.5cm) deep. If they're dwarf beans, plant the seeds 3–4 inches (7.5–10cm) apart in rows at least 18–24 inches (45–60cm) apart. Seeds of climbing beans should be planted 4–6 inches (10–15cm) apart in rows 30–39 inches (75–100cm) apart. Or plant in inverted hills—five or six seeds to a hill, and 30 inches (75cm) of space around each hill. When the seedlings are large enough to handle, thin the plants to 4–6 inches (10–15cm) apart. Cut the seedlings with scissors at ground level; be careful not to disturb the others. Beans don't mind being a little crowded—in fact, they'll use each other for support.

FERTILIZING AND WATERING

Beans set up a mutual exchange with soil microorganisms called nitrogen-fixing bacteria, which help them produce their own fertilizer. Some gardeners recommend that if you haven't grown beans in the plot the previous season, you should treat the bean seeds with a nitrogen-fixing bacteria inoculant to help them convert organic nitrogen compounds into usable organic compounds. This is a perfectly acceptable practice but it isn't necessary; the bacteria in the soil will multiply quickly enough once they've got a growing bean plant to work with.

Fertilize before planting and again at mid-season, at the same rate as the rest of the garden.

Keep the soil moist until the beans have pushed through the ground. Water regularly if there's no rain, but remember that water on the flowers can cause the flowers and small pods to fall off. When the soil temperature reaches 59°F (15°C) you can mulch to conserve moisture.

SPECIAL HANDLING

Don't touch bean plants when they're wet; handling or brushing against them when they're wet spreads fungus spores. Cultivate thoroughly but with care, so that you don't disturb the shallow root systems.

If planting climbing beans, set the trellis or support in position before you plant or at the same time. If you wait until the plants are established, you risk damaging the roots when you set the supports. Make sure the support will be tall enough for the variety you're growing.

PESTS

Beans may be attacked by aphids, bean beetles, leafhoppers and mites. Aphids, leafhoppers and mites can be controlled chemically by spraying with Malathion or Diazinon. Bean beetles can be controlled chemically by spraying with Carbaryl. Beans are almost always attacked by large numbers of pests that cannot be controlled by organic methods. This doesn't mean the organic gardener can't grow them, but yields may be lower if only organic controls are used.

DISEASES

Beans are susceptible to blight, mosaic, and anthracnose. You can cut down on the incidence of disease by planting disease-resistant varieties, maintaining the general health of your garden, and avoiding handling the plants when they're wet. If a plant does become infected, remove and destroy it so it cannot spread disease to healthy plants.

HARVESTING

Harvest dry beans when the plants have matured and the leaves have turned completely brown. At this time the seeds should be dry and hard—bite a couple of seeds; if you can hardly dent them they're properly dry and ready to harvest.

VARIETIES

Dry beans are so called because the mature seeds are generally dried before they're eaten. Horticultural beans, the genuine French flageolets, are a type of dry bean highly regarded by gourmets; they're usually eaten in the green-shell stage. Other varieties include: Jacob's Cattle, Midnight (black turtle), Montcalm, Drake (dark red kidneys), California Early (light red kidney), Red Kanner (light red kidney), Fleetwood (navy), Othello (pinto), Etna (cranberry).

STORING AND PRESERVING

Unshelled beans can be kept up to one week in the refrigerator. You can freeze, bottle, or dry the shelled beans, and they can also be sprouted. Dried shelled beans can be stored in a cool, dry place for 10–12 months.

Freezing
Shelled:
1. Choose well-filled pods of young, green, tender beans.

2. Wash, shell and wash again. Sort by size.

3. Blanch small beans 1 minute; medium beans 2 minutes; large beans 3 minutes. Cool; drain well.

4. Tray freeze or pack into containers. Seal, label and freeze.

5. Cook large beans 15 to 20 minutes; small beans 6 to 10 minutes.

Drying

If planning to sprout shelling beans, do not use this recipe, but use the recipe below for slow air-drying.

1. Choose fresh, just-mature beans.

2. Shell the beans; then wash and drain.

3. Blanch in boiling water 15 minutes. Drain well, chill and pat dry with paper towels.

4. Arrange the beans in a single, even layer on baking sheets or racks.

5. Dry until brittle, 4 to 12 hours.

6. Put the dried vegetables into a deep container, cover lightly with cheesecloth and condition, stirring once a day for a week to 10 days.

7. Pack into vapor/moistureproof, airtight containers or double plastic bags and store in a cool, dark, dry place for up to 12 months.

8. Rehydrate in 2½ cups of boiling water for each cup of beans, about 1½ hours.

Sprouting:

Beans to be sprouted must be dried slowly, without the blanching or heating used in the method above, because processing kills the seed. Only live seed can be sprouted.

1. Leave dry beans on the plants until the pods have matured and the leaves have turned brown. The seeds should be dry and hard.

2. Harvest the beans by pulling up the entire plant. Shake loose dirt from the roots.

3. Tie the plants in bundles and hang them to dry in a warm, dark, dry place; or spread them on clean newspaper on the floor in a dark, warm, dry room.

4. Let dry for 1 to 3 weeks, until beans are completely dry and hard. To test, shell a bean and bite it; you should hardly be able to dent the seed with your teeth.

5. When beans are completely dry, shell them. Discard the pods.

6. Pack into vapor/moistureproof, airtight containers or double plastic bags and store in a cool, dark, dry place for up to 12 months.

7. Use for sprouting or for planting the following year.

SERVING SUGGESTIONS

Dried beans are tremendously versatile and have the added advantage of being interchangeable in many recipes. They're also nourishing and figure prominently in vegetarian recipes. Chili and baked beans are two of the famous dishes that depend upon dried beans, and beans are essential to the famous French cassoulet—a hearty stew that combines beans with pork, chicken, sausage or a mixture of all three depending on the region the cook comes from. Add sausage or ham to a thick bean soup for a cheery winter supper.

Bean, Green or String

Common names: bean, green bean, string bean, French bean, wax bean, snake bean, runner bean, stringless bean

Botanic name: *Phaseolus vulgaris*

Origin: South Mexico, Central America

Beans are tender annuals. There are both dwarf and climbing types. Their leaves are usually composed of three leaflets; their flowers are pale yellow, lavender, or white. The size and color of the pods and seeds vary. They requite a short growing season—about 2½–3 months of moderate temperatures from seed to the first crop and are an encouraging vegetable for the inexperienced gardener. The immature pod is the part that's eaten. Dwarf beans are generally easier to handle; and they mature earlier. Climbing beans require a trellis for support; they grow more slowly, but produce more beans per plant.

PLANTING

Because many varieties have a short growing season, beans do well in most areas. They require warm soil to germinate and should be planted when all danger of frost is past. If you need to sow before, then start the seed indoors in peat pots and transplant the seedlings when the soil has warmed up. Time your planting so the beans will mature before very hot weather; they will not set pods at temperatures over 81°F (27°C). You can plant dwarf beans every 3 weeks to extend the harvest, or you can start with dwarf beans and follow up with climbers.

HOW TO PLANT

After the last frost is over, choose a bed in full sunlight; beans tolerate partial shade, but partial shade tends to mean a partial yield. Prepare the soil by mixing in 1lb (450g) of 5-10-10 fertilizer—don't use a high-nitrogen fertilizer, because too much nitrogen will promote growth of foliage but not of the beans. Work the fertilizer into the soil at the rate of 1lb per 95sq feet (450g per 9sq m).

Bean seeds may crack and germinate poorly when the moisture content of the soil is too high. Don't soak the seeds before planting, and don't overwater immediately afterwards.

Plant seeds of all varieties 1–2 inches (3–5cm) deep. If planting dwarf beans, sow the seeds 2 inches (5cm) apart in rows at least 18–24 inches (45–60cm) apart. Seeds of climbing beans should be planted 4–6 inches (10–15cm) apart in rows 15½ inches (40cm) apart. Or sow them in inverted hills, five or six seeds to a hill, about 3 ft. (1m) of space around each hill. For climbing varieties, set the supports or trellises at the time of planting.

When the seedlings are growing well, thin the plants to 4–6 inches (10–15cm) apart. Cut the seedlings with scissors at ground level; be careful not to disturb the others. Beans don't mind being a little crowded; in fact, they'll use each other for support.

FERTILIZING AND WATERING

Beans set up a mutual exchange with soil microorganisms called nitrogen-fixing bacteria, which help them produce their own fertilizer. Some gardeners recommend that if you haven't grown beans in the plot the

previous season, you should treat the bean seeds before planting with a nitrogen-fixing bacteria inoculant to help them convert organic nitrogen compounds into usable organic compounds. This is a perfectly acceptable practice but it isn't really necessary; the bacteria in the soil will multiply quickly enough once they've got a growing bean plant to work with.

Fertilize before planting and again at midseason, at the same rate as the rest of the garden.

Keep the soil moist until the beans have pushed through the ground. Water regularly if there is no rain, but remember that water on the flowers can cause the flowers and small pods to fall off. When the soil temperature reaches 59°F (15°C) you can mulch to conserve moisture.

SPECIAL HANDLING

Don't bother bean plants when they're wet or covered with heavy dew; handling or brushing against them when they're wet spreads fungus spores. Cultivate thoroughly but with care, so that you don't disturb the bean plants' shallow root systems. If you're planting climbing beans, set the trellis or support in position before you plant or at the same time. If you wait until the plants are established, you risk damaging the roots when you set the supports.

Make sure the support will be tall enough for the variety of beans you're growing.

PESTS

Beans may be attacked by aphids, bean beetles, leafhoppers, mites and Seedcorn maggots. Aphids, leafhoppers and mites can be controlled chemically by spraying with Malathion or Diazinon. Bean beetles can be controlled chemically by spraying with Carbaryl. Beans are almost always attacked by large numbers of pests that cannot be controlled by organic methods. This does not mean the organic gardener can't grow them, but yields may be lower if only organic controls are used. To prevent Seedcorn maggots, avoid heavy manure or organic matter in garden which attract maggot flies and encourages egg laying. Purchase insecticide-treated seed. Use gloves to plant.

DISEASES

Beans are susceptible to blight, mosaic, and white mold. You can cut down on the incidence of disease by planting disease-resistant varieties, maintaining the general health of your garden and avoiding handling the plants when they're wet. If a plant does become infected, remove and destroy it so it cannot spread disease to healthy plants.

HARVESTING

Time from planting to harvest is 2½–3½ months. Dwarf beans mature fairly quickly. Harvest the immature pods and continue removing the pods before they become mature, or the plant will stop producing. Once the seeds mature, the plant dies. Do not harvest when the weather is very hot or very cold.

VARIETIES

The most commonly grown beans are the green or string beans and the yellow or wax variety. Burpee introduced the Stringless Green Pod in 1894. Other varieties include: Ambra, Benchmark, Derby, Fastina, Kentucky Wonder, Provider, Strike, Romano, Blue Lake, Scarlet Runner, Tema, Tendercrop, Top Crop, Contender, Improved Tendergreen.

STORING AND PRESERVING

They'll keep up to one week in the refrigerator, but don't wash them until you're ready to cook them. You can also freeze, bottle, dry or pickle them.

Freezing

1. Choose young, tender beans that snap easily. The beans in the pods should not be fully formed.
2. Wash well, snip the ends, and sort by size.
3. Leave the beans whole, cut in even lengths, or cut French-style (lengthwise).
4. Blanch 2 to 3 minutes, depending on the size of the beans. Cool; drain well.
5. Tray freeze or pack into containers. Seal, label and freeze.
6. Cook frozen whole or cut beans 12 to 18 minutes; French-style beans 5 to 10 minutes.

Drying

1. Choose fresh, just-mature green beans.
2. Wash beans, then drain. Trim off ends and cut beans into 1–2 inch (2.5–5cm) pieces.
3. Blanch in boiling water 2 minutes; or in steam 2 to 2½ minutes. Drain well, chill and pat dry with paper towels.
4. Arrange in a single, even layer on baking sheets or racks.
5. Dry until brittle, 3 to 14 hours.
6. Put the dried vegetables into a deep container, cover lightly with cheesecloth and condition, stirring once a day for a week to 10 days.
7. Pack into vapor/moistureproof, airtight containers or double plastic bags and store in a cool, dark, dry place for up to 12 months.
8. Rehydrate in 2½ cups of boiling water for each cup of beans, about 1 hour.

SERVING SUGGESTIONS

Really fresh, tender green beans are delicious eaten raw; they make an unusual addition to a platter of crudites for dipping. They're also good lightly cooked and tossed with diced potatoes and a little onion and bacon for a delightful hot bean salad. Try them on toast with a light cheese sauce for lunch. And vary everyone's favorite bean dish by replacing the classic Amandine sauce with a Hollandaise or mushroom sauce. Or try tossing them with a few thinly sliced mushrooms and onions that have been lightly sautéed in butter.

You can also cut them in lengths and sauté them with diced potatoes, carrots and onions for an interesting vegetable dish. Purists will object that this means cooking the beans too long, but you can always add them halfway through the cooking time to preserve their crispness. Well-seasoned, this is a good, filling vegetable dish for a cold day. On their own, they take well to many spices, including basil, dill, marjoram and mint.

Bean, Lima

Common names: bean, lima bean, butter bean, civit bean

Botanic name: *Phaseolus lunatus*

Origin: South Mexico, Central America

Both dwarf and climbing type of this tender, large-seeded annual bean are available. With this type of bean the mature seed is eaten, not the entire pod.

Lima beans need warmer soil than green beans in order to germinate properly, and they need higher temperatures and a longer growing season for a good crop.

Dwarf lima beans are generally easier to handle than climbing varieties; bushes grow only 12–24 inches (30–60cm) tall and they mature earlier. Climbing

Lima bean

beans require a trellis for support; they grow more slowly, but produce more beans per plant.

GROWING

Lima beans require warm soil (five days at a minimum temperature of 64°F/18°C) to germinate. You can start the seed indoors in peat pots and transplant them when the soil has warmed up. Time your planting so the beans will mature before very hot weather; they will not set pods at temperatures over 81°F (27°C).

Plant bush beans every two weeks to extend the harvest, or start with bush beans and follow up with climbing beans. Because limas need a long stretch of pleasant weather, the slower-growing varieties are difficult to raise successfully where the growing season is short.

HOW TO PLANT

After the last frost is over, choose a bed in full sunlight; beans tolerate partial shade, but partial shade tends to mean a partial yield. Prepare the soil by mixing in 1lb (450g) of 5-10-10 fertilizer; don't use a high-nitrogen fertilizer, because too much nitrogen will promote growth of the foliage but not of the beans.

Plant seeds of all varieties 1 in. (2.5cm) deep. If you're planting bush limas, plant the seeds 2 in. (5cm) apart in rows at least 18–24 inches (45–60cm) apart. Seeds of

climbing beans should be planted 4–6 inches (10–15cm) apart in rows 2½–3 feet (0.75–1m) apart, or plant them in inverted hills, five or six seeds to a hill, with 30 inches (75cm) of space around each hill. For climbing varieties, set supports or trellises at the time of planting.

When the seedlings are growing well, thin the plants to 4–6 inches (10–15cm) apart. Cut the seedlings with scissors at ground level; be careful not to disturb the others. Beans don't mind being a little crowded; in fact, they'll use each other for support.

FERTILIZING AND WATERING

Beans set up a mutual exchange with soil microorganisms called nitrogen-fixing bacteria, which help them produce their own fertilizer. Some gardeners recommend that if you haven't grown beans in the plot before, you should treat the bean seeds before planting with a nitrogen-fixing bacteria inoculant to help them convert organic nitrogen compounds into usable organic compounds. This is a perfectly acceptable practice, but it isn't really necessary; the bacteria in the soil will multiply quickly enough once they've got a growing bean plant to work with.

Fertilize before planting and again at midseason, at the same rate as the rest of the garden.

Bean seeds may crack and germinate poorly when the moisture

content of the soil is too high. Don't soak the seeds before planting and don't water immediately afterwards. Keep the soil moist until the beans have pushed through the ground. Water regularly if there is no rain, but avoid getting water on the flowers; this can cause the flowers and the small pods to fall off. You can mulch to conserve moisture when the soil temperature reaches 59°F (15°C).

SPECIAL HANDLING

Don't handle bean plants when they're wet or covered with heavy dew; handling or brushing against them when they're wet spreads fungus spores. Cultivate thoroughly but with care, so you don't disturb the bean plants' shallow root systems.

If you're planting climbing beans, set the trellis or support in position before you plant or at the same time. If you wait until the plants are established, you risk damaging the roots when you set the supports. Make sure the support will be tall enough for the variety of beans you're planting.

The large lima bean seed sometimes has trouble pushing through the soil, although this should not happen if the soil is well worked. If your soil tends to cake, you can cover the seeds with sand, vermiculite, or a peatmoss/vermiculite mix instead.

PESTS

Beans may be attacked by aphids, bean beetles, leafhoppers and mites. Aphids, leafhoppers and mites can be controlled chemically by spraying with Malathion or Diazinon. Bean beetles can be controlled chemically by spraying with Carbaryl. Beans are almost always attacked by large numbers of pests that cannot be controlled by organic methods. This doesn't mean the organic gardener can't grow them, but yields may be lower if only organic controls are used.

DISEASES

Beans are susceptible to blight, mosaic, and anthracnose. You can cut down on the incidence of disease by planting disease-resistant varieties, maintaining the general health of your garden and avoiding handling the plants when they're wet. If a plant does become infected, remove and destroy it so it cannot spread disease to healthy plants.

HARVESTING

Time from planting to harvest is about 2–2½ months for bush limas and 3–3½ months for climbing limas. Harvest when the pods are plump and firm; if you leave them too long the beans will get tough and mealy. If you pick the pods promptly, limas will continue to yield until the first frost. In warmer climates, bush limas should give you two or three pickings.

VARIETIES

Bush lima: Burpee Improved Bush; Fordhook—both resistant to bean mosaic; Climbing lima: King of the Garden; Henderson Bush.

STORING AND PRESERVING

Unshelled lima beans can be kept up to one week in the refrigerator. Shelled lima beans freeze satisfactorily; they can also be bottled or dried. Dried shelled limas can be stored in a cool, dry place for 10 to 12 months.

Freezing.
Young:
1. Choose wide, flat beans that are tender, meaty and stringless.
2. Wash well, snip off the ends, and cut or break them into 1½ inch (3.5cm) pieces.
3. Blanch 3 minutes. Cool; drain well.
4. Tray freeze or pack into containers. Seal, label and freeze.
5. Cook frozen beans about 10 minutes.
Shelled:
1. Choose well-filled pods of young, green, tender beans.
2. Wash, shell and wash again. Sort by size.
3. Blanch small beans 1 minute; medium beans 2 minutes; large beans 3 minutes. Cool; drain well.
4. Tray freeze or pack into containers. Seal, label and freeze.
5. Cook large beans 15 to 20 minutes; small beans 6 to 10 minutes.

Drying
1. Choose fresh, just-mature beans.
2. Shell the beans; then wash and drain.
3. Blanch in boiling water 15 minutes. Drain well, chill and pat dry with paper towels.
4. Arrange the beans in a single, even layer on baking sheets or racks.
5. Dry until brittle, 4 to 12 hours.
6. Put the dried vegetables into a deep container, cover lightly with cheesecloth and condition, stirring once a day for a week to 10 days.
7. Pack into vapor/moistureproof, airtight containers or double plastic bags and store in a cool, dark, dry place for up to 12 months.
8. Rehydrate in 2½ cups of boiling water for each cup of beans, about 1½ hours.

SERVING SUGGESTIONS

Try limas raw for an unusual treat. Serve them in a salad with thinly sliced red onion, parsley, and a vinaigrette dressing, or marinate for 24 hours in oil, lemon juice and freshly chopped dill. Cook limas until just tender and serve with a creamy sauce. For a tangy taste bake them in a casserole with honey, mustard and yogurt.

Mung Bean

Common name: mung bean

Botanic name: *Phaseolus aureus*

Origin: India, Central Asia

The mung bean is a bushy annual that grows about 3ft. (1m) tall and has many branches with typical, hairy, beanlike leaves. The flowers are yellowish-green with purple streaks and produce long, thin, hairy pods containing nine to 15 small, yellow seeds. The seeds are used to produce bean sprouts.

GROWING

Mung beans can be grown in temperate to cool areas.

HOW TO PLANT

Mung beans grow best in full sun, in a rich, well-drained soil. When preparing the soil for planting, dig in a complete, well-balanced fertilizer at the rate of 1lb per 95sq feet (450g per 9sq m). Because the only seeds you may be able to get are not very reliable in growth, plant the seeds several at a time 1 inch (2.5cm) deep and 18–20 inches (45–50cm) apart in wide rows 18–24 inches (45–60cm) apart. When the seedlings are about 2 inches (5cm) tall, thin them to leave the strongest of each group growing. Cut off the extra seedlings at ground

level to avoid disturbing the survivor's roots.

FERTILIZING AND WATERING

Beans set up a mutual exchange with soil microorganisms called nitrogen-fixing bacteria, which help them produce their own fertilizer. Some gardeners recommend that if you haven't grown beans in the plot the previous season, you should treat the bean seeds before planting with a nitrogen-fixing bacteria inoculant to help them convert organic nitrogen compounds into usable organic compounds. This is a perfectly acceptable practice but it isn't really necessary; the bacteria in the soil will multiply quickly enough once they've got a growing bean plant to work with.

Fertilize before planting and again at midseason, at the same rate as the rest of the garden.

Mung beans don't like to dry out between waterings. If it doesn't rain, keep them well watered.

PESTS

Mung beans have no serious pest problems.

DISEASES

Mung beans have no serious disease problems.

HARVESTING

It usually takes about 3 months for mung beans to mature and you can expect 1–2lbs (0.5–1kg) of seeds from a 10-foot (3m) row. Harvest them as soon as a few of the pods begin to split. If the pods are picked when they are too young they won't store or sprout. Remove the seeds from pods when you harvest them.

VARIETIES

Few varieties are available. Grow whichever variety is available in your area, or plant the seeds sold for sprouting.

STORING AND PRESERVING

Mung beans are usually grown for sprouting. Unshelled beans can be kept up to one week in the refrigerator; shelled beans, naturally dried, can be stored in a cool, dry place for 10–12 months.

Drying

Beans to be sprouted must be dried slowly, without the blanching or heating used in the method above, because processing kills the seed. Only live seed can be sprouted.

1. Leave dry beans on the plants until the pods have matured and the leaves have turned brown. The seeds should be dry and hard.
2. Harvest the beans by pulling up the entire plant. Shake loose dirt from the roots.

3. Tie the plants in bundles and hang them to dry in a warm, dark, dry place; or spread them on clean newspaper on the floor in a dark, warm, dry room.

4. Let dry for 1 to 3 weeks, until beans are completely dry and hard. To test, shell a bean and bite it; you should hardly be able to dent the seed with your teeth.

5. When beans are completely dry, shell them. Discard the pods.

6. Pack into vapor/moistureproof, airtight containers or double plastic bags and store in a cool, dark, dry place for up to 12 months.

7. Use for sprouting or for planting the following year.

SERVING SUGGESTIONS

Bean sprouts turn up in all sorts of Chinese dishes. They're good in salads and sandwiches—vegetarians love them and rightly so, because they have a high Vitamin C content.

Bean, Soy

Common name: soybean

Botanic name: *Glycine max*

Origin: East Asia

The soybean is a tender, free-branching annual legume. Though it can grow 5 feet (1.5m) tall, it's usually only 3 feet (1m) tall. The stems and leaves are hairy; the flowers are white with lavender shading, and the pods are one to four inches long and grow in clusters. The soybean is extremely high in protein and calcium and is a staple of a vegetarian diet. It's also very versatile and can be used to make milk, oil, tofu, or a meat substitute. The ancient Chinese considered the soybean their most important crop.

GROWING

Soybeans are sensitive to cold and most varieties have a narrow

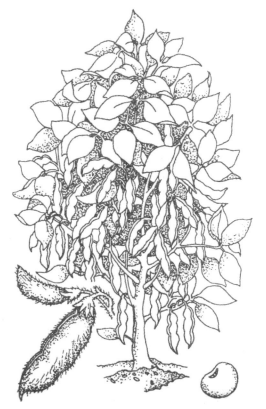

latitude range in which they will mature properly and produce a good crop. Plant a variety suited to your area after the soil has warmed up.

HOW TO PLANT

After the last frost is over, choose a bed in full sunlight; soybeans tolerate partial shade, but partial shade tends to mean a partial yield. Prepare the soil by mixing in a pound of 5-10-10 fertilizer— don't use a high-nitrogen fertilizer, because too much nitrogen will promote growth of foliage but not of the beans. Work the fertilizer into the soil at the rate of 1lb per 95sq feet (450g per 9sq m). The seeds may crack and germinate poorly when the moisture content of the soil is too high. Don't soak the seeds before planting and don't over-water immediately afterwards.

Plant seeds 1 inch (2.5cm) deep, 1–2 inches (2.5–5cm) apart in rows 24–28 inches (60–70cm) apart. When the seedlings are growing well, thin the plants to 2 inches (5cm) apart. Cut the seedlings with scissors at ground level; be careful not to disturb the others. Soybeans don't mind being a little crowded; in fact, they'll use each other for support.

FERTILIZING AND WATERING

Soybeans set up a mutual exchange with soil microorganisms called nitrogen-fixing bacteria, which help them produce their own fertilizer. Some gardeners recommend that if you haven't grown soybeans or beans in the plot the previous season, you should treat the seeds before planting with a nitrogen-fixing bacteria inoculant to help them convert organic nitrogen compounds into usable organic compounds. This is a perfectly acceptable practice, but it isn't really necessary; the bacteria in the soil will multiply quickly enough once they've got a growing plant to work with.

Fertilize before planting and again at midseason, at the same rate as the rest of the garden.

Keep the soil moist until the soybeans have pushed through the ground. Water regularly if there's no rain, but remember that water on the flowers can cause the flowers and small pods to fall off. When the soil temperature reaches 59°F (15°C) you can mulch to conserve moisture.

SPECIAL HANDLING

Don't handle soybean plants when they're wet or covered with heavy dew; handling or brushing against them when they're wet spreads fungus spores. Cultivate thoroughly but with care, so that you don't disturb the plants' shallow root systems.

PESTS

Soybeans do not have many pest problems.

DISEASES

Soybeans have no serious disease problems.

HARVESTING

Time from planting to harvest is 1½–2 months and a 10-foot (3m) row will supply 1–2lbs (0.5–1kg) of beans. The yield is not generous, so except for novelty value, soybeans are not the ideal crop for a small home garden. Harvest when the pods are about 4 inches (10cm) long or when they look plump and full.

VARIETIES

A number of varieties have been bred to adapt to certain types of climate, such as Vinton or Verde.

STORING AND PRESERVING

Store fresh unshelled soybeans in the refrigerator up to one week. Shelled soybeans can be frozen or dried. They can also be sprouted. Dropping the pods into boiling water for a minute or two makes shelling easier. Dried, shelled soybeans can be stored in a cool, dry place for 10–12 months.

Freezing
1. Choose well-filled pods of young, tender green beans.
2. Wash pods well.
3. Blanch beans in pods 5 minutes. Cool; drain well.
4. Squeeze beans out of pods and pick over, discarding any bad beans.

5. Tray freeze or pack into containers. Seal, label and freeze.
6. Cook frozen soybeans 10 to 20 minutes.

Drying
1. Choose very fresh, evenly sized beans.
2. Wash, but don't shell.
3. Blanch in boiling water 10 minutes; or in steam 12 to 15 minutes. Drain, chill and pat dry with paper towels, then shell.
4. Arrange in a single, even layer on baking sheets or racks.
5. Dry until brittle, usually more than 12 hours. Tap a single bean with a hammer; if done, it will shatter easily.
6. Put the dried vegetables into a deep container, cover lightly with cheesecloth and condition, stirring once a day for a week to 10 days.
7. Pack into vapor/moistureproof, airtight containers or double plastic bags and store in a cool, dark, dry place for up to 12 months.
8. Rehydrate in 2½ cups of boiling water for each cup of beans, about 1½ hours.

SERVING SUGGESTIONS

The Japanese cook soybeans in salted water, serve them in the shell, and then squeeze out the seeds and eat them. Soybeans are extremely versatile; they can be made into oil, milk or tofu—a major foodstuff among vegetarians. Soybeans are also used as a high-protein meat substitute or ground into flour.

Beet

Common name: beet

Botanic name: *Beta vulgaris*

Origin: Southern Europe

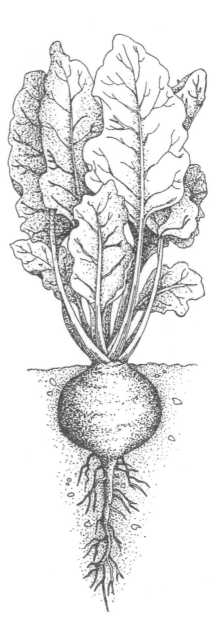

The beet is grown as an annual, although technically it's a biennial. It originated in the Mediterranean, where it existed first as a leafy plant, without the enlarged root we grow it for these days. Swiss chard, which is a bottomless beet, is an improved version of the early, leafy beets. The modern beet has a round or tapered swollen root—red, yellow or white—from which sprouts a rosette of large leaves. The leaves as well as the root can be eaten.

GROWING

Beets can tolerate frost and do best in the cooler areas of the country, but they'll go to seed without making roots if the plants get too cold when they're young. If you live in a hot climate you'll need to pay special attention to watering and mulching to give seedlings a chance to establish themselves. In very hot weather the roots become woody. Sow — S.T.-all seasons. T-spring to autumn. C-spring to early autumn.

HOW TO PLANT

Beets can tolerate shade and thrive in well-worked, loose soil high in organic matter. They don't like a very acid soil, and need a lot of potassium. Before planting, work a complete, well-balanced fertilizer into the soil at the rate of 1lb per 95sq feet (450g per 9sq m). Remove stones and other obstacles, and break up any lumps in the soil that might cause the roots to become malformed.

Beets are grown from seed clusters that are slightly smaller than a pea and contain several seeds each. Plant the clusters 1 inch (2.5cm) deep and 1 inch (2.5cm) apart in rows spaced 8–10 inches (20–45cm) apart. The seedlings may emerge over a period of time so that you've got a group of seedlings of different sizes. Since several seedlings will emerge from each seed cluster, they must be thinned to 2–3 inches (5–7.5cm) apart when the seedlings develop true leaves. Eat thinned seedlings like spinach; they do not transplant well. Use all the seed cluster—most seeds store well, but these clusters have only a short period of viability.

FERTILIZING AND WATERING

Fertilize before planting and again at midseason, at the same rate as the rest of the garden.

Be sure to provide plenty of water for the tender young roots—lack of moisture will result in stringy, tough vegetables.

SPECIAL HANDLING

Cultivate by hand regularly; beets do not like competition from weeds. Take care, because the roots are shallow and easily damaged.

PESTS

Leafminer— Cover plants with fine netting or cheesecloth or floating row cover to protect them from adult flies. Handpick and destroy infested (mined) leaves. Control weeds.

DISEASES

Beets have no serious disease problems.

HARVESTING

Time from planting to harvest is about 2½–3 months. Pull them up when they're the size you want. Twist the leaves off rather than cutting them off; this prevents "bleeding," which causes less intense color and, some people claim, less flavor.

VARIETIES

Early Wonder, Burpee's Golden, Little Ball, Warrior (hybrid),

Crosby Green Top, Long Season, Formanova, Lutz Green, Ruby Queen, Red Ace, Crosby Green-top, Cylindra.

STORING AND PRESERVING

You can store beets in the refrigerator for one to three weeks; store the greens in a plastic bag in the refrigerator up to one week.

Beets will keep for five to six months in a cold, moist place. You can also freeze, dry and bottle both the root and the greens (use the recipe for "greens"). You can even pickle the root. So there's never any problem figuring what to do with the excess crop.

Freezing
1. Choose young, tender, evenly colored beets no more than 3 inches (7.5cm) in diameter.
2. Remove tops, leaving ½ inch (1cm) of stem. Wash.
3. Cook in boiling water to cover, 25 to 30 minutes for small beets; 45 to 50 minutes for medium.
4. Cool and slip off skins. Leave whole or slice, cube or dice. Pack into containers. Seal, label and freeze.
5. Cook frozen beets just until heated through.

Drying
1. Choose firm, undamaged beets.
2. Remove tops and roots.
3. Blanch in boiling water about 45 minutes, or until tender. Drain well, chill and pat dry with paper towels. Slip off skins and cut into ⅛ inch (0.5cm) slices or strips.
4. Arrange in a single, even layer on baking sheets.
5. Dry until brittle, 3 to 12 hours.
6. Put the dried vegetables into a deep container, cover lightly with cheesecloth and condition, stirring once a day for a week to 10 days.
7. Pack into vapor/moistureproof, airtight containers or double plastic bags and store in a cool, dark, dry place for up to 12 months.
8. Rehydrate in 2¾ cups of boiling water for each cup of beets, about 1½ hours.
Greens:
1. Choose very fresh, perfect leaves.
2. Wash leaves well; shake dry. Remove any large, tough stalks.
3. Blanch in boiling water about 1½ minutes; or in steam about 2½ minutes, until completely wilted. Drain very well, chill and pat dry with paper towels.
4. Arrange leaves in a single layer on baking sheets or racks.
5. Dry until brittle, 2½ to 8 hours or more.
6. Put the dried vegetables into a deep container, cover lightly with cheesecloth and condition, stirring once a day for a week to 10 days.
7. Pack into vapor/moistureproof, airtight containers or double plastic bags and store in a cool, dark, dry place for up to 12 months.
8. Rehydrate in 1 cup of boiling water for each cup of greens, about ½ hour.

SERVING SUGGESTIONS

Beets are more versatile than they're often given credit for. Eat them raw, or serve the tops raw as a salad green—if you don't cook them, you'll retain some of the vitamins normally lost in cooking. If you cook beets in their skins, the skins will slip off readily at the end of the cooking time. Hot, try them dressed with orange juice and topped with a few slivers of green onion, or glaze them with orange marmalade. Or keep the dressing simple: just a little butter, lemon juice and seasoning. Beets are the basis of the thick, delicious Russian soup called borscht. Serve borscht with a dollop of sour cream.

Broad Bean

See Bean, Broad

Broccoli

Common names: broccoli, Italian broccoli, Calabrese

Botanic name: *Brassica oleracea italica*

Origin: Mediterranean

The hardy biennial, grown as an annual, is a member of the cabbage family. It grows 16–24 inches (40–60cm) tall and looks a bit like a cauliflower that hasn't quite got itself together. The flower stalks are green, purple or white; the flowers are yellow. Broccoli is eaten while the flowers are in bud.

Broccoli has four stages of growth: (1) rapid growth of leaves; (2) formation of the head (which is the part you eat); (3) a resting period while the embryonic blossoms are being formed; and (4) development of the stalk, flowers and seeds. The head formation stage is essential for the production of the vegetable but not at all necessary for the survival of the plant. Broccoli held in check by severe frost, lack of moisture, or too much heat will go directly to seed without bothering to form a head.

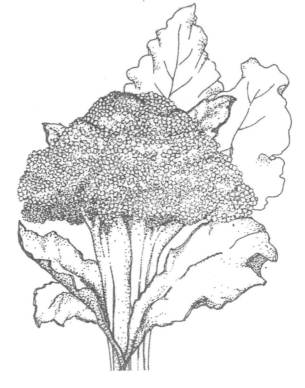

As with other cabbage family crops, you can grow broccoli in a container on the patio or indoors—a single broccoli plant in a flower pot might make a novel house plant. You can also grow broccoli as an accent in a flowerbed.

GROWING

Broccoli is frost-hardy. It's a cool season crop and does best with day temperatures under 77°F (25°C) and night temperatures of 59°F (15°C). Weather too cold or too warm will cause the plants to bolt without forming a head. It is not a suitable crop for very hot climates. Sow— S.T.- summer. T&C- summer–early autumn.

HOW TO PLANT

Broccoli likes fertile, well-drained soil with a pH within the 6.5 to 7.5 range—this discourages disease and lets the plant make the most of the nutrients in the soil.

When preparing the soil for planting, work in a complete, well-balanced fertilizer at the rate of 1lb per 95sq feet (450g per 9sq m). If you have sandy soil or your area is subject to heavy rains, supplement the nitrogen to the soil. Use about 1lb (450g) nitrogen fertilizer for a 10-foot (3m) row.

Plant out seedlings that are four to six weeks old with four or five true leaves. If they are leggy or have crooked stems, plant them deeply (up to the first leaves) so they won't grow to be top-heavy. Plant the seedlings 18–24 inches (45–60cm) apart, in rows 24 inches (60cm) apart. Plan for only a few heads at a time, or plant seeds and seedlings at the same time for succession crops—you'll get the same result by planting early and midseason varieties at the same time. Set seeds ½ inch (1.5cm) deep and 3 inches (7.5cm) apart, and thin them when they're big enough to lift by the true leaves. You can transplant the thinned seedlings.

FERTILIZING AND WATERING

Fertilize before planting and again at midseason, at the same rate as the rest of the garden.

Broccoli needs abundant soil moisture and cool moist air for the best growth. Cut down on watering as the heads approach maturity.

PESTS

The cabbage family's traditional enemies are cutworms and caterpillars. However, cutworms, cabbage loopers and cabbage worms can all be controlled by spraying with bacillus thuringiensis, an organic product sold as Dipel.

DISEASES

Such cabbage family vegetables as broccoli are susceptible to fungal, bacterial and virus diseases, especially clubroot and downy mildew. Planting resistant varieties, rotating crops from year to year and maintaining the general health of your garden will cut down on the incidence of disease. Remove infected plants before disease spreads.

HARVESTING

Broccoli grown from seed will take 3½–4 months to mature. Harvesting can continue over a relatively long period. Cut the central head with 5–6 inches (12–15cm) of stem, when the head is well developed and before it begins to loosen and separate—if the small yellow flowers have started to show, it's past the good-eating stage. Leave the base of the plant and some outer leaves to encourage new growth. In many varieties small clusters will grow in the angles of the leaves and can be harvested later.

VARIETIES

Green Valiant, Liberty, Waltham 29, DeCicco, Calabrese, Premium Crop, Packman, Arcadia, Emporer, Goliath, Marathon, Green Duke Hybrid*, Skiff*.
*Good in colder areas.

STORING AND PRESERVING

Broccoli can be stored, refrigerated, for up to one week, or in a cold, moist place for two to three weeks.

Freezing
1. Choose compact, dark green heads. Stalks should be tender, not woody.
2. Wash well, then soak heads of broccoli in 1 cup salt per gallon of water for ½ hour to get rid of bugs. Rinse in fresh water; drain.
3. Cut stalks to fit into containers. Split stalks so that heads are about 1 inch (2.5-3cm) in diameter.
4. Blanch 3 minutes. Cool; drain well.
5. Pack into containers. Seal, label and freeze.
6. Cook frozen broccoli 5 to 8 minutes.

SERVING SUGGESTIONS

The good taste of broccoli has always been appreciated. Pliny the Elder wrote in the second century that it was much in favor with the Romans. Serve broccoli with a cheese or Hollandaise sauce, au gratin, or in casseroles. It's also delicious raw, broken into flowerets and used in a salad or with a dipping sauce; the small flowerets are decorative on a platter of raw vegetables. If you have stalks left over after using the head for salads, parboil them and then sauté them in oil with a little onion and garlic. To make sure the stems cook adequately without overcooking the tender tops, cook broccoli like asparagus—upright in a tall pot so that the stems boil and the tops steam.

Brussels Sprouts

Common names: Brussels sprouts, sprouts

Botanic name: *Brassica oleracea gemmifera*

Origin: Europe, Mediterranean

Miniature cabbage-like heads, 2 inches (5cm) or so in diameter, sprout from a tall, heavy main stem, nestled in among large green leaves. Brussels sprouts belong to the cabbage family and are similar to cabbage in their growing habits and requirements. They're hardy, grow well in fertile soils, and are easy to grow in the home garden if you follow correct pest control procedures.

Brussels sprouts have four stages of growth: (1) rapid growth of leaves; (2) formation of the heads (which is the part you eat); (3) a resting period while the embryonic blossoms are being formed; and (4) development of the stalk, flowers and seeds. The head formation stage is essential for the production of the vegetable, but not at all necessary for the survival of the plant. Brussels sprouts held in check by severe frost, lack of moisture, or too much heat will bolt, which means that they'll go directly to seed without bothering to form a head at all.

GROWING

Brussels sprouts are frost-hardy—in fact, they're the most cold-tolerant of the cabbage family. They do best in a cool growing season with day temperatures around 77°F (25°C) and night temperatures around 50°F (10°C). Weather too cold for too long or too warm will make them taste bitter; if the sprouts develop in hot weather, they may not form compact heads, but will remain loose tufts of leaves. Brussels sprouts are not a suitable crop for very hot climates. S.T.- not suitable. T- mid-summer and early autumn. C- early–mid-summer.

HOW TO PLANT

Brussels sprouts like fertile, well-drained soil with a pH within the 6.5 to 7.5 range—this discourages disease and lets the plant make the most of the nutrients in the soil.

When preparing the soil for planting, work in a complete, well-balanced fertilizer at the rate of 1lb per 95sq feet (450g per 9sq m). If you have sandy soil or your area is subject to heavy rains, you'll probably need to supplement the nitrogen content of the soil. Use about 1lb (450g) of nitrogen fertilizer for a 10-foot (3m) row.

Plant out seedlings that are four to six weeks old, with four to five true leaves. If they are leggy or have crooked stems, plant them deeply (up to the first leaves) so they won't grow to be top-heavy.

Seedlings should be planted out 18 inches (45cm) apart in rows 24 inches (60cm) apart when they are about 3 inches (7.5cm) tall. Sow seeds ½ inch (1cm) deep, 3 inches (7.5cm) apart in rows 24–35 inches (60–90cm) apart and transplant to the recommended distance when large enough.

FERTILIZING AND WATERING

Fertilize before planting and again at midseason, at the same rate as the rest of the garden.

Brussels sprouts need abundant soil moisture and cool moist air for the best growth. Cut down on watering as they approach maturity.

SPECIAL HANDLING

If you live in an area with cold winters, pick off the top terminal bud when the plant is 12–20 inches (30–50cm) tall. This encourages all of the sprouts to mature at once. Some gardeners believe that Brussels sprouts develop better if the lower leaves are removed from the sides of the stalk as the sprouts develop. A few more leaves can be removed each week, but the top leaves should be left intact.

PESTS

The cabbage family's traditional enemies are cutworms and caterpillars. Aphids are particularly troublesome. Cutworms, cabbage loopers and cabbage worms can all be controlled by spraying with bacillus thuringiensis, an organic product known as Dipel. It's especially important to control insects on Brussels sprouts; if they insinuate themselves into the tightly curled sprouts, you'll have a lot of trouble dislodging them.

DISEASES

Cabbage family vegetables are subject to fungal, bacterial and virus diseases, particularly clubroot, or downy mildew. Lessen the incidence of disease by planting disease-resistant varieties, maintaining the general health of your garden and avoiding handling the plants when they're wet. If a plant does become infected, remove and destroy it so it cannot spread disease to healthy plants.

They are subject to attack by the caterpillars of the cabbage moth and cabbage butterfly and by aphids. Dust with Carbaryl dust or spray with Malathion.

HARVESTING

Time from planting to harvest is 3½–4 months. The sprouts mature from the bottom of the stem upwards, so start from the bottom and remove the leaves and sprouts as the season progresses. Harvesting can continue until all the sprouts are gone. The leaves can be cooked like collards or cabbage.

VARIETIES

Long Island Improved, Jade Cross, Rearguard, Top Score Hybrid, Prince Marvel Hybrid, Rubine Red, Lunet Hybrid, Oliver, Valiant, Fieldstar Number 1.

STORING AND PRESERVING

If you have sprouts still on the stem in early winter, remove all the leaves from the plant, and hang it in a cool dry place; it will give you a late harvest. The plant can be kept up to one month in a cold, moist place. Sprouts can keep for about a week in the refrigerator. Remove loose or discolored outer leaves before you store them, but don't wash them until you're ready to use them. You can also freeze or dry sprouts.

Freezing

1. Choose firm, compact, dark green heads.
2. Wash thoroughly, then soak in salt water as for broccoli. Rinse in fresh water; drain. Sort by size.
3. Blanch small sprouts 3 minutes; medium sprouts 4 minutes; large sprouts 5 minutes. Cool; drain well.
4. Tray freeze or pack into containers. Seal, label and freeze.
5. Cook frozen sprouts 4 to 9 minutes.

Drying

1. Choose perfect, evenly sized sprouts. Remove any discolored leaves.
2. Wash sprouts well; drain. Slice lengthwise, ½ inch (1cm) thick.
3. Blanch 4½ to 5 minutes in boiling water or 6 to 7 minutes in steam. Drain very well, chill and pat dry with paper towels.
4. Arrange slices in a single, even layer on racks.
5. Dry until brittle, 4 to 12 hours.
6. Put the dried vegetables into a deep container, cover lightly with cheesecloth and condition, stirring once a day for a week to 10 days.
7. Pack into vapor/moistureproof, airtight containers or double plastic bags and store in a cool, dark, dry place for up to 12 months.
8. Rehydrate in 3 cups of boiling water for each cup of Brussels sprouts, about 1 hour.

SERVING SUGGESTIONS

Sprouts are traditionally served with turkey at Christmas dinner. They're also good lightly steamed and served with a lemon-butter sauce. Don't overcook them; young sprouts should be slightly crunchy, and light cooking preserves their delicate flavor. Older sprouts have a stronger taste. Brussels sprouts can also be french fried, baked, or pureed. When you trim them for cooking, cut an X in each stem so that the sprouts cook evenly; be careful not to trim the stem ends too closely or the outer leaves will fall off when you cook them. A walnut in the pot when you cook Brussels sprouts should cut down on the cabbagey smell.

Cabbage

Common name: cabbage

Botanic name: *Brassica oleracea capitata*

Origin: South Europe

Cabbage, a hardy biennial grown as an annual, has an enlarged terminal bud made of crowded and expanded overlapping leaves shaped into a head. The leaves area smooth or crinkled in shades of green or purple, and the head can be round, flat or pointed. The stem is short and stubby, although it may grow to 20 inches (50cm) if the plant is left to go to seed.

Cabbage is a hardy vegetable that grows well in fertile soils, and it's easy to grow in the home garden if you choose suitable varieties and follow correct pest control procedures. Like other members of the cabbage family (broccoli and kale are among them), cabbage is a cool-weather crop that can tolerate frost but not heat.

Cabbages have four stages of growth: (1) rapid growth of leaves (2) formation of the head (which is the part you eat); (3) a resting period while the embryonic blossoms are being formed; and (4) development of the stalk, flowers

and seeds. The head formation stage is essential for the production of the vegetable, but not at all necessary for the survival of the plant. Cabbages held in check by severe frost, lack of moisture, or too much heat will bolt, which means that they will go directly to seed without forming a head. And even if the cabbage does make a head, if the weather gets too hot once it reaches that stage, the head can split.

Cabbages are decorative in the flower garden; purple cabbages and savoys look good in a mixed border. Flowering cabbages look like enormous variegated blossoms. In small spaces, grow cabbages as an accent in each corner of a flowerbed or as a border. Decorative cabbages can be grown in containers on the patio or even indoors. Try growing a single cabbage in a 8-inch (20cm) flowerpot; choose a flowering cabbage or a small early variety.

PLANTING

Cabbages are frost-hardy. They do best in a cool growing season with day temperatures around 77°F (25°C) and night ones of 59°F (15°C). If the plants are cold for too long a period or if the weather is warm, they will bolt without forming a head. If the head has already formed, it will split in hot weather—splitting happens when the plant takes up water so fast that the excess cannot escape

through the tightly overlapped leaves and the head bursts. The cabbage is not a suitable crop for very hot climates. Time planting so that you harvest cabbage during cool weather. If your area has cold winters, plant for summer to early autumn harvest. In mild climates, plant for late spring or autumn harvest. S.T.- autumn and winter. T&C- summer, autumn and spring.

HOW TO PLANT

Cabbages like fertile, well-drained soil with a pH within the 6.5 to 7.5 range—this discourages disease and lets the plant make the most of the nutrients in the soil. When you're preparing the soil for planting, work in a complete, well-balanced fertilizer at the rate of 1lb per 95sq feet (450g per 9sq m). If you have sandy soil or your area is subject to heavy rains, you'll probably need to supplement the nitrogen content of the soil. Use about 1lb (450g) of nitrogen fertilizer for a 10-foot (3m) row. Cabbages are sown in seedbeds and the seedlings are transplanted to their growing position when they are four to six weeks old with four or five true leaves. If the transplants are leggy or have crooked stems, plant them deeply (up to the first leaves) so they won't grow to be top-heavy. Plant the seedlings 24 inches (60cm) apart in rows 30 inches (75cm) apart. Plan for only a few heads at a time, or plant seeds and seedlings at the same time for succession crops; you'll get the same result by planting early and midseason varieties at the same time. If you're planting seeds, set them ½ inch (1cm) deep and space them 3 inches (7.5cm) apart. Thin them to 24 inches (60cm) apart when they're big enough to lift by the true leaves and transplant the thinned seedlings.

FERTILIZING AND WATERING

Fertilize before planting and again at midseason, at the same rate as the rest of the garden.

Cabbages need abundant soil moisture and cool air for best growth. Cut down the watering as the heads approach maturity to prevent splitting.

PESTS

The cabbage family's traditional enemies are cutworms and caterpillars. Cutworms, cabbage loopers and cabbage worms can all be controlled by spraying with bacillus thuringiensis, an organic product also known as Dipel.

Dust with Carbaryl dust or spray with Malathion every two weeks.

DISEASES

Virus, clubroot fungus and black rot may attack cabbage. Cut down on the incidence of disease by planting disease-resistant varieties, maintaining the general health of your garden and avoiding handling the plants when they're wet. If a plant does become infected, remove and destroy it so it cannot spread disease to healthy plants.

To prevent clubroot lime ground with 1lb (500g) to 10 feet square (1 square meter) 10 to 12 months before planting cabbage.

To protect mildew dust the seed with Thiram—1 teaspoonful to 1 pound (0.5kg). Spray young plants with Zineb or Maneb.

HARVESTING

Cabbages mature in 4–5 months. A 10-foot (3m) row should give you five to eight heads. Start harvesting when the head is firm. To harvest, cut off the head, leaving the outer leaves on the stem. Often a few small heads will grow on the stalk, and you can harvest them later.

VARIETIES

Early—Green Cup Hybrid, Early Jersey Wakefield, First Early Improved, Head Start, Golden Acre, Market Victor Hybrid, Regal Red, Salarite, Stonehead, Sugarloaf, Supercite, Savoy King (warmer areas); Middle—Savoy Chieftain, Gourmet, Market Prize Hybrid, Ruby Ball, Red Acre, Ruby Perfection Hybrid, Red Head Hybrid, Savoy Ace Hybrid, Savoy King Hybrid, Lennox, Morris (67D); Late—Danish Ballhead, Huron Hybrid, Michihli, Rio Verde, Ruby Perfection, Savoy King.

STORING AND PRESERVING

Cabbage stores well in the refrigerator for one to two weeks, and can be kept for three to four months in a cold, moist place. Cabbage can also be dried, and freezes fairly well; it can be bottled as sauerkraut. Cabbage seeds can also be sprouted.

Freezing

Frozen cabbage can only be used as a cooked vegetable, not in slaw.
1. Choose fresh, solid heads with crisp leaves.
2. Trim the coarse outer leaves.
3. Cut medium-coarse shreds, thin wedges, or separate into leaves.
4. Blanch 1 to 1½ minutes for shreds; 3 minutes for wedges or leaves. Cool; drain well.
5. Pack into containers, leaving ⅛ inch (0.5cm) head space. Seal, label and freeze.
6. Cook frozen cabbage about 5 minutes, or thaw leaves to use for stuffed cabbage or cabbage rolls.

Drying

1. Choose firm, compact heads with unblemished leaves.
2. Wash, remove the outer leaves, then quarter and core the cabbage. Cut cabbage into slices ⅛ inch (½cm) thick or less.
3. Blanch 2 minutes in water; 2½ to 3 minutes in steam, until leaves are wilted. Drain very well, chill and pat dry with paper towels.
4. Arrange in a single, even layer on baking sheets or racks.
5. Dry until brittle, 1 to 12 hours.
6. Put the dried vegetables into a deep container, cover lightly with cheesecloth and condition, stirring once a day for a week to 10 days.
7. Pack into vapor/moistureproof, airtight containers or double plastic bags and store in a cool, dark, dry place for up to 12 months.
8. Rehydrate in 3 cups of boiling water for each cup of cabbage, about 1 hour.

SERVING SUGGESTIONS

Steamed or boiled cabbage is an excellent dish—the secret is to cut it into small pieces before you cook it so that it cooks fast and evenly. Or try braising it in a heavy-bottomed pan with butter and just a little water; toss a few caraway seeds over it before serving. Sweet and sour red cabbage is an interesting dish. Stuffed cabbage leaves are delicious, and cabbage makes a good addition to soup—the leaves add an additional texture to a hearty, rib-sticking winter soup. The Irish traditionally serve cabbage with corned beef, and a British combination of cooked cabbage and mashed potatoes sautéed together is known as "bubble-and-squeak." French country cooks stuff a whole cabbage with sausage, then simmer it with vegetables—a version known as chou farci. One way or another, there's a lot more to cabbage than coleslaw.

Cardoon

Common name: cardoon

Botanic name: *Cynara cardunculus*

Origin: Europe

Cardoon is a tender perennial grown as an annual for its young leafstalks, which are blanched and eaten like celery. It looks like a cross between burdock and celery but is actually a member of the artichoke family and has the same deeply cut leaves and heavy, bristled flower head. Cardoon can grow to 5 feet (1½m) tall and 3 feet (1m) wide, so it will need plenty of space in your garden.

GROWING

Not commonly grown here. Needs warmth and shelter. Sow indoors in spring and transplant when soil has warmed up. Cardoon prefers full sun but can tolerate partial shade and grows quickly in any well-drained fertile soil.

When preparing the soil, dig in a complete, well-balanced fertilizer at the rate of 1lb per 95sq feet (450g per 9sq m). Space the young plants 14–16 inches (30–45cm) apart, with 3–5 feet (1–1.5m) between the rows.

FERTILIZING AND WATERING

Fertilize before planting and again at midseason, at the same rate as the rest of the garden.

Allow the plants to dry out between waterings.

SPECIAL HANDLING

Cardoon is usually blanched to improve the flavor and to make it more tender—the stalks can be very tough. Blanch when the plant is about 3 feet (1m) tall, four to six week before harvesting. Tie the leaves together in a bunch and wrap water-resistant paper around the stems, or hill up the soil around the stem.

PESTS

Aphids may be a problem. Pinch out infested foliage or hose the aphids off the cardoon plants. Control aphids chemically with Malathion or Diazinon.

DISEASES

Cardoon has no serious disease problems.

HARVESTING

Harvest the plants four to six weeks after blanching. Cut them off at ground level and trim off the outer leaves.

VARIETIES

Verde de Peralta, Tafalla.

STORING AND PRESERVING

Keep stalks on root, wrap and refrigerate; they will keep for one to two weeks. The plants can be kept for two to three months in a cold, moist place. Cardoon freezes fairly well and can be bottled or dried; handle it like celery.

SERVING SUGGESTIONS

Cut the stalks into sections and parboil them until tender—the time will depend on the size of the stalks. Serve cardoon stalks cut into pieces and chilled with an oil and vinegar dressing, or hot with a cream sauce. Dip chunks into batter and deep-fry them. The Italians are fond of cardoon.

Carrot

Common name: carrot

Botanic name: *Daucus carota*

Origin: Europe, Asia

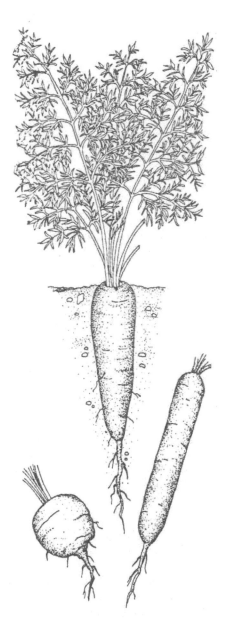

Carrots are hardy biennials grown as annuals. They have a rosette of finely divided fernlike leaves growing from a swollen, fleshy taproot. The root, which varies in size and shape, is generally a tapered cylinder that grows up to 10 inches (25cm) long in different shades of orange. They are cool-weather crops that tolerate the cold and are easy to grow. The carrots we grow today originated in the Mediterranean. By the 13th century the Europeans were well aware of the carrot's food value.

There are all sorts of carrots— long, short, fat, thin—but basically they differ only in size and shape. However, the sort of soil you have will influence which variety you choose. The shorter varieties will better tolerate heavy soil; the long types are more particular about their environment. Finger carrots can be satisfactorily grown in containers.

PLANTING

Carrots are a cool-weather crop and fairly adaptable. Although tolerant of cold, the seeds take a long time to germinate, and when they're

planted in cold, raw weather they
may give up before they come up.
Plant them in spring and early
summer for a continuous crop
making sowings every 2–3 weeks.
S.T.- spring to autumn. T- spring
to early autumn. C- Early spring
to late summer.

HOW TO PLANT

Carrots need a cool bed. They
prefer full sun but will tolerate
partial shade. Before planting,
work half a cup of low-nitrogen
(5-10-10) fertilizer into the soil,
and turn the soil thoroughly to a
depth of about 10 inches (25cm).
This initial preparation is vital for
a healthy crop; soil lumps, rocks or
other obstructions in the soil will
cause the roots to split, fork, or
become deformed.

Sow the seeds in rows 14–16
inches (30–45cm) apart. Wide-row
planting of carrots gives a good
yield from a small area. When
planting in early spring, cover
the seeds with ½ inch (1–2cm) of
soil. Later, when the soil is drier
and warmer, they can be planted
a little deeper. When the seedlings
are growing well, thin to ½ inch
(1–2cm) apart.

FERTILIZING AND WATERING

Fertilize before planting and again
at midseason, at the same rate as
the rest of the garden.

Carrots need well-worked soil, free of rocks and lumps that can cause the roots to fork or split.

To keep carrots growing
quickly, give them plenty of water.
As they approach maturity, water
less—too much moisture at this
stage will cause the roots to crack.

SPECIAL HANDLING

In areas with high soil temperatures, mulch to regulate the soil
temperature; otherwise, the roots
will grow short and pale. Carrot
seedlings grow slowly while
they're young, and it's important
to control weeds especially during
the first few weeks. Shallow cultivation is necessary to avoid
damaging the roots.

PESTS AND DISEASES

Aphids spread a virus disease—
leaves yellow and wilt and roots

stunt. Spray with Malathion. Carrot weevil. Spray with Malathion during warm weather. Root nematodes give yellowing of leaves and swellings in the roots. Destroy all diseased plants. Fumigate the ground.

HARVESTING

Time from planting to harvest is 4–4½ months, depending on the variety. Small finger carrots are usually ready to harvest in 2 months. When you think they're ready, pull a few samples to check on their size. If they're ½–1 inch (2cm) thick or more (for regular varieties), they're ready to harvest. Pull them up by hand, or use a spading fork to lift them gently out of the ground. Pull carrots when the soil is moist—if you try to pull them from hard ground, you'll break the roots.

VARIETIES

Danvers Half-Long, Avenger, Dominater, Nantes, Premium, Royal Chantenay, Pioneer Hybrid, A-Plus, Rumba, Kinko, Healthmaster, Gold Pak, Orlando Gold, Kundulus, Oxheart, Little Finger, Lady Finger, Short 'n' Sweet.

STORING AND PRESERVING

Carrots are most obliging vegetables when it comes to preservation—most methods can be used. They'll store for one to three weeks in plastic bags or aluminum foil in the refrigerator, or for four to five months in a cold, moist place. They can also be bottled, frozen or dried.

Freezing
1. Choose tender, small to medium, mild-flavored carrots.

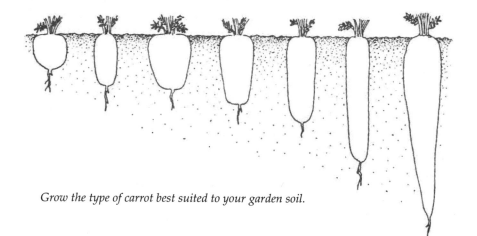

Grow the type of carrot best suited to your garden soil.

2. Remove tops, wash well and peel or scrape.

3. Cut in cubes, slices or lengthwise strips, or leave small carrots whole.

4. Blanch small whole carrots 5 minutes; blanch diced or sliced carrots and lengthwise strips 2 minutes. Cool; drain well.

5. Tray freeze or pack into containers, leaving ⅛ inch (0.5cm) head space. Seal, label and freeze.

6. Cook frozen carrots 5 to 10 minutes.

Drying

1. Choose crisp, young, tender carrots.

2. Wash well, scrape and cut off tops and ends.

3. Slice very thin, crosswise or lengthwise. Or shred and put shreds into a cheesecloth bag.

4. Blanch in boiling water or steam about 3½ minutes. If using carrot shreds, blanch about 1½ to 2 minutes. Drain well, chill and pat dry with paper towels.

5. Arrange the slices in a single, even layer on baking sheets or racks.

6. Dry until very tough and leathery, 4 to 12 hours. If using carrot shreds, dry until shreds are brittle.

7. Put the dried vegetables into a deep container, cover lightly with cheesecloth and condition, stirring once a day for a week to 10 days.

8. Pack into vapor/moistureproof, airtight containers or double plastic bags and store in a cool, dark, dry place for up to 12 months.

9. Rehydrate in 2 cups of boiling water for each cup of carrots, about 1 hour.

SERVING SUGGESTIONS

Carrots fresh from the garden are wonderful raw. Shredded raw carrots are delicious with a touch of oil and lemon; or add raisins and fresh pineapple for an exotic flavor. Add shredded carrots to a peanut butter sandwich. Try carrot cake with a cream cheese frosting. There are any number of ways to cook carrots; perhaps the best treatment for very young fresh carrots is to boil them and toss with a respectful touch of butter. You can also try them boiled, then rolled in breadcrumbs and deep-fried, or served with a marmalade glaze. Most herbs complement the taste of carrots; parsley is the most common, but try cooked carrots and peas with a touch of mint to enhance the flavor.

Cauliflower

Common name: cauliflower

Botanic name: *Brassica oleracea botrytis*

Origin: Europe, Mediterranean

Cauliflower is a single-stalked, half-hardy, biennial member of the cabbage family. It's grown as an annual, and the edible flower buds form a solid head (sometimes called a curd) which may be white, purple or green. Cauliflower and broccoli are easy to tell apart until you meet a white-flowered broccoli or a green cauliflower. Both also come in purple. Cauliflowers are prima donnas and need a lot of attention. Mark Twain described a cauliflower as a cabbage with a college education.

Cauliflower has four stages of growth: (1) rapid growth of leaves; (2) formation of the head (which is the part you eat); (3) a resting period while the embryonic blossoms are formed; and (4) development of the stalk, flowers and seeds. The head formation stage is essential for the production of the vegetable, but not at all necessary for the survival of the plant. Cauliflower held in check by severe frost, lack of moisture or too much heat will bolt, which means that it will go directly to seed without forming a head.

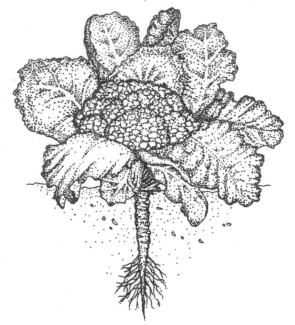

PLANTING

Cauliflower is more restricted by climatic conditions than other family vegetables like cabbage or broccoli. It's less adaptable to extremes of temperature; it doesn't like cold weather, won't head properly if it's too hot and doesn't tolerate dry conditions as well as broccoli.

Cauliflower needs two cool months in which to mature and is planted for spring and autumn crops in most areas. Plant for a winter crop if your winters are mild. S.T.- autumn. T- summer and autumn. C- late spring to early autumn.

Sow in seedbeds or boxes and transplant into permanent position later.

HOW TO PLANT

Cauliflower likes fertile, well-drained soil with a pH within the 6.5 to 7.5 range—this discourages disease and lets the plant make the most of the nutrients in the soil. When you're preparing the soil for planting, work in a complete, well-balanced fertilizer at the rate of 1lb per 95sq feet (450g per 9sq m). If you have sandy soil or your area is subject to heavy rains, you will probably need to supplement the nitrogen content of the soil. Use about 1lb (450g) of high-nitrogen fertilizer for a 10-foot (3m) row. Transplant seedlings when four to six weeks old, with four or five true leaves. If they are leggy or have crooked stems, plant them deeply (up to the first leaves) so they won't grow to be top-heavy.

Plant the seedlings 30 inches (75cm) apart in rows 30 inches (75cm) apart. Plan for only a few heads at a time, or plant seeds and seedlings at the same time for succession crops; you'll get the same result by planting early and midseason varieties at the same time. Set seeds ⅓ inch (1cm) deep and space them 3 inches (7.5cm) apart. Thin them when they're big enough to lift by the true leaves, and transplant the thinned seedlings.

FERTILIZING AND WATERING

Fertilize before planting and again at midseason, at the same rate as the rest of the garden.

Abundant soil moisture and cool moist air are needed for the best growth; do not let the ground dry out. The plants must be kept growing vigorously; if growth is interrupted by heat, cold, damage, or lack of water, the head will not form properly.

SPECIAL HANDLING

Cultivate cauliflower regularly to diminish weed competition and prevent a crust from forming on the soil's surface. Take care not to damage the roots.

The objective with cauliflower is to achieve a perfect head, with all the flowerets pressed tightly together. Unless it's supposed to be green or purple, the color should be untinged creamy-white, and too much sun or rain can damage the head. To prevent this, blanch (whiten) it. Blanch the cauliflower when it gets to be about the size of an egg, by gathering three or four leaves and tying them together over the head. If you secure the leaves with colored rubber bands you can keep track of cauliflowers tied at different times. Check the heads occasionally for pests that may be hiding inside. The self-blanching cauliflower doesn't need to be tied, but it will not blanch in hot weather.

Blanching cauliflower is a cosmetic procedure; the flavor is not significantly improved, as is celery's, by blanching.

PESTS

The cabbage family's traditional enemies are cutworms and caterpillars, and cauliflower is particularly susceptible to them. However, cutworms, cabbage loopers and cabbage worms can all be controlled by spraying with bacillus thuringiensis, an organic product known as Dipel.

DISEASES

Cauliflower may be susceptible to root rots; the first indication of this disease is yellowing of the leaves. Cut down on the incidence of disease by planting disease-resistant varieties, maintaining the general health of your garden and avoiding handling the plants when they're wet. If a plant does become infected, remove and destroy it so it cannot spread disease to healthy plants.

HARVESTING

Time from planting to harvest is 4–5 months. Under good growing conditions the head develops rapidly to about 6–8 inches (15–20cm) in diameter. The mature head should be compact, firm, and white. Cut the whole head from the main stem. The leaves can be cooked like cabbage.

VARIETIES

Snowball, Snow King, Super Snowball, Self-blanche, Purple Head, Snow Crown, White Sails, Alert, Amazing, Violet Queen.

STORING AND PRESERVING

Unwashed and wrapped in plastic, cauliflower can be stored for up to one week in the refrigerator, or for two to three weeks in a cold, moist place. Cauliflower freezes satisfactorily and can also be dried or used in relishes or pickled.

Freezing

1. Choose compact, white, tender heads.
2. Break into flowerets about 1 inch (2.5cm) in diameter.
3. Wash well, then soak in salt water as for broccoli. Rinse with fresh water; drain.
4. Blanch 3 minutes. Cool; drain well.
5. Tray freeze or pack into containers. Seal, label and freeze.
6. Cook frozen cauliflower 5 to 8 minutes.

Drying

1. Choose perfect, firm heads. Break into small flowerets.
2. Blanch in boiling water or in steam about 4 to 5 minutes, or until just tender. Drain well, chill and pat dry with paper towels.
3. Cut into slices, if you wish.
4. Arrange slices or flowerets in a single, even layer on baking sheets or racks.
5. Dry until crisp, 4 to 12 hours.
6. Put the dried vegetables into a deep container, cover lightly with cheesecloth and condition, stirring once a day for a week to 10 days.
7. Pack into vapor/moistureproof, airtight containers or double plastic bags and store in a cool, dark, dry place for up to 12 months.
8. Rehydrate in 3 cups of boiling water for each cup of flowerets, about 1 hour.

SERVING SUGGESTIONS

Boil the whole cauliflower head until the base yields to the touch of a fork. Add lemon juice to the boiling water to preserve the curd's whiteness. Coat the head with a light cheese sauce or simply with melted butter and parsley. Tartar sauce is an original accompaniment to cauliflower, or sprinkle it with browned breadcrumbs for a crunchy texture. The flowerets can be separated and french fried. Raw cauliflower lends a distinctive flavor to salads and is good served with other raw vegetables with a mustard- or curry-flavored dip. Cauliflower pickles are good, too.

Celeriac

Common names: celeriac, turnip-rooted celery, celery root, knob celery

Botanic name: *Apium graveolens rapaceum*

Origin: Europe and Africa

Celeriac is a form of celery, a member of the same family, and similar in growing habits and requirements. Its physical characteristics and culinary uses, however, are quite different. The edible root of celeriac is large and swollen, like a turnip, and develops at soil-level; a rosette of dark green leaves sprouts from the root. The stems are hollow.

PLANTING

Celeriac does best in cool weather and especially enjoys cool nights. The seeds are very slow to germinate. Sow the seeds ½ in. (1cm) deep in rows 2½ feet (0.75m) apart, and when the seedlings are large enough to handle, thin them to 5–6 inches (12–15cm apart).

HOW TO PLANT

Celeriac tolerates light shade and prefers rich soil high in organic matter, well able to hold moisture but with good drainage. It needs constant moisture and does well in wet locations. It's a heavy feeder and needs plenty of fertilizer to keep it growing quickly. When preparing the soil for planting, work in a complete, well-balanced fertilizer at the rate of 1lb per 95sq feet (450g per 9sq m).

Sow seeds indoors two to four months before your estimated

planting date—from September to January. Cover the seeds very lightly and then lay a material like sacking over the containers to keep the moisture in. Transplant carefully. To give the seedlings a good start, plant them in a trench ½–4 inches (1–10cm) deep. Space the seedlings 8–10 inches (20–25cm) apart in rows 24 inches (60cm) apart.

FERTILIZING AND WATERING

Fertilize before planting and again at midseason, at the same rate as the rest of the garden.

Frequent watering is important; celeriac, like celery, is shallow-rooted and a lack of soil moisture can stop its growth. Keep the top inch (few centimeters) of soil moist at all times.

SPECIAL HANDLING

Celeriac cannot compete with weeds. Cultivate conscientiously, but be careful not to disturb the shallow roots. As the tuber develops, snip off the side roots and hill up the soil over the swollen area for a short time to blanch the tubers. The outer surface will be whitened, but the interior will remain a brownish color.

PESTS AND DISEASES

Celeriac is subject to the same pests and diseases as celery.

HARVESTING

Time from planting to harvest is 3–4 months from seed. A 10-foot (3m) row should give you 16 to 20 roots. Pick off the lower leaves—you can use them to flavor soups and stews. Harvest celeriac when the swollen root is 3–4 inches (7–10cm) wide. In warmer climates, harvest the roots when they're about the size of a tennis ball. Celeriac increases in flavor after the first frost, but should be harvested soon after.

VARIETIES

Brilliant, Giant Prague, Monarch.

STORING AND PRESERVING

You can dry the leaves to use as an herb in soups and stews. Keep the roots in the refrigerator up to one week, or store them in a cold, moist place for two to three months. They will keep in the ground in areas where freezing weather is not a problem. You can also freeze the roots; handle them like turnips.

SERVING SUGGESTIONS

Peel, dice and cook celeriac roots; then marinate them in vinegar and oil, seasoned to your taste. Or shred the raw roots, dress them with a light vinaigrette, and add them to a salad. Celeriac makes an interesting addition to any luncheon.

Celery

Common name: celery

Botanic name: *Apium graveolens dulce*

Origin: Europe

Celery is a hardy biennial grown as an annual. It has a tight rosette of 8–10 inches (20–25cm) stalks, topped with many divided leaves. The flowers look like coarse Queen Anne's lace and are carried on tall stalks. Celery is a more popular vegetable in this country than its cousin celeriac (which it doesn't resemble at all in looks or taste). Both are members of the parsley family, to which dill and fennel also belong, and probably originated in Mediterranean countries. Celery had been used earlier for medicinal purposes, but the French were probably the first to use it as a vegetable somewhere around 1600. It's a versatile vegetable—you can eat the stalks, leaves and seeds—but it needs a lot of attention, and it's not an easy crop for the home gardener.

PLANTING

Celery does best in cool weather and especially enjoys cool nights. Cold weather will inhibit growth. Celery seeds are very slow to germinate, so it's usually more satisfactory to transplant seedlings. S.T.- spring and summer. T&C- spring to mid-summer.

HOW TO PLANT

Celery tolerates light shade and prefers rich soil high in organic matter, well able to hold moisture but with good drainage; it does well in wet, almost boggy locations. It's a heavy feeder and needs plenty of fertilizer for continuous quick growth. When preparing the soil for planting, work in a complete, well-balanced fertilizer at the rate of 1lb per 95sq feet (450g per 9sq m). Sow seeds for transplanting two to four months before your estimated planting date—they germinate slowly. Cover the seeds very lightly and then lay a material like sacking over the containers to keep the moisture in. Transplant seedlings into trenches 3–4 inches (7–10cm) deep and 24 inches (60cm) apart. Space the seedlings 8–10 inches (20–25cm) apart, and as they grow mound the soil up around them to blanch the stems. Having the plants fairly close together will also help blanching.

FERTILIZING AND WATERING

Fertilize before planting and again at midseason, at the same rate as the rest of the garden.

Make sure that the plants get plenty of water at all stages of growth. Celery is a moisture-loving plant, and lack of water may slow growth and encourage the plant to send up flower stalks—it will also get very stringy.

SPECIAL HANDLING

Celery does not like competition from weeds during the slow early growth stage, so cultivate regularly, taking care to avoid damage to the roots close to the soil surface. Unlike cauliflower, which is not much affected in flavor by blanching or whitening, celery will be bitter if it isn't blanched. Blanching is achieved by covering the plants to protect them from the sun, which encourages them to produce chlorophyll and turn green. This should be started 10 days to two weeks before harvesting.

There are a number of blanching methods to choose from, but none of them should be left on more than 10 days to two weeks or the celery stalks will become pithy and rot. Soil can be mounded around each side of the celery row and built up to the tops of the stalks. Or use boards tilted to shade the celery plants. Heavy paper—freezer paper or layers of newspaper—can also be used; wrap it around each plant and fasten with a rubber band. You can also place milk cartons with the top and bottom cut out over the plant, or gather the stalks together and fit cylinder-shaped tiles over the tops of the plants.

PESTS

Use Carbaryl dust or Malathion against aphids.

DISEASES

Septoria, Leaf-spot. Spray with Benlate. Magnesium and calcium in the soil discourage these conditions, and with adequate fertilizing you shouldn't have a problem. If you do, check the mineral content of your soil.

HARVESTING

Time from planting to harvest is about 5 months. A 10-foot (3m) row should yield about 20 heads of celery. Start harvesting before hard frost, when the head is about 3–4 inches (5–7.5cm) in diameter at the base. Cut off the head at or slightly below soil level.

VARIETIES

Golden Self-blanching, Summer Pascal, Utah 52-70, Florida 683, Giant Pascal, Alabaster, Giant Prague.

STORING AND PRESERVING

You can refrigerate celery for up to two weeks; or if you cut the leaves to use as herbs, you can keep the leaves in the refrigerator up to one week. Celery can be dried or bottled and it freezes fairly well; or you can store it for two to three months in a cold, moist place.

Freezing
Use frozen celery in cooked dishes only.
1. Choose crisp, tender stalks without coarse strings.
2. Wash well, trim and cut into 1-inch (2.5cm) lengths.
3. Blanch 3 minutes. Cool; drain well.
4. Tray freeze or pack into containers.
5. Cook frozen celery with other vegetables in soups, stews or casseroles.

Drying
1. Choose young, tender stalks with tender, green leaves.

2. Wash the stalks and leaves well; shake dry. Trim the ends.

3. Slice the stalks thinly.

4. Blanch in boiling water or in steam about 2 minutes. Drain well, chill and pat dry with paper towels.

5. Spread the slices in a single, even layer on baking sheets or racks. Spread leaves in a single, even layer.

6. Dry until brittle, 3 to 12 hours.

7. Put the dried vegetables into a deep container, cover lightly with cheesecloth and condition, stirring once a day for a week to 10 days.

8. Pack into vapor/moistureproof, airtight containers or double plastic bags and store in a cool, dark, dry place for up to 12 months.

9. Rehydrate in 2 cups boiling water for each cup of celery, about 1 hour.

SERVING SUGGESTIONS

Celery is versatile. You can eat the stems, the leaves and the seeds. The stems can be boiled, braised, fried, or baked; most people are more accustomed to celery as a raw salad vegetable or relish, but celery is great creamed or baked au gratin. And what could be more elegant than cream of celery soup? The leafy celery tops that most people throw out can be made into a refreshing drink. Boil and strain them, chill the liquid, and drink it by itself or combined with other vegetable juices.

Chard

See Swiss Chard

Chayote

Common names: choko, alligator pear, one-seeded cucumber

Botanic name: *Sechium edule*

Origin: Central America

The chayote is a tender perennial vine that grows from a tuber and can climb to 33 feet (10m). It's a member of the gourd family, and it has hairy leaves the size and shape of maple leaves; male and female flowers are borne on the same vine. The fruit looks like a greenish or whitish flattened pear. You can eat the young shoots, the fruit, and, if the plant lives long enough, the tubers.

PLANTING

The chayote prefers warm to hot temperatures and cannot survive temperatures below freezing. In areas where the season is short, a chayote can be grown in a pot

inside and then set out in the soil or kept in a pot and brought back inside when the weather turns cold. S.T.- spring. T&C- late spring

HOW TO PLANT

You plant the whole fruit with the fat side placed at an angle halfway down in the soil so that the stem area is level with the soil surface. Before planting, work a complete, well-balanced fertilizer into the soil at the rate of 1lb per 95sq feet (450g per 9sq m). The chayote likes well-drained soil with a high content of organic matter and will tolerate partial shade. Space the plants about 1½ inches (3–3.5cm) apart. You don't need to provide a support for the vine unless you want to save space. It will happily run wild. The vine is usually enough for the average family.

FERTILIZING AND WATERING

Fertilize before planting and again at midseason, at the same rate as the rest of the garden.

Give the chayote plants plenty of water to keep them growing strongly.

PESTS

Aphids may visit your chayote vines. Handpick or hose them off, or control them chemically by spraying with Malathion or Diazinon.

DISEASES

Chayotes have no serious disease problems.

HARVESTING

Time from planting to harvest is about 5 months. Cut while the fruit is young and tender; don't wait until the flesh gets hard. Cut old vines down in winter, leaving 2–4 shoots for next year.

VARIETIES

Green or cream fleshed. No named varieties. You can use the vegetable bought from a shop.

STORING AND PRESERVING

Chayotes will keep in the refrigerator up to one week. Freeze extra ones either diced or stuffed like squash.

SERVING SUGGESTIONS

Chayotes can be prepared any way you prepare squash and are best eaten young and tender. If it over-ripens, scoop out the flesh, remove the seed (a large seed, in what looks like a terry cloth bag), mash the flesh with cheese or meat, re-stuff the empty shell and bake. The tubers of very mature plants are edible and filling, but not very flavorsome.

Chick Pea

Common names: chick pea, gram, garbanzo

Botanic name: *Cicer arietinum*

Origin: Southern Europe and India

Chick peas or garbanzos are regarded as beans, but their botanic place is somewhere between the bean and the pea. They're tender annuals and grow on a bushy plant, rather like green beans but they have a longer growing season. Chick peas have puffy little pods that contain one or two seeds each. In some areas they're grown as a field crop as a food for horses, but they're good food for people too.

PLANTING

Chick peas are tender plants and can't tolerate much cold—a hard frost will damage the immature beans. You can grow them anywhere that has 90 to 100 frost-free days. Sow chick peas from seed in spring.

HOW TO PLANT

Choose a bed in full sunlight; chick peas tolerate partial shade, but partial shade tends to mean a partial yield. Prepare the soil by mixing in 1lb (450g) of 5-10-10 fertilizer—don't use a high-

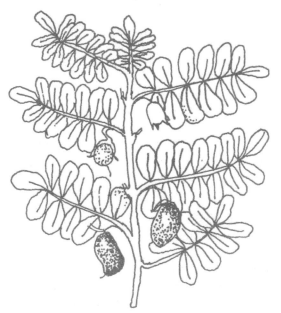

nitrogen fertilizer, because too much nitrogen will promote growth of foliage but not of the pods. Work the fertilizer into the soil at the rate of 1lb per 95sq feet (450g per 9sq m). The seeds may crack and germinate poorly when the moisture content of the soil is too high. Don't soak the seeds before planting and don't overwater immediately afterwards. Plant seeds 1 inch (2.5cm) deep and 2 inches (5cm) apart in rows at least 18–24 inches (45–60cm) apart. When the seedlings are growing well, thin the plants to 4–6 inches (10–15cm) apart. Cut the seedlings with scissors at ground level; be careful not to disturb the others. They don't mind being a little crowded; in fact, they'll use each other for support.

FERTILIZING AND WATERING

Chick peas set up a mutual exchange with soil microorganisms called nitrogen-fixing bacteria, which help them produce their own fertilizer. Some gardeners recommend that if you haven't grown beans in the plot the previous season, you should treat the seeds before planting with a nitrogen-fixing bacteria inoculant to help them convert organic nitrogen compounds into usable organic compounds. This is a perfectly acceptable practice but it isn't really necessary; the bacteria in the soil will multiply quickly enough once they've got a growing plant to work with.

Fertilize before planting and again at midseason, at the same rate as the rest of the garden.

Keep the soil moist until the chick peas have pushed through the ground. Water regularly if there's no rain, but remember that water on the flowers can cause the flowers and small pods to fall off. When the soil temperature reaches 59°F (15°C) you can mulch to conserve moisture.

SPECIAL HANDLING

Don't bother the plants when they're wet or covered with heavy dew; handling or brushing against them when they're wet spreads fungus spores. Cultivate thoroughly but with care, so that you don't disturb the shallow root systems.

PESTS

Chick peas may be attacked by aphids, bean beetles, leafhoppers and mites. Aphids, leafhoppers and mites can be controlled chemically by spraying with Malathion or Diazinon. Bean beetles can be controlled chemically by spraying with Carbaryl. Chick peas are almost always attacked by large numbers of pests that cannot be controlled by organic methods. This doesn't mean the organic gardener can't grow them, but yields may be lower if only organic controls are used.

DISEASES

Chick peas are susceptible to blight, mosaic and anthracnose. You can cut down on the incidence of disease by planting disease-resistant varieties, maintaining the general health of your garden, and avoiding handling the plants when they're wet. If a plant does become infected, remove and destroy it so it cannot spread disease to healthy plants.

HARVESTING

If you want to eat them raw, pick chick peas in the green shell or immature stage. For drying, harvest the chick peas when the plants have matured and the leaves have turned completely brown. At this time the seeds should be dry and hard—bite a couple of seeds; if you can hardly dent them they're properly dry and ready to harvest.

VARIETIES

Amit, Sierra.

STORING AND PRESERVING

Unshelled chick peas can be kept up to one week in the refrigerator. You can freeze, bottle or dry the shelled chick peas, and they can also be sprouted. Dried shelled chick peas can be stored in a cool, dry place for 10 to 12 months.

Freezing

1. Choose pods of young, tender chick peas.
2. Wash, shell and wash again.
3. Blanch chick peas 2 to 3 minutes. Cool, drain well.
4. Tray freeze or pack into containers. Seal, label and freeze.
5. Cook frozen chick peas for 10 to 15 minutes.

Drying

1. Choose fresh, just-mature chick peas.
2. Shell the peas; then wash and drain.
3. Blanch in boiling water about 15 minutes. Drain well, chill and pat dry with paper towels.
4. Arrange the peas in a single, even layer on baking sheets or racks.
5. Dry until brittle, 4 to 12 hours.
6. Put the dried vegetables into a deep container, cover lightly with cheesecloth and condition, stirring once a day for a week to 10 days.
7. Pack into vapor/moistureproof, airtight containers or double plastic bags and store in a cool, dark, dry place for up to 12 months.
8. Rehydrate in 2½ cups of boiling water for each cup of peas, about 1½ hours.

SERVING SUGGESTIONS

Shelled chick peas can be steamed or boiled like peas, or roasted like peanuts. Vegetarian cooks often use chick peas with grains as a protein-rich meat substitute. In the Middle East they're pureed with garlic, lemon juice, and spices.

Chicory

Common names: chicory, witloof, French endive, Belgian endive, succory

Botanic name: *Cichorium intybus*

Origin: Asia, Europe

Chicory is a hardy perennial with a long, fleshy taproot and a flower stalk that rises from a rosette of leaves. It looks much like a dandelion except that the flowers grow on a branched stalk and are pale blue.

Chicory is grown either for its root, which can be roasted to produce a coffee substitute, or for its tender leaf shoots. This plant is not to be confused with endive, which is grown as a salad green. Both chicory and endive belong to the same family, and the names are often used interchangeably, but they aren't the same plant. If you want to produce the chicory root or the Belgian endive, you grow chicory (*Cichorium intybus*). If you're growing specifically for greens, you grow endive (*Cichorium endivia*).

Chicory has two stages of development. The first produces the harvestable root. In the second stage, you harvest the root and bury it upright in damp sand or soil until it produces sprouts or heads of pale, blanched leaves; these heads are the Belgian endives. Once you've harvested the heads, you can still use the roots, although they won't be as satisfactory as roots grown specifically for their own sake.

PLANTING

Chicory tolerates cold. Since the second stage that produces the heads takes place after harvesting, climate is not an issue. Sow chicory seeds in the garden in early spring.

HOW TO PLANT

Chicory tolerates partial shade. The soil should be well drained, high in organic matter, and free of lumps that might cause the roots to fork or split. Work a complete, well-balanced fertilizer into the soil before planting, at the rate of 1lb per 95sq feet (450g per 9sq m). Sow the seeds 1 inch (2.5cm) deep in rows 24–35 inches (60–90cm) apart, and thin them to 12–18 inches (30–45cm) apart when the seedlings are 4 inches (10cm) tall. You can eat the thinnings.

FERTILIZING AND WATERING

Fertilize before planting and again at midseason, at the same rate as the rest of the garden. Keep the plants evenly moist.

SPECIAL HANDLING

If chicory is planted in well-cultivated soil rich in organic matter, it should develop large roots. If you grow the plants for the roots alone, they'll be ready to harvest about 120 days after planting. If you want to produce the blanched heads, follow this procedure. Before the ground freezes, dig up the chicory roots and cut off the tops about 2 inches (5cm) above the crown or top of the root. Store the roots in a cool, humid place. In winter and spring, bury the roots to "force" them and produce the blanched sprouts—for a continuous supply, repeat the procedure every few weeks.

To prepare the roots for forcing, cut off the tips so that the roots are 6–8 inches (15–20cm) long, and pack them upright in a box, pot or other container filled with fine sand or a mixture of sand and peatmoss. Cover the tops of the roots with about 8 inches (20cm) of sand or sawdust, water thoroughly and keep at a temperature of 59–68°F (15–20°C). Put them in a cold frame or trench in the garden. You may need to water occasionally during the three or four weeks the heads take to develop. When the heads break the surface, remove the potting material and cut the heads with a knife where they meet the root.

PESTS

Chicory has no serious pest problems. It's a good crop for the organic gardener who doesn't mind doing the extra work that chicory requires in its second stage of growth.

DISEASES

Chicory has no serious disease problems.

HARVESTING

It takes more than 100 days to produce a mature chicory root. For the traditional blanched endive, you'll have to wait three or four weeks after starting the forcing procedure. You should be able to get 30 to 50 blanched heads from a 10-foot (3m) row of chicory plants.

VARIETIES

Frisée (curly Endive), Escarole (also called Batavian), Pan di Zucchero (Italian for "Sugarloaf," a very mild chicory with a huge, swirling head of green), Chioggia Radicchio (most common type of radicchio, with baseball-sized red and white heads), Treviso Radicchio (romaine-shaped heads of red and white), Castelfranco Radicchio (baseball-sized heads of red and green), Puntarelle, Dentarelle.

STORING AND PRESERVING

Refrigerate the cut heads until you're ready to serve them, up to one week. You can keep the entire plant—root and all—for two to three months in a cold, moist place, or you can dig up the roots and store them for 10 to 12 months.

SERVING SUGGESTIONS

The roots of chicory are sometimes roasted and ground to add to coffee or used as a coffee substitute. Wash and dice the root, then dry it and roast it before grinding. Blanched endive heads are good braised or in salads. Mix endive with peppers, artichoke hearts and sardines for an Italian-style salad, or with olives, cucumbers, anchovies and tomato wedges in the Greek manner.

Chinese Cabbage

Common names: Bok Choy, Wong Bok, Kim Chee, celery cabbage, Pakchoy, Michihli, Napa cabbage, Pe-tsai

Botanic name: *Brassica chinensis*

Origin: China

Chinese cabbage is a hardy biennial grown as an annual and is not a member of the cabbage family. It has broad, thick, tender leaves; heavy midribs; and can be either loosely or tightly headed and grow 14–18 inches (35–45cm) tall. The variety with a large compact heart is called celery cabbage, pakchoy, or Michihli. In Chinese, call it pe-tsai; in Japanese, say hakusai. Despite the name, the appearance and taste of Chinese cabbage are closer to lettuce than to regular cabbage.

PLANTING

Chinese cabbage can be grown only in cold weather, because it bolts (goes to seed) quickly in hot weather and long days—it bolts much faster than the cabbage family vegetables. It can be started inside and transplanted outside in the spring, but Chinese cabbage shocks easily, and transplanting sometimes shocks it into going to seed.

HOW TO PLANT

Chinese cabbage is difficult to grow in the home garden unless you can give it a long, cool growing season. Plant seedlings in mid-late summer in warm areas and in spring in cool districts. Chinese cabbage will tolerate partial shade. The soil should be well worked and well fertilized, high in organic matter and able to hold moisture. When preparing the soil for planting, work in a complete, well-balanced fertilizer at the rate of 1lb per 95sq feet (450g per 9sq m). Sow seeds in rows 18–39 inches (45–100cm) apart, and when the seedlings are large enough to handle, thin them to stand 8–12 inches (20–30cm) apart. Don't even attempt to transplant Chinese cabbage unless you've started the seeds in peat pots or other plantable containers.

FERTILIZING AND WATERING

Fertilize before planting and again at midseason, at the same rate as the rest of the garden.

Water frequently to help the young plants grow fast and become tender. They'll probably go to seed if their growth slows down.

PESTS

Aphids and cabbage worms make Chinese cabbage difficult to grow without spraying. Aphids can be partially controlled without chemicals by handpicking or hosing, and cabbage worms can be controlled by spraying with bacillus thuringiensis, which is an organic product sold as Dipel. Carbaryl will control cabbage loopers.

DISEASES

Purple blotch, clubroot and black rot may attack Chinese cabbage. Cut down on the incidence of disease by planting disease-resistant varieties, maintaining the general health of your garden, and avoiding handling the plants when they're wet. If a plant does become infected, remove and destroy it so it cannot spread disease to healthy plants.

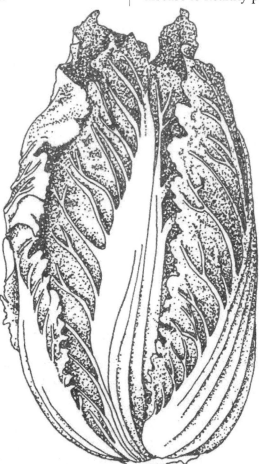

HARVESTING

Time from planting to harvest is 1½–2½ months and a 10-foot (3m) row should give you 10 or more heads. Harvest when the heads are compact and firm and before the seed stalks form. With an autumn crop, harvest before frost. To harvest, cut off the whole plant at ground level.

STORING AND PRESERVING

Chinese cabbage stays fresh in the refrigerator up to one week, or in a cold, moist place for two to three months. You can also freeze or dry it and the seeds of Chinese cabbage can be sprouted.

Freezing

Use frozen Chinese cabbage in cooked dishes only.
1. Choose fresh, solid heads with crisp leaves.
2. Trim coarse or shriveled leaves.
3. Cut into medium-coarse shreds, thin slices, or separate into leaves.
4. Blanch 1 to 1½ minutes for shreds; 3 minutes for slices or leaves. Cool; drain well.
5. Pack into containers, leaving ⅛ inch (0.5cm) head space. Seal, label and freeze.
6. Cook frozen Chinese cabbage about 5 minutes, or thaw leaves to stuff.

Drying

1. Choose very fresh, perfect leaves.
2. Wash the leaves well; shake dry.

Remove any large, tough stalks.
3. Blanch in boiling water about 1½ minutes; or in steam about 2½ minutes, until completely wilted. Drain very well, chill and pat dry with paper towels.
4. Arrange leaves in a single layer on baking sheets or racks.
5. Dry until brittle, 2½ to 8 hours or more.
6. Put the dried vegetables into a deep container, cover lightly with cheesecloth and condition, stirring once a day for a week to 10 days.
7. Pack into vapor/moistureproof, airtight containers or double plastic bags and store in a cool, dark, dry place for up to 12 months.
8. Rehydrate in 1 cup of boiling water for each cup of chinese cabbage, about ½ hour.

SERVING SUGGESTIONS

Chinese cabbage has a very delicate, mild flavor, more reminiscent of lettuce than of cabbage. It makes an interesting slaw, with a sour cream dressing and a little chopped pineapple. Or serve it in wedges like cabbage. Of course, the ideal use is in Chinese stir-fry dishes and soups. Try shredding the Chinese cabbage with a bit of carrot, flavoring it with ginger and soy sauce, and dropping it in spoonfuls into oil in the wok. It's crunchy and delicious. You can also butter-steam Chinese cabbage as an accompaniment to roast pork, or use the leaves to make cabbage rolls.

Collard

Common name: collard

Botanic name: *Brassica oleracea acephalo*

Origin: Europe

A hardy biennial grown as an annual, the collard grows 3–6 feet (1–1.75m) tall and has tufts or rosettes of leaves growing on sturdy stems. Collard is a kind of kale, a primitive member of the cabbage family that does not form a head. The name collard is also given to young cabbage plants that are harvested before they have headed. Collards were England's main winter vegetable for centuries.

PLANTING

Like other members of the cabbage family, collards are hardy and can tolerate low 23°F (-5°C) temperatures. They can take more heat than cabbage and more cold than cauliflower.

HOW TO PLANT

Collards like fertile, well-drained soil with a pH within the 6.5 to 7.5 range—this discourages disease and lets the plant make the most of the nutrients in the soil. Sow seeds direct in spring and in late summer in mild weather areas. Thin to 12

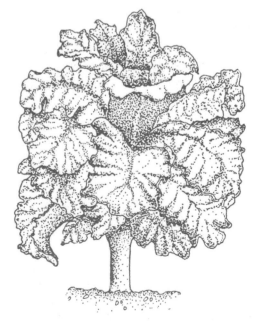

inches (30cm) apart with 16 inches (40cm) between the rows. Seedlings can be raised in boxes or seedbeds and easily transplanted.

When preparing the soil for planting, work in a complete, well-balanced fertilizer at the rate of 1lb per 95sq feet (450g per 9sq m). If you have sandy soil or your area is subject to heavy rains, you'll probably need to supplement the nitrogen content of the soil. Use about 1lb (450g) of nitrogen fertilizer for a 10-foot (3m) row.

Set seeds 1 inch (2.5cm) deep and space them 3 inches (7.5cm) apart. Thin them when they're big enough to lift by the true leaves. You can transplant the thinned seedlings. If planting seedlings they should be four to six weeks old with four or five true leaves. If the transplants are leggy or have crooked stems, plant them deeply (up to the first leaves) so that they won't grow to be top heavy. Plant the seedlings 12 inches (30cm) apart in rows 16 inches (40cm) apart.

FERTILIZING AND WATERING

Fertilize before planting and again at midseason, at the same rate as the rest of the garden.

Water them regularly to keep the leaves from getting tough.

SPECIAL HANDLING

If collard plants get too heavy you may need to stake them.

PESTS

The cabbage family's traditional enemies are cutworms and caterpillars. Cutworms, cabbage loopers and cabbage worms can all be controlled by spraying with bacillus thuringiensis, an organic product also known as Dipel. Generally, collards have fewer pest problems than other cabbage crops. They are one of the best and most prolific crops for the organic gardener.

DISEASES

Some diseases include Clubroot, Black rot, Black leg, and Alternaria.

HARVESTING

Time from planting to harvest is approximately 2½–3 months from seedlings and 3–3½ months from seed. A 10-foot (3m) row should yield 8lbs (3.5kg) or more of collard greens. Collards become sweeter if harvested after a frost, but you should harvest them before a hard freeze. In warmer areas, harvest the leaves from the bottom up before they get old and tough.

VARIETY

Blue Max, Georgia, Vates, Champion, Hicrop.

STORING AND PRESERVING

Collards can be stored in the refrigerator up to one week, or in a cold, moist place for two to three weeks. Collards can be frozen, bottled or dried; use the recipes for greens.

Freezing

1. Choose young, tender leaves.
2. Wash well in several changes of water.
3. Remove tough stems or bruised leaves.
4. Blanch each pound (450g) of greens in 2½ gallons (9 liters) boiling water for 2 minutes; collard greens, 3 minutes. Stir to keep greens from sticking together. Cool, drain well.
5. Pack into containers, leaving ⅛ in. (0.5cm) head space. Seal, label and freeze.
6. Cook frozen greens 8 to 15 minutes.

Drying

1. Choose very fresh, perfect leaves.
2. Wash leaves well; shake dry. Remove any large, tough stalks.
3. Blanch in boiling water about 1½ minutes; or in steam about 2½ minutes, until completely wilted. Drain very well, chill and pat dry with paper towels.
4. Arrange leaves in a single layer on baking sheets or racks.
5. Dry until brittle, 2½ to 8 hours or more.
6. Put the dried vegetables into a deep container, cover lightly with cheesecloth and condition, stirring once a day for a week to 10 days.
7. Pack into vapor/moistureproof, airtight containers or double plastic bags and store in a cool, dark, dry place for up to 12 months.
8. Rehydrate in 1 cup of boiling water for each cup of greens, about ½ hour.

SERVING SUGGESTIONS

Collards can be steamed or boiled; serve them alone or combine them with ham or salt pork. Corn bread is a nice accompaniment.

Corn

Common names: corn, sweet corn

Botanic name: *Zea mays*

Origin: Central America

Corn, a tender annual that can grow up to 17 feet (5m) tall, is a member of the grass family. It produces one to two ears on a stalk, of which only one may be harvestable. The pollen from the tassels must fall into the cornsilk to produce kernels, and if pollination does not occur, all that will grow is the cob. The kernels of sweet corn can be yellow, white, black, red or a combination of colors. With rice, wheat and potatoes, corn is one of the top four crops in the world. It is not the easiest crop to grow in the home vegetable garden, and it doesn't give much return for the space it occupies. Don't be taken in by all that lush foliage—you will generally get only one harvestable ear of corn from a stalk, although some dwarf varieties will produce two or three.

PLANTING

The time it will take to reach maturity depends on the amount of heat it gets; corn doesn't really get into its stride until the weather warms up. You may get two crops, depending on which variety you plant.

HOW TO PLANT

Corn likes well-worked, fertile soil with good drainage, and it must have full sun. Fertilize the soil before planting, using 5 oz. (150g) of a complete, well-balanced fertilizer on each side of a 30-foot (9m) row. Place the fertilizer 1 inches (2.5cm) below and 2 inches (5cm) away from where you plan to put the seed.

Sow seed direct at end of March, April and May in rows 35 inches (90cm) apart and plants 12–14 inches (30–35cm) apart. Make two sowings during each month with a late sowing at the beginning of June. Sow corn when the soil temperature reaches 59°F (15°C)—usually end of March. Sow the seeds 2–4 inches (5–10cm) apart, in rows (short rows in a block, rather than one long row) or inverted hills. Planting in clumps or blocks ensures pollination. For a continuous supply, plant a dozen seeds of the same variety every two weeks (or when the previous planting shows three leaves), or plant early, midseason and late varieties at the same time. When the corn is about 6 inches (15cm) tall, thin short varieties to 24 inches (60cm) apart, tall varieties to 35 inches (90cm) apart. Corn can be grown closer together than this, but the roots are more crowded and more watering and feeding are needed.

FERTILIZING AND WATERING

Corn is a heavy user of nitrogen. Fertilize in spring, again when the corn is 8 inches (20cm) tall and again when it's 18 inches (45cm) tall. Sidedress between the rows, using 4 ounces (115g) of complete, well-balanced fertilizer on each side of a 10-foot (3m) row.

Watering is very important. Keep the soil evenly moist. Corn often grows so fast in hot weather that the leaves wilt because the roots can't keep the leaves supplied with moisture. Although corn requires so much water, rain or water on the tassels at the time of pollination can reduce the number of kernels on a cob—and sometimes can destroy the whole crop. When watering corn, avoid getting water on the tassels.

SPECIAL HANDLING

Keep competition down. Weed early and keep the weeds cut back, but remember that corn has very shallow roots; a vigorous attack on the weeds may destroy the corn. Be sure to thin the crop—crowding stimulates lots of silage, but no cobs. Protect the ears with paper bags after pollination if you have trouble with birds.

PESTS

Corn is attacked by many pests—notably corn earworms, corn

borers, and Seedcorn maggots—and they usually attack in numbers too large to control by physical methods. Be prepared to use the appropriate insecticide at the first signs of insect damage. The corn earworm deposits its eggs on the developing silks of the corn, and the small caterpillars follow the silks down into the ears, where they feed on the tips. Once they get inside the ear there is no effective control, so watch out for them and spray with Carbaryl before the earworms get inside the protective cover of the ear. Corn borers damage stalks, ears and tassels. They tunnel into the plant and can cause such severe damage that the stalks fall over. Watch for them, and spray with Carbaryl every five days, starting when the first eggs hatch. To prevent Seedcorn maggots, avoid heavy manure or organic matter in garden, which attract adults and encourage egg laying. Do not overwater. Use insecticide-treated seed. Wear gloves when planting.

Rodents love corn and know exactly when to harvest it—usually the day before you plan to. Removing the offenders' homes and fencing in the garden are about the only ways to deter them. Because it takes up so much room and has so many pest problems, corn is not the ideal choice for either the organic gardener or the novice gardener. But for the experienced gardener with lots of room and a good spray tank, there's

Protect corn from birds by tying paper pags over the ears.

nothing like the taste of fresh, homegrown sweet corn.

DISEASES

Corn smut and Rust are the two main disease problems. Corn smut is a fungus disease that attacks the kernels—which turn gray or black and become four times larger than normal. Destroy the affected plants, and plant your corn in a new part of the garden next time. Smut spores can survive in the soil for two years. To prevent Rust, avoid wetting foliage if possible. Water in the morning so aboveground plant parts will dry as quickly as possible. Avoid crowding plants, space allows more air circulation.

HARVESTING

From planting to harvest takes approximately 2½–3 months depending on the variety and, to some extent, the weather. Your harvest won't be generous— maybe five to eight ears from a 10-foot (3m) row. Harvest your corn when the kernels are soft and plump and the juice is milky. Have the water boiling when you go out to harvest and rush the corn from the stalk to the pot, then to the table. The goal is to cook the corn before the sugar in the kernels changes to starch. A delay of even 24 hours between harvesting and eating will cause both flavor and texture to deteriorate noticeably.

VARIETIES

Improved Golden Bantam, Mandan Bride, Reid's Yellow Dent, Polar Vee, Earlivee, Early Sunglow, Butter and Sugar, Seneca Chief, Merit, Silver Queen, Iochief, Kandy Korn, White Lightning, Miracle, Early Xtra-sweet, How Sweet It Is, Illini Xtra Sweet, Golden Midget, Golden Jubilee, Northern Xtra-sweet, Ornamental Indian Corn, Calico, Strawberry, Japanese Hulless, White Cloud.

STORING AND PRESERVING

If you must keep corn before eating, wrap the whole thing, ear and husk, in damp paper towels; store in the refrigerator for four to eight days. Corn can be sprouted and it also freezes, bottles and dries satisfactorily.

Freezing
Whole Kernel:
1. Choose well-developed ears with plump, tender kernels and thin, sweet milk. Press a kernel with a thumbnail to check the milk. Corn must be fresh to freeze.
2. Husk, remove the silk and trim the ends. Sort by size.
3. Blanch small ears (1½ in. [3.5cm] or less in diameter) 1 minute; medium ears (2 inches/5cm in diameter) 8 minutes; large ears (more than 2 inches/5cm in diameter) 10 minutes. Cool; drain well.
4. Cut kernels from the cob at ⅔ the depth of the kernel.
5. Tray freeze or pack in containers, leaving ⅛ inch (0.5cm) head space. Seal, label and freeze.
6. Cook frozen corn 3 to 4 minutes.
Cream-style:
1. Prepare as for whole-kernel corn, but cut the kernels from cob at ½ the depth of the kernel. Then scrape the cob with the back of a knife to remove the milk and heart of the kernel.
2. Pack with liquid in containers as for whole-kernel coin. Seal, label and freeze.

3. Cook as for whole-kernel corn.
Precooked:
1. Choose, husk and sort corn. Don't blanch.
2. Cut corn from cob as for cream-style corn.
3. Heat corn with about ¼ cup water for each 2 cups (½ liter) of corn over low heat, stirring frequently, just until thick.
4. Pour hot corn into another pan, and set pan into ice water to cool. Stir frequently to hurry cooling.
5. Pack in containers, leaving ⅛ inch (0.5cm) head space.
6. Seal, label and freeze.
7. Cook just until heated to serving temperature. Note: Don't cook more than a gallon of corn at one time.
Corn-on-the-Cob:
1. Choose corn and prepare as for whole kernel corn.
2. Blanch small ears (1½ inch/ 3.5cm or less in diameter) 6 minutes; medium ears (2 inches/ 5cm in diameter) 8 minutes; large ears (more than 2 inches/5cm) 10 minutes. Cool thoroughly; drain well.
3. Pack in containers or wrap ears individually or in family-size amounts in freezer paper, plastic wrap or foil, then in plastic freezer bags. Seal, label and freeze.
4. Thaw frozen corn-on-the-cob before cooking, then cook about 4 minutes.

Drying
1. Choose young, tender ears of very fresh corn.

2. Husk the ears, remove the silk and then wash the corn.
3. Blanch in boiling water about 1½ minutes; or in steam about 2 to 2½ minutes, or until milk doesn't come out of the cut kernels. Drain, chill and pat dry with paper towels.
4. Cut the kernels from ears and spread them in a single, even layer on baking sheets or racks.
5. Dry until very brittle, 2 to 10 hours. Tap a single kernel with a hammer; if done, it will shatter easily.
6. Put the dried vegetables into a deep container, cover lightly with cheesecloth and condition, stirring once a day for a week to 10 days.
7. Pack into vapor/moistureproof, airtight containers or double plastic bags and store in a cool, dark, dry place for up to 12 months.
8. Rehydrate in 2¼ cups boiling water for each cup of corn, about ½ hour.

SERVING SUGGESTIONS

After you've given your home-grown corn all that care and attention—to say nothing of a good deal of your garden space—you can do more with it than steaming it and anointing it with a dab of butter. You can roast it in the husks in a hot oven or on the barbecue grill or make a delicate corn soup or a delicious and different soufflé.

Cress (Mustard)

Common names: cress, garden cress, peppergrass

Botanic name: *Lepidium sativum*

Origin: Asia

Cress is a hardy annual with finely divided tiny green leaves that have a biting flavor. You can grow cress from seed indoors or out—it will even sprout on water-soaked cotton. It takes only 15 to 20 days from planting to harvest, which means more or less instant gratification for the least patient gardener. Children love to grow it.

Cress has a peppery flavor that gives a lift to salads. There are several kinds available, but the Triple Curled variety is the most common.

Other types of cress are upland or winter cress (*Barbarea vernapraecox*) and watercress (*Nasturtium officinale*). Upland or winter cress is a hardy biennial from Europe. You can sow it in the garden in early spring and harvest soon after midsummer. The plants are tough and will survive a cold winter if you mulch them.

Watercress is a trailing perennial of European origin with dark green peppery leaves and is usually grown in water. It's easily grown from seed but is usually propagated in temperate climates from stem-pieces, which root easily in wet soil. If you're fortunate enough to have a stream running through your garden, you can try growing watercress on the bank. You can also grow it indoors in pots set in a tray of water. Watercress adds a kick to salads and makes a pretty garnish. It's full of vitamin C and minerals.

PLANTING

Garden cress, which is the one you're most likely to grow, is started from seeds sown every two weeks starting early in spring and continuing through the year.

Mustard is grown in the same way as cress and the two can usually be sown together.

HOW TO PLANT

When sown outdoors, cress likes well-drained soil with good drainage. It will flourish in shade or semi-shade and can tolerate a wide range of temperatures. When preparing the soil, dig in a complete, well-balanced fertilizer at the rate of 1lb per 95sq feet (450g per 9sq m). Sow the seeds thickly, ⅕ inch (0.5cm) deep in wide rows, 18–24 inches (45–60cm) apart, and for a continuous crop repeat the planting every 10 to 14 days.

FERTILIZING AND WATERING

Fertilize before planting and at midseason, at the same rate as the rest of the garden.

Cress needs even moisture. Try not to wet the leaves more than necessary since the soil that lodges on wet leaves is impossible to wash out without damage. Cress grown indoors must have good drainage or it tends to rot.

PESTS

Watercress can be attacked by a small fly which rises in clouds when disturbed. Dust with Carbaryl dust. Watercress may also become victim to flea beetles. To avoid this, use row covers to help protect plants from early damage. Put in place at planting and remove when temperatures get too hot. Control weeds.

HARVESTING

Often the plants are eaten at their very early seed-leaf stage. Cut off the cress with scissors and enjoy in salads or sandwiches.

VARIETIES

Watercress, upland cress, curly cress, land cress.

STORING AND PRESERVING

Cress does not store well, but it can be kept in the refrigerator up to one week. The seeds can be sprouted.

SERVING SUGGESTIONS

The English nibble "small salads" of cress and mix the young sprouts with mustard for dainty cress sandwiches. Use it in salads or for a garnish. The peppery taste is a good foil to more bland salad greens. Watercress, with thin bread and butter, is as much an English delicacy as cucumber sandwiches.

Cucumber

Common name: cucumber

Botanic name: *Cucumis sativus*

Origin: Asia

Cucumbers are weak-stemmed, tender annuals that can sprawl on the ground or be trained to climb. Both the large leaves and the stems are covered with short hairs; the flowers are yellow. Some plants have both male and female flowers on the same vine, and there may be 10 males to every female flower, but only the female flowers can produce cucumbers. The expression "cool as a cucumber" has long been used to describe a person who is always calm in a crisis, and cucumbers do seem to give off a cool feeling. They're tender plants, however, and not at all tolerant to cold themselves.

Gulliver, in the report of his voyage to Brobdingnag, told of a project for extracting sunbeams from cucumbers, sealing them in jars, and letting them out to warm the air on raw days. Long before Gulliver, the Emperor Tiberius was so fond of cucumbers that the first greenhouses—sheets of mica in window sashes—were developed to keep the plants growing happily indoors when it was too cold to take them outside. You can

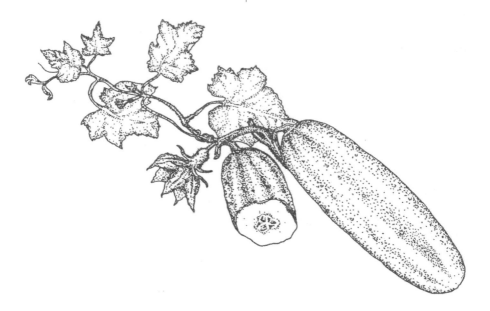

grow cucumbers in a large pot or hanging basket, or train them up a fence or over a trellis.

PLANTING

The cucumber is a warm-weather vegetable and very sensitive to frost. It has a very short growing season—and most areas can provide it with sufficient sunshine. Cucumbers like night temperatures of 59–64°F (15–18°C) and day temperatures up to 90°F (32°C). Plant them when the soil has warmed up in mid-spring to early summer.

HOW TO PLANT

Cucumbers will tolerate partial shade, and respond to a rich, well-worked, well-drained soil high in organic matter. When preparing the soil, dig in a complete, well-balanced fertilizer at the rate of 1lb per 95sq feet (450g per 9sq m). Plant cucumbers in inverted hills, by removing an inch (a few centimeters) of soil from a circle 12 inches (30cm) across and use this soil to make a rim around the circle. This protects the young plants from heavy rains that might wash away the soil and leave their shallow roots exposed. Plant six or eight seeds in each hill, and when the seedlings are growing strongly, thin them, leaving the three hardiest plants standing 6–12 inches (15–30cm) apart. Cut the thinned seedlings off with scissors

at soil level to avoid disturbing the roots of the remaining plants.

FERTILIZING AND WATERING

Fertilize before planting and again at midseason, at the same rate as the rest of the garden.

Cucumbers are 95 percent water and need plenty of water to keep them growing fast. Don't let the soil dry out. In hot weather the leaves may wilt during the day, even when soil moisture is high, because the plant is using water faster than its roots can supply. This is normal; just be sure that the plant is receiving regular and sufficient water. Mulch to avoid soil compaction caused by heavy watering.

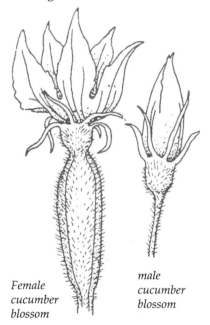

Female cucumber blossom

male cucumber blossom

In a small garden, save space by growing cucumbers on a fence.

SPECIAL HANDLING

Cultivate to keep weeds down. If you are growing cucumbers inside, or in an area where there are no insects to pollinate the female flower, you may need to help with pollination. Take a soft-bristled brush and dust the inside of a male flower (the one without an immature fruit on the stem), then carefully dust the inside of the female flowers. Harvest promptly; mature cucumbers left on the vine suppress the production of more flowers.

PESTS

Aphids and cucumber beetles are the pests you're most likely to encounter. To control aphids, pinch out infested vegetation or hose them off the vines, or spray with Malathion or Diazinon. Cucumber beetles may not do much feeding damage, but they carry cucumber bacterial wilt. Handpick them off the vines promptly, or spray them with Carbaryl. Also be aware of the squash vine borer. Remove borers by hand and destroy. Be sure to destroy crop residues after harvest. Cucumbers are so prolific that the organic gardener who doesn't want to use chemical controls can afford to lose a few to the bugs.

DISEASES

Cucumber plants are susceptible to bacterial wilt, scab, mosaic, and mildew. Planting disease-resistant varieties and maintaining the general cleanliness and health of your garden will help cut down the incidence of disease. If a plant does become infected, remove and destroy it before it can spread disease to healthy plants. Cucumbers will not tolerate air pollution; a high ozone level may affect their development. For plants infected with bacterial wilt, remove and discard or destroy infested plants. Control cucumber beetles that spread the bacteria. Control as soon as they appear. Some varieties are less susceptible to bacterial wilt but may not be readily available.

HARVESTING

Time from planting to harvest is 2½–3 months and a 10-foot (3m) row should give you as many cucumbers as you can use. Pick the cucumbers while they're immature—the size will depend on the variety. When the seeds start to mature the vines will stop producing.

VARIETIES

There are dozens of varieties of cucumber, including "burpless" ones, which are supposed to be more digestible than regular cucumbers, and round yellow lemon cucumbers. Marketmore 70, Burpee Hybrid, Supersett, Slicemaster, Sweet Success, Wisconsin SMR 18, Ohio MR17, Weest India Gherkin, Bush Champion, Spacemaster, Bush Pickle, Patio Pik, Pot Luck, Extra Early Express, Victory, Yard-long, Lemon. Among the Burpless: Burpless, Tastygreen Burpless, Sweet Slice Hybrid.

STORING AND PRESERVING

Cucumbers can be stored in the refrigerator up to one week, but if the temperature is too low they'll freeze and turn soft. You can pickle them or use them for relish if they're the right variety.

SERVING SUGGESTIONS

In England sandwiches are cut into small squares or triangles. Slice cucumbers thinly and dress them with plain yogurt and a little dill. Don't peel them—cucumbers are mostly water anyway, and most of the vitamins they contain are in the skin. You can also make them into a refreshing face cleanser—cucumbers are an ingredient in many cosmetic products.

Dandelion

Common name: dandelion

Botanic name: *Taraxacum officinale*

Origin: Europe and Asia

The dandelion is a hardy perennial that's grown as an annual for its foliage and as a biennial for its roots. The jagged green leaves grow in a short rosette attached by a short stem to a long taproot. Bright yellow flowers 1–2 inches (2–5cm) wide grow on smooth, hollow flower stalks. The dandelion is best known—and feared—by gardeners as a remarkably persistent lawn weed, but its leaves are actually high in vitamin A and four times higher in vitamin C than lettuce. It's also versatile: Dandelion leaves are used raw in salads or boiled like spinach, and the roots can be roasted and made into a coffee-like drink.

PLANTING

Dandelions grow well in any soil anywhere. They prefer full sun but will do fine in partial shade. They're very hardy and will survive both the hottest summers and the coldest winters. Plant the seeds in early spring, four to six weeks before the average date of last frost.

HOW TO PLANT

Dandelions grow best in a well-drained fertile soil from which you've removed all the stones and rubble. If you're growing dandelions for their foliage only, they'll tolerate soil in poorer physical condition. When you're preparing the soil, dig in a complete, well-balanced fertilizer at the rate of

1lb per 95sq feet (450g per 9sq m). Plant seeds in the garden ⅕ inch (0.5cm) deep in rows or wide rows 12–18 inches (30–45cm) apart. Thin plants 6–10 inches (15–25cm) apart after the true leaves appear.

FERTILIZING AND WATERING

Don't bother to fertilize dandelions at midseason.

Keep the plants supplied with water; the dandelion's foliage may become even more bitter than it is naturally if it's subjected to long periods of drought.

PESTS

Pests don't bother dandelions. If you let the dandelions produce their delicate clocklike seed heads, however, they may well become pests themselves by seeding all over you and your neighbors' lawns.

DISEASES

Dandelions have no serious disease problems.

HARVESTING

Harvest dandelion greens at your pleasure throughout the growing season. Harvest the roots in the fall of the second year; pull the whole root from the ground—or lift the roots with a fork to avoid breaking them.

VARIETIES

Thick-leaved; Improved Thick-leaved.

STORING AND PRESERVING

You can refrigerate the greens up to one week, or store the roots for 10 to 12 months in a cold, moist place, as you do with chicory.

SERVING SUGGESTIONS

Dandelion wine is a brew much beloved of do-it-yourself vintners. Or make dandelion tea, and drink it well chilled. Remove the stalks from the dandelions and toss the leaves in a vinaigrette dressing. Or try a hot dressing, as for a wilted spinach salad. Cook the leaves quickly and serve them with lemon and oregano, Greek-style. To use the roots, wash and dice them, then dry and roast them before grinding.

Eggplant

Common names: eggplant, aubergine, guinea squash

Botanic name: *Solanum melongena*

Origin: East Indies, India

Eggplant is a very tender perennial plant with large grayish-green hairy leaves. The star-shaped flowers are lavender with yellow centers, and the long, slender or round, egg-shaped fruit is creamy-white, yellow, brown, purple or sometimes almost black. Eggplants will grow 24–59 inches (60–150cm) tall, depending on the variety. They belong to the solanaceous family, and are related to tomatoes, potatoes and peppers, being first cultivated in India.

PLANTING

Eggplant is very sensitive to cold and needs a growing season with day temperatures between 77–86°F (25–30°C) and night temperatures between 72–77°F (22–25°C). Don't plant eggplant seedlings until daytime temperatures reach 72°F (22°C).

HOW TO PLANT

You can grow eggplant from seed, but you'll wait 5 months for a harvest. It's easier to grow from seedlings, started indoors about two months before your outside planting date. Don't put your seedlings into the garden until the soil is warm—eggplants won't be rushed, and if you plant them too early they won't develop. Eggplants must have full sun. They'll grow in almost any soil, but they do better in rich soil that is high in organic matter, with excellent drainage. When preparing the soil, dig in a complete, well-balanced fertilizer at the rate of 1lb per 95sq feet (450g per 9sq m). Set the plants 18–24 inches (45–60cm) apart in rows 24–35 inches (60–90cm) apart.

FERTILIZING AND WATERING

Fertilize before planting and again at midseason, at the same rate as the rest of the garden.

Eggplants are very fussy about temperature and moisture and must be treated with solicitude until they're well established. Try to maintain even soil moisture to ensure even growth; eggplants are susceptible to rootrot if there's too much moisture in the soil.

SPECIAL HANDLING

If you live in an area where an unpredictable late frost may occur, provide protection at night until all danger of frost is past. In hot climates the soil temperature may become too warm for the roots; in this case, mulch the plants about a month after you set them outside. Plants that are heavy with fruit may need to be staked.

PESTS

Eggplants are almost always attacked by one pest or another, so they're not the ideal crop for the organic gardener. The pests you're most likely to encounter are cutworms, aphids, spider mites, flea beetles, colorado potato beetles and tomato caterpillars. Control aphids and beetles by handpicking or hosing them off the plants and pinching out infested areas. Collars set around the plants at the time you transplant will discourage cutworms. Spider mites are difficult to control even with the proper chemicals; spray the underside of the foliage with Diazinon before the populations get too large.

DISEASES

Fungus and bacterial diseases may attack eggplants. Planting disease-resistant varieties and maintaining the general cleanliness and health of your garden will help lessen the incidence of disease. Verticillium wilt is the most serious disease of the eggplant. If a plant does become infected, remove it before it can spread disease to healthy plants. Remove and destroy entire infested plant along with immediately surrounding soil and soil clinging to roots. Set into soil never planted to tomatoes, peppers, or strawberries. If you cannot, locate new plants in a part of the garden different from previous year's location, remove infested soil and replace with fresh soil. Protect the plants against soil-borne diseases by rotating your crops and planting vegetables from a different plant family in the eggplants' spot the following season.

HARVESTING

Time from planting to harvest is 4–4½ months. Harvest the fruit young, before the flesh becomes pithy. The fruit should be firm and shiny, not streaked with brown. The eggplant fruit is on a sturdy stem that does not break easily from the plant; cut it off with a sharp knife instead of expecting it to fall into your hand.

VARIETIES

Black Beauty, Black Magic, Early Beauty Hybrid, Burpee Hubrid Dusky Hybrid, Tycoon, Orient Express, Long Tom Hybrid, Black Jack, Super Hybrid, Florida Market, Easter Egg, White Beauty, Ghostbuster, Round de Valence, Small Round Italian.

STORING AND PRESERVING

Whole eggplant will store up to one week at 50°F (10°C); don't refrigerate it. You can also freeze or dry it.

Freezing

1. Choose plump, firm, evenly and darkly colored eggplant and harvest before inner seeds mature.
2. Wash, peel and slice ⅛ inch (0.75cm) thick. Work quickly because eggplant discolors if allowed to stand.
3. Blanch 4 minutes. Add ½ cup lemon juice or 4½ teaspoons citric acid to 1 gallon (4 ½ liters) blanching water. Cool; drain well.
4. Tray freeze or pack into containers. Seal, label and freeze. To make slices easier to separate, pack with a piece of freezer wrap between them.
5. Cook frozen eggplant about 5 to 10 minutes. It's best cooked in a sauce, or thawed to be coated and fried, or used as an ingredient in Ratatouille or Moussaka.

Drying

1. Select perfect, plump, well-colored eggplant.
2. Wash, trim and cut into ⅛ inch (0.5cm) thick slices.
3. Blanch 3 minutes in boiling water; or 3½ minutes in steam. Drain well, chill and pat dry with paper towels.
4. Spread slices in a single, even layer on baking sheets or racks.
5. Dry until leathery, 3½ to 12 hours.
6. Put the dried vegetables into a deep container, cover lightly with cheesecloth and condition, stirring once a day for a week to 10 days.
7. Pack into vapor/moistureproof, airtight containers or double plastic bags and store in a cool, dark, dry place for up to 12 months.
8. Rehydrate in 2½ to 3 cups of boiling water for each cup of dried eggplant, about 1 hour.

SERVING SUGGESTIONS

Eggplant is very versatile and combines happily with all kinds of other foods—cheese, tomatoes, onions and meats all lend distinction to its flavor. The French use it in a vegetable stew called ratatouille, with tomatoes, onions, peppers, garlic and herbs. Ratatouille is a good hot side dish or can be served cold as a salad. Eggplant is also a key ingredient of the Greek moussaka, layered with ground meat and topped with a Bechamel sauce. Or coat slices in egg and breadcrumbs and deep-fry them. To remove excess moisture from eggplant slices before you cook them, salt them liberally, let them stand about half an hour, wash them and pat them dry. Or weight the slices with a heavy plate to squeeze out the moisture.

Endive

Common names: endive, escarole

Botanic name: *Cichorium endivia*

Origin: South Asia

Endive is a half-hardy biennial grown as an annual, and it has a large rosette of toothed curled or wavy leaves that are used in salads as a substitute for lettuce. Endive is often known as escarole but escarole has broader leaves.

Endive should not be confused with Belgian endive, which is the young blanched sprout of the chicory plant. Both endive and chicory, however, belong to the genus Cichorium.

PLANTING

Like lettuce, endive is a cool-season crop, although it's more tolerant of heat than lettuce. Grow it from seed planted in your garden in late summer to early autumn (August-September) for winter harvest. Sow in July and August for summer and early autumn crop. Long hot summer days will force the plant to bolt and go to seed. If your area has a short, hot growing season, start endive from seed indoors and transplant it as soon as possible so that the plants will mature before the weather gets

really hot. Sow succession crops, beginning in mid-summer. In a mild winter climate, you can grow spring, autumn and winter crops.

HOW TO PLANT

Endive needs well-worked soil with good drainage and moisture retention. When preparing the soil, dig in a complete, well-balanced fertilizer at the rate of 1lb per 95sq feet (450g per 9sq m). Sow seeds ⅕ inch (0.5cm) deep in wide rows 18–24 inches (45–60cm) apart, and when the seedlings are large enough to handle, thin them to 10–12 inches (25–30cm) apart. Thinning is important because the plants may bolt if they're crowded. Plant seedlings 10–12 inches (25–30cm) apart in rows 18–24 inches (45–60cm) apart.

FERTILIZING AND WATERING

Fertilize before planting and again at midseason, at the same rate as the rest of the garden.

Water regularly to keep the plants growing quickly; lack of water will slow growth and cause the leaves to become bitter.

SPECIAL HANDLING

Endive tastes better in salads if you blanch it to remove some of the bitter flavor. Blanching deprives the plants of sunlight and discourages the production of chlorophyll.

Blanch two to three weeks before you're ready to harvest the plants. You can do this in several ways: Tie string around the leaves to hold them together; lay a board on supports over the row; or put a flowerpot over each plant. If you tie the endive plants, do it when they're dry; the inner leaves may rot if the plants are tied up while the insides are wet.

PESTS

Cutworms, slugs and snails can be troublesome. You may also have to deal with aphids. Put a collar around each plant to discourage cutworms and trap slugs and snails with a saucer of stale beer set flush to the soil. To control aphids, pinch out infested foliage, or hose the aphids off the plants. You can also spray them with Malathion or Diazinon, taking care to spray the undersides of the leaves.

DISEASES

Endive has no serious disease problems.

HARVESTING

Time from planting to harvest is 2–3 months. To harvest, cut off the plant at soil level.

STORING AND PRESERVING

Like lettuce, endive can be stored for up to two weeks in the refrigerator, but you can't freeze, bottle or dry it. Share your harvest with friends.

SERVING SUGGESTIONS

Chill endive and serve it with an oil-and-vinegar dressing; add chunks of blue cheese or croutons. Mix it with other salad greens to add a distinctive flavor. The French use endive in a salad with heated slices of mild sausage, diced bacon and croutons.

Fennel

Common names: fennel, Florence fennel, finocchio, fenucchi

Botanic name: *Foeniculum vulgare dulce*

Origin: Mediterranean

Florence fennel or finocchio is the same as the common or sweet fennel grown for use as an herb. The leaves and seeds of both are used the same way for seasoning, but Florence fennel is grown primarily for its bulbous base and leaf stalks, which are used as vegetables. Florence fennel is a member of the parsley family. It's a stocky perennial grown as an annual, and looks rather like celery with very feathery leaves. The plant grows 47–59 inches (120–150cm) tall and has small, golden flowers, which appear in flat-topped clusters in summer. The whole plant has an anise flavor.

PLANTING

Fennel tolerates both heat and cold, but should mature in cold weather. Grow it from seed sown in early spring.

HOW TO PLANT

Fennel needs well-drained soil high in organic matter. When preparing the soil for planting, work in a complete, well-balanced fertilizer at the rate of 1lb per 95sq feet (450g per 9sq m).

Sow the seeds ⅛ (0.5cm) deep, in rows 24–35 inches (60–90cm) apart, in full sun. When the seedlings are growing strongly, thin them to 12 inches (30cm) apart.

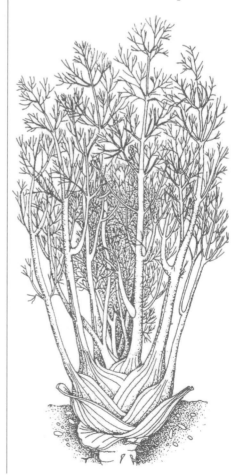

FERTILIZING AND WATERING

Fertilize before planting and again at midseason, at the same rate as the rest of the garden. Keep fennel on the dry side.

SPECIAL HANDLING

Fennel plants grow 47–59 inches (120–150cm) tall; you may need to stake them if they become unwieldy. It's not often necessary, so don't bother to set stakes at the time of planting.

PESTS

Since fennel is a member of the parsley family, the parsley caterpillar may appear. Remove it by hand. It has no other serious pest problems, so fennel is a good bet for the organic gardener.

DISEASES

Fennel has no serious disease problems.

HARVESTING

You can start harvesting a few sprigs as soon as the plant is well established and growing steadily; use them for flavoring. Harvest the bulbous stalk when it is 3 in (8cm) or more in diameter; cut the whole stalk like celery, just below the point where the individual stalks join together.

STORING AND PRESERVING

Fennel leaves can be frozen or dried as herbs; crumble the dried leaves and store them in an airtight container. You'll probably want to eat the stalks fresh; store them in the refrigerator up to one week or in a cold, moist place for two to three months. The stalks can also be frozen or dried; handle them like celery.

SERVING SUGGESTIONS

Fennel is featured in many Italian dishes. The leaves add flavor to soups and casseroles, and fennel goes well with fish. You can prepare Florence fennel in many ways as you do celery. Cut the fennel stalks into slices, simmer them in water or stock until tender, and serve buttered. Bake slices of fennel with cheese and butter as an accompaniment to a roast, or eat the stalks raw as a dipping vegetable. French and Italian cooks have been using fennel for generations—hence the variety of names by which it's known. The French serve grilled sea bass on a bed of flaming fennel stalks and the dried stalks can be used for barbecuing, too.

Garbanzo

See Chick Pea

Garden Pea

See Pea

Gourd

See Squash, Winter

Green Bean

See Bean, Green or String

Greens

See Beet, Swiss chard, Collard, Kale, Turnip

Honey-dew Melon

See Melon

Horseradish

Common name: horseradish

Botanic name: *Armoracia rusticana*

Origin: Eastern Europe

Horseradish looks like a giant radish but in fact it's a hardy perennial member of the cabbage family. Horseradish has a very strong flavor and—like the animal for which it's named—can deliver a powerful kick.

PLANTING

Horseradish is a hardy plant. Grow it from crowns or roots planted in early spring.

HOW TO PLANT

Horseradish tolerates partial shade and needs rich, well-drained soil. Turn over the soil to a depth of 12 inches (30cm) and remove stones and lumps that might cause the roots to split. When preparing the soil, dig in a complete, well-balanced fertilizer at the rate of 1lb per 95sq feet (450g per 9sq m). Plant the roots, narrow end down, 24 inches (60cm) apart in a trench. Fill in the trench until the thicker end is just covered.

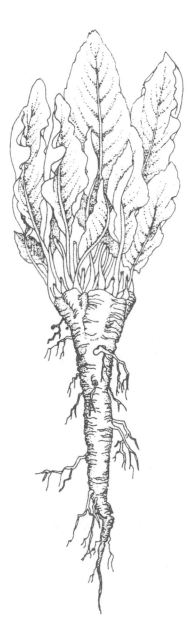

FERTILIZING AND WATERING

Fertilize before planting and again at midseason, at the same rate as the rest of the garden.

Keep the soil evenly moist so that the roots will be tender and full of flavor; horseradish gets woody in dry soils.

PESTS

Horseradish has no serious pest problems.

DISEASES

Horseradish has no serious disease problems.

HARVESTING

Plants grown from roots cannot be harvested until the second year. A 10-foot (3m) row should give you six to eight roots. Horseradish makes its best growth in late summer and autumn, so delay harvesting until October or later. Dig the roots as needed, or in areas where the ground freezes hard, dig them in the autumn. Leave a little of the root in the ground so that you'll have horseradish the following year, too.

STORING AND PRESERVING

Store in a glass jar in the refrigerator one to two weeks. To freeze, grate the roots and mix with vinegar and water. You can also dry horseradish or store the roots in a cold, moist place for 10–12 months.

Freezing

1. Choose tender small to medium roots.
2. Wash well and remove small roots and stubs.
3. Pare and grate root outdoors, if possible; or if you must work indoors, peel, cube and grate the root in a blender or food processor with tap water to cover or with a couple of ice cubes. Add water until horseradish reaches desired consistency. Add 2 to 3

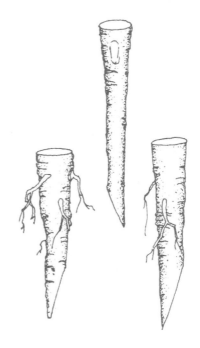

Plant horseradish roots narrow end down.

tablespoons of white vinegar and ½ teaspoon salt to each cup of grated horseradish to stop enzyme action. (The earlier in the grating process you add vinegar, the milder horseradish will be.)

4. Pack into jars, screw on lids and freeze. Horseradish prepared in this fashion can also be kept in jars in the refrigerator for a long time. To use frozen horseradish, thaw to desired temperature.

Drying

Horseradish doesn't require blanching. Add dried shreds as desired when cooking.

1. Select firm, unblemished roots.
2. Wash well and remove small roots and stubs; then peel and grate.
3. Spread grated horseradish in a single, even layer on baking sheets or racks.
4. Dry until brittle, 3 to 10 hours.
5. Put the dried vegetables into a deep container, cover lightly with cheesecloth and condition, stirring once a day for a week to 10 days.

6. Pack into vapor/moistureproof, airtight containers or double plastic bags and store in a cool, dark, dry place for up to 12 months.

SERVING SUGGESTIONS

Horseradish is a classic accompaniment to roast beef and steaks. Serve it solo, freshly grated, to brave souls who appreciate its full flavor. For the less stern of stomach, calm the flavor with whipped or sour cream. Serve it as one of the dipping sauces with a beef fondue. Since the fumes are very strong, grate horseradish outdoors if you can. If you must do it indoors, use a blender.

Hot Pepper

See Pepper

Kale

Common names: kale, borecole, collards, green cabbage, German greens

Botanic name: *Brassica oleracea acephala*

Origin: horticultural hybrid

Kale is a hardy biennial plant grown as an annual. It's a member of the cabbage family and looks like cabbage with a permanent wave. Scotch kale has gray-green leaves that are extremely crumpled and curly; Siberian or blue kale usually is less curly and is a bluer shade of green. There are also decorative forms with lavender and silver variegated leaves.

PLANTING

Kale is a cool-weather crop that grows best in the autumn and will last through the winter. Frost even improves the flavor. Kale doesn't tolerate heat as well as the collard—which it resembles in being one of the oldest members of the cabbage family. All crops of the family are frost-hardy and can tolerate sub-zero temperatures. Kale does best in a cool growing season with day temperatures under 81°F (27°C). Time plantings so that you can harvest kale during cool weather. If your area has cold winters, plant to harvest in summer to autumn.

In mild climates, plant for late spring or early autumn harvest. Plant seedlings early in the spring and again in the mid-summer if your summers aren't too hot. Direct-seed in autumn.

Flowering varieties of kale can be planted in containers or as accent points in a flowerbed. The leaves are attractive, and their color is at its best in the cool autumn weather. S.T.- not suitable. C- summer.

HOW TO PLANT

Kale likes fertile, well-drained soil with pH within the 6.5 to 7.5 range; this discourages disease and lets the plant make the most of the nutrients in the soil. Kale is usually grown from seedlings except where there is a long cool period, in which case seed can be sown directly in the garden in autumn for winter harvest.

When preparing the soil for planting, work in a complete, well-balanced fertilizer at the rate of 1lb per 95sq feet (450g per 9sq m). If you have sandy soil or your area is subject to heavy rains, you'll probably need to supplement the nitrogen content of the soil. Use about 1lb (450g) of nitrogen fertilizer for a 10-foot (3m) row.

Plant seedlings that are four to six weeks old, with four or five true leaves. If they are leggy or have crooked stems, plant them deeply (up to the first leaves) so they won't grow to be top-heavy.

Plant the seedlings 8–12 inches (20–30cm) apart, in rows 18–24 inches (45–60cm) apart. Set seeds ⅓ inch (1cm) deep and space them 3 inches (7.5cm) apart. Thin them when they're big enough to lift by the true leaves, and either transplant the thinned seedlings or eat them right away.

FERTILIZING AND WATERING

Fertilize before planting and again at midseason, at the same rate as the rest of the garden.

Abundant soil moisture and cool moist air are needed for the best growth. Regular watering keeps kale growing strongly and prevents it from getting tough.

PESTS

The cabbage family's traditional enemies are cutworms and caterpillars. Cutworms, cabbage loopers and cabbage worms can all be controlled by spraying with bacillus thuringiensis, an organic product known as Dipel. Kale does not suffer too much from pests, so it's a good choice for the organic gardener.

DISEASES

Kale may be infected by clubroot, black rot, black leg, or alternaria. To help reduce disease, do not plant kale or other cole crops in the same location more than once every three or four years.

HARVESTING

Time from planting to harvest is 2½–3 months. A 10-foot (3m) row will produce about 10 plants. Leave kale in the garden until needed. As the plants mature, take outside leaves, leaving the inner ones to grow, or cut off the entire plant. Harvest kale before it gets old and tough.

VARIETIES

Dwarf Blue Curled Scotch (Vates), Siberian Improved, Dwarf Greed Curled Vates, Ornamental Flowering Kale, Blue Knight Hybrid, Winterbor Hybrid, Red Russian.

STORING AND PRESERVING

If possible, leave kale in the garden until you want to eat it. It will store in the refrigerator in a plastic bag for up to one week, or in a cold, moist place for up to three weeks. You can also freeze, bottle, or dry it; use the recipes for greens.

Freezing

1. Choose young, tender leaves.
2. Wash well in several changes of water.
3. Remove tough stems or bruised leaves.

4. Blanch each pound (450g) of greens in 2½ gallons (9 liters) boiling water for 2 minutes; collard greens, 3 minutes. Stir to keep greens from sticking together. Cool, drain well.
5. Pack into containers, leaving ⅛ inch (0.5cm) head space. Seal, label and freeze.
6. Cook frozen greens 8 to 15 minutes.

Drying

1. Choose very fresh, perfect leaves.
2. Wash leaves well; shake dry. Remove any large, tough stalks.
3. Blanch in boiling water about 1½ minutes; or in steam about 2½ minutes, until completely wilted. Drain very well, chill and pat dry with paper towels.
4. Arrange leaves in a single layer on baking sheets or racks.
5. Dry until brittle, 2½ to 8 hours or more.
6. Put the dried vegetables into a deep container, cover lightly with cheesecloth and condition, stirring once a day for a week to 10 days.
7. Pack into vapor/moistureproof, airtight containers or double plastic bags and store in a cool, dark, dry place for up to 12 months.
8. Rehydrate in 1 cup of boiling water for each cup of greens, about ½ hour.

SERVING SUGGESTIONS

Young kale makes a distinctive salad green; dress it simply with oil and vinegar. You can also cook it in a little water and serve it with butter, lemon juice and chopped bacon. Instead of boiling, try preparing it like spinach steamed with butter and only the water that clings to the leaves after washing. The Italians steam kale until tender, then add olive oil, a little garlic and breadcrumbs and sprinkle it with Parmesan cheese in the last minute or two of cooking. You can also prepare kale Chinese-style, stir-fried with a few slices of fresh gingerroot.

Kohlrabi

Common names: kohlrabi, turnip-rooted cabbage, stem turnip, turnip cabbage

Botanic name: *Brassica caulorapa*

Origin: horticultural hybrid

Kohlrabi is a hardy biennial grown as an annual and is a member of the cabbage clan. It has a swollen stem that makes it look like a turnip growing on a cabbage root. This swollen stem can be white, purple or green and is topped with a rosette of blue-green leaves. In German, kohl means cabbage and rabi means turnip—a clue to the taste and texture of kohlrabi, although it is milder and sweeter than either of them.

PLANTING

All cabbage crops are hardy and can tolerate sub-zero temperatures. Kohlrabi tolerates heat better than other members of the cabbage family, but planting should be timed for harvesting during cool weather. Kohlrabi has a shorter growing season than cabbage. It grows best in cool weather and produces better with marked differences between day and night temperatures. If your area has cold winters, plant for summer to early autumn harvest. In warmer areas plant for harvest in late autumn or winter. With spring plantings, start kohlrabi early so that most growth will occur before the weather gets too hot.

HOW TO PLANT

Kohlrabi likes fertile, well-drained soil with a pH within the 6.5 to 7.5 range; this discourages disease and lets the plant make the most of the nutrients in the soil. The soil should be high in organic matter. When preparing the soil for planting, work in a complete, well-balanced fertilizer at the rate of 1lb per 95sq feet (450g per 9sq m). Kohlrabi can be grown directly from seed in the garden. Sow seeds in rows 18–24 inches (45–60cm) apart and cover them with ⅕–½ inch (0.5–1cm) of soil. When the seedlings are growing well, thin them to 5–6 inches (12–15cm) apart—you can transplant the thinnings. Cultivate carefully to avoid harming the shallow roots.

FERTILIZING AND WATERING

Fertilize before planting and again at midseason, at the same rate as the rest of the garden.

Kohlrabi should have even moisture or it will become woody.

PESTS

The cabbage family's traditional enemies are cutworms and caterpillars. Cutworms, cabbage loopers and cabbage worms can all be controlled by spraying with bacillus thuringiensis, an organic product known as Dipel.

DISEASES

Cabbage family crops are sus-ceptible to fungal, bacterial and virus diseases, particularly clubroot, black rot, black leg and downy mildew. Lessen the incidence of disease by planting disease-resistant varieties; main-taining the general health of your garden; and avoiding handling the plants when they're wet. If a plant does become infected, remove and destroy it so it cannot spread disease to healthy plants.

VARIETIES

Grand Duke Hybrid, Early White Vienna, Early Purple Vienna, Kossak, Eden, Rapid.

STORING AND PRESERVING

Kohlrabi will store for one week in a refrigerator or for one or two months in a cold, moist place. Kohlrabi can also be frozen.

Freezing

1. Choose young, tender small to medium kohlrabi.
2. Cut off tops and roots and wash well.
3. Pare, leave whole, or slice ⅛ inch (0.5cm) thick or dice into ½ inch (1cm) cubes.
4. Blanch whole kohlrabi 3 minutes; blanch diced or sliced kohlrabi 1 to 2 minutes.
5. Tray freeze or pack in containers, leaving ⅛ inch (0.5cm) head space.
Seal, label and freeze.
6. Cook frozen kohlrabi 8 to 10 minutes.

SERVING SUGGESTIONS

Small, tender kohlrabi are delicious steamed, unpeeled. As they mature you can peel off the outer skin, dice them, and boil them in a little water. Kohlrabi can also be stuffed like squash.

Try young kohlrabi raw, chilled and sliced; the flavor is mild and sweet, and the vegetable has a nice, crisp texture. You can also cook kohlrabi then cut it into strips and marinate the strips in an oil-and-vinegar dressing; chill this salad to serve with cold cuts. Cooked kohlrabi can be served just with seasoning and a little melted butter or mashed with butter and cream. For a slightly different flavor, cook it in bouillon instead of water.

Leek

Common name: leek

Botanic name: *Allium porrum*

Origin: Mediterranean, Egypt

T he leek is a hardy biennial grown as an annual. It's a member of the onion family, but has a stalk rather than a bulb and flat, strap-like leaves. The Welsh traditionally wear a leek on St. David's Day (March 1) to commemorate King Cadwallader's victory over the Saxons in A.D. 640, when the Welsh pulled up leeks and wore them as ID's. The more decorous now wear a daffodil instead.

PLANTING

Leeks are a cool-weather crop. They'll tolerate warm temperatures, but you'll get better results if the days are cool; temperatures under 75°F (24°C) produce the best yields. Plant seedlings in spring if

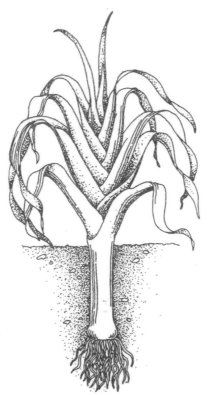

you want to speed up the crop to avoid a hot summer and in autumn for a late crop. S.T.- autumn. T&C- spring and autumn.

HOW TO PLANT

Leeks like a place in full sun and thrive in rich, well-worked soil with good drainage. When preparing the soil, dig in a complete, well-balanced fertilizer at the rate of 1lb per 95sq feet (450g per 9sq m). Plant the seeds ⅛ inch (0.3cm) deep in rows 12–18 inches (30–45cm) apart, and thin them 6–9 inches (15–22cm) apart. To plant seedlings, make holes 6 inches (15 cm) deep, about 6–9 inches (15–22cm) apart, in well-worked soil. Double rows save space; to make them, stagger the plants with their leaves growing parallel to the rows so they will not grow into the pathway. Drop the leeks in the holes, but do not fill in with soil. Over a period of time, watering will slowly collapse the soil around the leeks and settle them in.

SPECIAL HANDLING

In order to grow a large, white, succulent leek, blanch the lower part of the stem by hilling the soil up around the stalk as it develops.

FERTILIZING AND WATERING

Fertilize before planting and again at midseason, at the same rate as the rest of the garden.

Give leeks plenty of water to keep them growing strongly.

PESTS

Onion maggots, slugs, snails. For maggots, use floating row covers to prevent infestations. Onion thrips may show up on leeks in dry weather. Discourage them by hosing them off the plants, or spray them with Malathion or Diazinon. Leeks will do well in the organic garden despite the thrips.

DISEASES

Leeks may be infected by Purple blotch (Alternaria porri) and Botrytis leaf blight.

HARVESTING

Time from planting to harvest is about 3 months from seedlings and 4–5 months from seed. A 10-foot (3m) double row should give you about 20 leeks. Around midsummer, start removing the top half of the leaves. This will encourage greater growth of the leek stalk. Pull the leeks as you need them, but harvest them all before frost.

VARIETIES

London Flag, Giant Musselburgh, King Richard, Electra, American Flag, Pancho, Broad London.

STORING AND PRESERVING

Store leeks in the refrigerator for up to one week or in a cold, moist place for two to three months. You can also freeze them.

Freezing

1. Select fresh, firm leeks. Trim off the roots and all but 2 inches (5cm) of the leaves.
2. Wash leeks well, then split lengthwise and wash again.
3. Slice leeks or chop them.
4. Package in recipe-size amounts. Or tray freeze them and then pack or bag the leeks so you can pour out what you need. Leeks don't require blanching, but they shouldn't be stored in the freezer more than 3 months.

SERVING SUGGESTIONS

Leeks don't develop bulbs as onions do, but they belong to the same family and have a delicate onion flavor. Grit and sand get trapped in the wrap-around leaves, so slice the leeks or cut them lengthwise and wash them thoroughly under running water before you cook them. Serve leeks steamed or braised, chilled in a salad, or in a hot leek and potato soup—keep the soup chunky or puree it for a creamy texture. The French call leeks the "asparagus of the poor."

Lentil

Common name: lentil

Botanic name: *Lens culinaris*

Origin: Mediterranean region

Lentils are a hardy annual member of the pea family. They grow on small weak vines 18–24 inches (45–60cm) tall and the small whitish to light purple pea-like flowers are followed by flat, two-seeded pods.

PLANTING

Lentils need a cool growing season of 2½–3 months. Plant them early in spring.

HOW TO PLANT

Lentils grow best in a sunny area with a fertile, well-drained soil. When preparing the soil, dig in a complete, well-balanced fertilizer at the rate of 1lb per 95sq feet (450g per 9sq m). Sow seeds 1 inch (2.5cm) apart and ⅓ inch (1cm) deep in rows 18–24 inches (45–60cm) apart. Thin to 1–2 inches (3–5cm) apart.

FERTILIZING AND WATERING

Lentils will probably be harvested before your midseason fertilizing of the vegetable garden. Keep the lentils fairly moist.

SPECIAL HANDLING

Give your lentil plants a low trellis for support.

PESTS

Aphids may show interest in your lentils. Control them by pinching out infested areas of the plants or, if there are a lot of them, hose them off the vines. You can also spray them with Malathion or Diazinon.

DISEASES

Lentils have no serious disease problems.

HARVESTING

The growing season for lentils is about 2½ months. Harvest them when the pods are plump and full.

VARIETIES

There are three varieties of lentil seeds: flat brown ones, small yellow ones, and larger pea-shaped ones. Choose the variety that tastes best to you.

STORING AND PRESERVING

Store fresh lentils in the refrigerator, unshelled, for up to one week. Or dry the shelled lentils and store them in a cool, dry place for 10 to 12 months. Lentils can also be sprouted.

Freezing
1. Choose pods of young, tender lentils.
2. Wash, shell and wash again.
3. Blanch lentils 1 minute. Cool; drain well.
4. Pack into containers. Seal, label and freeze.
5. Cook frozen lentils 6 to 10 minutes.

Drying
1. Choose fresh, just-mature lentils.
2. Shell the lentils; then wash and drain.
3. Blanch in boiling water 15 minutes. Drain well, chill and pat dry with paper towels.
4. Arrange the lentils in a single, even layer on baking sheets or racks.
5. Dry until brittle, 4 to 12 hours.
6. Put the dried vegetables into a deep container, cover lightly with cheesecloth and condition, stirring once a day for a week to 10 days.
7. Pack into vapor/moistureproof, airtight containers or double plastic bags and store in a cool, dark, dry place for up to 12 months.
8. Rehydrate in 2½ cups of boiling water for each cup of lentils, about 1½ hours.

SERVING SUGGESTIONS

Cooked lentils with a little onion and seasonings, chilled, make a good salad. You can also serve them in a hearty soup with tomatoes using thyme and marjoram for a delicate and unusual flavor combination. Try lentils curried with apples and raisins.

Lettuce

Common names: lettuce, crisp-head lettuce, butterhead lettuce, stem lettuce (celtuce), leaf lettuce, cos, mignonette (miniature)

Botanic name: *Lactuca sativa*

Origin: Near East

Lettuce is a hardy, fast-growing annual with either loose or compactly growing leaves that range in color from light green through reddish-brown. When it bolts, or goes to seed, the flower stalks can grow up to 3 feet (1m) tall, with small, yellowish flowers on the stalk. The lettuce most commonly found in supermarkets is the most difficult to grow in the home vegetable garden. Butter-head and bibb lettuces are easier to grow. Butter-head lettuces have loose heads and delicate crunchy leaves. Stem lettuce (celtuce) might fool you into thinking you're eating hearts of palm and makes a crunchy addition to a salad. Celtuce is grown in the same way as lettuce, except that you want celtuce to bolt or go to seed, because you're going to harvest the thickened stem. You use the leaves of celtuce as you would regular lettuce; the heart of the stem is used like celery. Cos or romaine lettuce forms a loose, long head.

Leaf lettuce and butterhead lettuce make attractive borders or accents in a flower garden, and either kind can be grown singly in a 4-inch (10cm) pot or in a window box. With a little planning you can grow an entire salad garden in containers on a balcony or terrace.

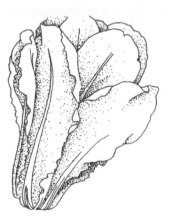

Romaine lettuce

Leaf lettuce

Historically, King Nebuchadnezzar grew lettuce in his gardens in ancient Babylon. The Romans used lettuce as a sedative.

PLANTING

Lettuce is a cool-season crop, hardy and frost-resistant. Long, hot summer days will make the plants bolt, or go to seed; when this happens the plant sends up a flower stalk and becomes useless as a vegetable. If your area has a short, hot growing season, start lettuce from seed in early spring and transplant it as soon as possible so that the plants will mature before the weather gets really hot. From end March to early March sow direct in soil 12 inches (30cm) apart and thin. Sow every 3–4 weeks for succession crops. In a mild winter climate, grow spring, autumn and winter crops.

HOW TO PLANT

Lettuce needs well-worked soil with good drainage and moisture retention. When preparing the soil, dig in a complete, well-balanced fertilizer at the rate of 1lb per 95sq feet (450g per 9sq m). If you are direct-seeding lettuce in the garden, sow seeds ⅕ inch (0.5cm) deep in wide rows and when the seedlings are large enough to handle, thin cos lettuce to 6–8 inches (15–20cm) apart and head lettuce 12 inches (30cm) apart. Thinning is important; lettuce won't heart and may bolt if the plants are crowded. Transplant the thinnings.

FERTILIZING AND WATERING

Give the entire garden a mid-season application of fertilizer. Your successive crops of lettuce

Crisphead lettuce

Celtuce

will benefit from it, even though you will already have harvested an early crop.

Always keep the soil evenly moist but not soggy, and don't let the shallow-rooted lettuce plants dry out. Lettuce needs careful watering when the heart is forming. Try not to splash muddy water on the lettuce plants—the cleaner they are, the easier they are to prepare for eating. Use a light mulch of straw or hay to keep soil off the leaves.

PESTS

Cutworms, slugs and snails can be troublesome. You may also have to deal with aphids: Put a collar around each plant to discourage cutworms and trap slugs and snails with a saucer of stale beer flush to the soil. To control aphids, pinch out infested foliage, or hose the aphids off the plants. Control aphids chemically with Malathion or Diazinon, taking care to spray the undersides of the leaves.

DISEASES

Leaf rot, Botrytis, downy mildew, mosaic and Fusarium. Prevent soil-borne fungi that causes leaf rot by mulching, rotating your crops and cleaning up all debris promptly.

HARVESTING

As the lettuce grows, either pick the outer leaves and let the inner leaves develop, or harvest the whole plant at once by cutting it off at ground level. Try to harvest when the weather is cool; in the heat of the day the leaves may be limp. Chilling will crisp up the leaves again.

Head lettuce

Butterhead or Bibb lettuce

VARIETIES

Crisphead lettuce varieties with good solid hearts: Ithaca, Burpee Iceburg, Great Lakes, Vanguard, King Crown, Buttercrunch, Dark Green Boston, Bibb, Summer Bibb, Tom Thumb, Kagran Summer.

Looseleaf varieties: Salad Bowl, Prizehead, Slobolt, Four Seasons, Oakleaf, Ruby Red, Red Sails, Black Seeded Simpson, Parris Island Cos.

Other varieties: Frosty, Green Wave, Little Gem, Sierra, Cosmo, Green Towers.

Lettuce varieties are basically of two types—one forms a tight head and the other has a head of loose, more open leaves. A less usual type is stem lettuce, which has thicker stems and far less prominent leaves.

STORING AND PRESERVING

Don't harvest lettuce until you're ready to use it. It can be stored for up to two weeks in the refrigerator, and everyone has a favorite way of keeping it crisp. Some suggest washing the lettuce first, then wrapping it in a cotton or linen towel and keeping it in the refrigerator. Others suggest storing the whole lettuce in a plastic bag. You can't freeze, dry or bottle lettuce, but you can sprout lettuce seeds. If you've got lots, share your bounty with friends.

SERVING SUGGESTIONS

Yes, salads, of course—but there are other ways to serve lettuce. Braise it in butter with seasoning to taste—the French use nutmeg. Make a wilted salad or cream of lettuce soup, or stir-fry it with mushrooms and onions. Cook peas and shredded lettuce together in a little butter—throw in the lettuce just before you take the peas off the heat. Use several varieties of lettuce together for an interesting combination of shades and textures. Serve a very plain salad—a few leaves of lettuce dressed with oil and a good wine vinegar—to cleanse the palate between courses of a fancy dinner.

Lima Bean

See Bean, Lima

Melon

The melon is a trailing annual that belongs to the cucumber family. The word cantaloupe means "song of the wolf" and was the name of a famous Italian castle.

The honeydew is sometimes referred to as a winter melon, but the name is inaccurate—the true winter melon is a Chinese vegetable. Honeydews have a smoother surface than rock melons and lack their distinctive odor. They ripen later and require a longer growing season, which means that they will not ripen fully in short-season areas. The following growing information applies to honeydews and rock melons.

PLANTING

Melons are tender, warm-weather plants that will not tolerate even the slightest frost. They have a long growing season, which means that you must be careful to select a variety suited to your area's climate. In cool areas you'll do better with small-fruited varieties; in warmer areas, where you can accommodate their need for a longer season, you can grow the large varieties. In cool areas grow cantaloupe from seedlings, using individual, plantable containers at least 4 inches (10cm) in diameter so that the root systems are not disturbed when you plant them.

Set the plants in the garden when the ground is thoroughly warm.

HOW TO PLANT

Melons must have full sun and thrive in well-drained soil high in organic matter. When preparing the soil, dig in a complete, well-balanced fertilizer at the rate of 1lb per 95sq feet (450g per 9sq m). Grow in inverted hills spaced 5 ft (1.5–1.75m) apart. If planting from seed, sow six to eight seeds in each hill; when the seedlings have developed three or four true leaves, thin them to leave the strongest two or three seedlings in each hill. Cut the thinned seedlings with scissors at soil level to avoid damaging the survivors' root systems. Where cucumber beetles, other insects or weather are a problem, wait before making the final selection. If you use seedlings, put two or three in each hill.

FERTILIZING AND WATERING

Fertilize before planting and again at midseason, at the same rate as the rest of the garden.

Melons need a lot of water while the vines are growing. Be generous with water until the melons are mature, then stop watering while the fruit ripens.

SPECIAL HANDLING

To keep competitive plants weeded out, cultivate carefully until the vines cover the ground. The roots are very shallow and extend quite a distance, so proceed with caution. You can grow melons 3 ft. (1m) apart on fences instead of in inverted hills. As the fruits develop, they may need support if grown on a fence. A net or bag will do the job—try using old pantihose. If the melons are growing in a hill, put a board under each melon to keep it off the ground.

PESTS

Aphids and cucumber beetles are the pests you're most likely to encounter. To control aphids, pinch out infested vegetation, hose them off the vines, or spray the aphids with Malathion or Diazinon. Cucumber beetles may not do much feeding damage, but they carry cucumber bacterial wilt. Handpick them off the vines promptly, or spray them with Carbaryl.

DISEASES

The vines are susceptible to wilt, blight, mildew, root rot, fungal leaf spot and cucumber mosaic virus. Planting disease-resistant varieties when possible and maintaining the general cleanliness and health of your garden will help cut down the incidence of disease. If a plant does become infected, remove and destroy it before it can spread disease to healthy plants. To prevent fungal leaf spot avoid wetting foliage if possible. Water early in the day so aboveground plant parts will dry as quickly as possible. Avoid crowding plants. Space apart to allow air circulation. Eliminate weeds around plants and garden area to improve air circulation. In autumn, rake and dispose of all diseased leaves or fruit. To prevent cucumber mosaic virus remove and destroy infested plants. Eliminate perennial weeds such as milkweed, marshcress and yellow rocket and avoid planting next to susceptible ornamentals.

HARVESTING

Time from planting to harvest is 3–3½ months, depending on type, and in a good season you might get 10 melons from a 10-foot (3m) row. Leave melons on the vine until ripe; there is no increase in sugar after harvesting. Mature melons slip easily off the stem; a half-ripe melon needs more pressure to remove than a ripe melon, and often comes off with half the stem attached.

VARIETIES

There are canteloupe (Rock-melon), Cassaba (Honeydew melon) and Watermelon.

Burpee Hybrid, Hale's Best, Classic Hybrid, Mainstream, Rocky Sweet, Jenny Lind, Ambrosia, Saticoy, Earligold, Earli-Sweet, Alaska. Minnesota Midget, Bush Musketeer, Early Hybrid Crenshaw, Crenshaw, Earli-Dew (an early honeydew).

Watermelon (see following section).

STORING AND PRESERVING

You can store melons up to one week in the refrigerator or, if you have a lot, for two to three weeks in a cool, moist place. You can also freeze your extras or make pickles with them.

Freezing
1. Select fully ripe but firm melons.
2. Cut in half, scoop out seeds and cut off rind.
3. Cut into 1-inch (2cm) cubes, slices or balls. Pack into freezer containers or freezer bags, seal and freeze.
4. Thaw only until still slightly frozen and serve.

SERVING SUGGESTIONS

Cantaloupe or honeydew melon is delicious by itself. A squeeze of lemon or lime juice brings out the flavor nicely. Or fill the halves with fruit salad, yogurt or ice cream. You can also scoop out the flesh with a melon-baller, and freeze the balls for future use. Mix balls or chunks of different types of melon for a cool dessert. Serve wedges of honeydew melon with thinly sliced prosciutto as an appetizer.

Watermelon

Common name: watermelon

Botanic name: *Citrullus vulgaris*

Origin: Tropical Africa

The watermelon is a spreading, tender annual vine related to the cucumber. It produces round, oval or oblong fruits that can weigh 11–99lbs (5–45kg) and have pink, red, yellow, or grayish-white flesh. Male and female flowers appear on the same vine. Watermelon was Dr. Livingstone's favorite African fruit. Although smaller varieties are now available, you still need to give watermelons a lot of headroom. They're space-consuming, and they take a lot of nutrients from the soil, so they're still not the ideal crop.

PLANTING

Watermelons require warm soil and warm days; night temperatures below 50°F (10°C) will cause the flavor of the fruit to deteriorate. In warm areas, direct-seed watermelons in spring. In cold areas, start from seedlings grown in peat pots; watermelons don't transplant easily.

HOW TO PLANT

Watermelons must have full sun, and prefer well-drained soil that holds moisture well. When preparing the soil for planting, work in a complete, well-balanced fertilizer at the rate of 1lb per 95sq feet (450g per 9sq m). Grow watermelons in inverted hills, made by removing

1 inch (2.5cm) of soil from a circle 12 inch (30cm) across and using the soil to form a rim around the circle. Space the hills 6½ feet (2m) apart and plant four to five seeds in each hill. When the seedlings have developed three or four true leaves, thin them to leave the strongest one or two seedlings in each hill. Cut the thinned seedlings with scissors at soil level to avoid damaging the survivor's root systems. Where cucumber beetles, other insects, or weather are a problem, wait before making the final selection. If using seedlings, put two or three in each hill.

FERTILIZING AND WATERING

Fertilize before planting and again at midseason, at the same rate as the rest of the garden.

Watermelons are 95 percent water, so make sure they have enough to keep them growing well. Do not let the soil dry out, and use a mulch to keep the soil moisture even.

SPECIAL HANDLING

As the watermelons develop, provide a support for the fruit. If they're growing on a fence or trellis, support the fruit with a net. If the vines are trailing on the ground, put a board under the fruit to keep it off the ground. Mulch helps keep the fruit clean as well as regulating soil moisture.

PESTS

Cucumber beetles may visit your watermelon vines. They don't cause much feeding damage, but they carry cucumber bacterial wilt; handpick them off the vines as soon as they appear. Watermelons are a good crop for the organic gardener who has lots of space.

DISEASES

Watermelons are susceptible to anthracnose, wilt, powdery mildew, cucumber mosaic virus and scab. Planting disease-resistant varieties when available and maintaining the general cleanliness and health of your garden will help cut down the incidence of disease. Don't handle the vines when they're wet. If a plant does become infected, remove it before it can spread disease to healthy plants. To prevent powdery mildew avoid wetting plants if possible. Water early in the day so aboveground plant parts dry as quickly as possible. Avoid crowding plants. Space apart to allow air circulation. Eliminate weeds around plants and garden area to improve air circulation. To prevent cucumber mosaic virus remove and destroy infested plants. Control cucumber beetles and aphids as soon as they appear. To prevent scab avoid wetting foliage if possible. Water early in day so aboveground plant parts dry as quickly as possible. Avoid crowding plants. Space apart for air circulation.

HARVESTING

If one watermelon gets an early start on a vine it can suppress all further activity until it matures. Some people suggest pinching out this first watermelon to encourage more melons, but this is a gamble because, sometimes, no more watermelons will set. It's easier to judge when a watermelon is ripe than it is with some other types of melon; a watermelon is ready to harvest when the vine's tendrils begin to turn brown and die off. A ripe watermelon will also sound dull and hollow when you tap it with your knuckles.

VARIETIES

Crimson, Sweet, Charleston Gray, Charelston Gray #5, Calhoun gray, Sweet Favorite Hybrid, Sugar Baby, Bush Jubilee, New Hampshire Midget, Family Fun, Yellow Doll, Black Diamond, Cannonball, Florida Giant, Burpee Seedless Hybrid.

STORING AND PRESERVING

A watermelon will store for up to one week in the refrigerator—it takes about 12 hours to chill a large one thoroughly before you eat it. If you have a lot of melons, store them in a cool, moderately moist place for two to three weeks.

You can freeze the flesh of the watermelon and make pickles with the rind.

Freezing
1. Select fully ripe but firm melons.
2. Cut in half, scoop out seeds and cut off rind.
3. Cut into 1-inch (2cm) cubes, slices or balls. Pack into freezer containers or freezer bags, seal and freeze.
4. Thaw only until still slightly frozen and serve.

SERVING SUGGESTIONS

Slices of fresh watermelon make a wonderful summer cooler. Scoop out the flesh with a melon baller and add to other types of melon for a cool fruit salad—pile the fruit into a honeydew half. For a great party dish, serve a big fruit salad in the scooped out half-shell of the watermelon—or carve the shell into a basket. Make pickles with the rind.

Mung Bean

See Bean, Mung

Mushroom

Common name: mushroom

Botanic name: *Agaricus species*

Origin: Mushrooms are found all over the world

Mushrooms are the fruiting bodies of a fungus organism and there are between 60,000 and 100,000 species of fungus that produce mushrooms. Because many mushrooms are poisonous, and it's extremely difficult to tell the edible variety from the poisonous kind, gathering wild mushrooms to eat is a very risky pastime. There are many good books on the market that will help you recognize the edible varieties that grow wild; so if you want to go mushroom-hunting, do a little homework first.

You can also grow mushrooms at home from prepared trays, kits and spawn available commercially.

PLANTING

Because you're growing them indoors, the type of climate you live in is a matter of indifference to your mushrooms. You can grow them at any time of the year the trays or kits are available.

HOW TO PLANT

Mushrooms grow best in dark, humid, cool areas. In most homes the best places are the basement and the cabinet under the kitchen sink. A little light won't hurt the mushrooms, but they do need high humidity—80 to 85 percent—

and a cool temperature—54–59°F (12–15°C). Mushrooms for growing at home are available in two different forms—in kits or as spawn. You can buy prepared trays and kits already filled with the growing medium and the mushroom spores. All you have to do is remove the tray from the package, add 1 inch (2.5cm) of topsoil, and water. Keep them in a dark, humid, cool place and you should be harvesting mushrooms within about four weeks.

Many seed companies also sell mushroom spawn; growing from spawn is less expensive, but it does require a little more care. Plant ½ inch (1cm) pieces of the spawn about 2 inches (5cm) deep and 8–10 inches (20–25cm) apart in a well-rooted strawy horse or cow manure. Keep the planted spawn in a dark, humid room with the temperature at about 54°F (22°C) for the first 21 days; then lower the temperature to about 59°F (15°C) and cover the bed with a 1-inch (2.5cm) layer of good, sterilized topsoil. If the conditions are right, you should be able to start harvesting in about four weeks.

FERTILIZING AND WATERING

You don't need to fertilize mushrooms.

Keep them moist; don't let the mushrooms dry out, but don't allow water to stand on the soil.

PESTS

Pests present no serious problems when you're growing mushrooms at home.

DISEASES

Mushrooms grown at home have no serious disease problems.

HARVESTING

Whether growing mushrooms from a kit or from spawn, you'll wait about four weeks for results. You can harvest the mushrooms as immature buttons, before the caps open, or when the cap is fully open and the gills exposed—at this stage the mushrooms are ripe and their flavor is at its highest level. Never pull the mushrooms out of the soil; cut them off at soil level with a sharp knife. Check and harvest your mushrooms every day; if you leave mature mushrooms in the planting bed your yield will be lower, but if you pick them regularly the bed will produce continuously for as long as six months.

STORING AND PRESERVING

Mushrooms can be stored in the refrigerator up to one week. You can also freeze, bottle or dry them.

Freezing
1. Choose young, firm, medium mushrooms with tightly closed caps.

2. Wash well, trim off ends and sort by size. Slice larger mushrooms, if desired.

3. Blanch small mushrooms 3 minutes; large mushrooms 4 minutes. Add 1 tablespoon lemon juice to each liter of blanching water. Cool; drain well. Or cook mushrooms in a frying pan with a small amount of butter until almost done. Cool.

4. Pack in containers. Seal, label and freeze.

5. Cook frozen mushrooms just until heated through.

Drying

1. Mushrooms don't require blanching. Choose young, fresh, evenly sized, tender mushrooms with tightly closed heads.

2. Wash very well. Remove and discard any tough or woody stalks and trim off the ends of any remaining stalks.

3. Slice large mushrooms and leave medium and small mushrooms whole, as you wish.

4. Arrange the slices or whole mushrooms in a single, even layer on baking sheets or racks.

5. Dry until leathery and hard, usually 3 to 12 hours. Small pieces may be brittle.

6. Put the dried vegetables into a deep container, cover lightly with cheesecloth and condition, stirring once a day for a week to 10 days.

7. Pack into vapor/moistureproof, airtight containers or double plastic bags and store in a cool, dark, dry place for up to 12 months.

8. Rehydrate in 2 cups boiling water for each cup of dried mushrooms, about 1 hour.

SERVING SUGGESTIONS

Fresh mushrooms are wonderful raw, sliced thinly and eaten alone or tossed in a green salad. Simmer them in red wine and tomatoes with parsley and herbs for a delicious vegetarian supper dish. Stuff them with herbed breadcrumbs and broil them, or sauté them lightly and toss them in with a dish of plain vegetables—try them with zucchini. Use mushrooms in your stir-fry Oriental dishes; the quick cooking preserves their flavor and texture. You can also fold them into an omelet topped with sherry sauce for an elegant lunch dish.

Mustard Greens

Common names: mustard, Chinese mustard, leaf mustard, spinach greens

Botanic name: *Brassica juncea*

Origin: Asia

This is not the mustard eaten with cress. Mustard is a hardy annual with a rosette of large light or dark green crinkled leaves that grow up to 3 feet (1m) in length. The leaves and leaf stalks are eaten. The seeds can be ground and used as a condiment. If you had lived in ancient Rome, you would have eaten mustard to cure your lethargy and any pains you suffered.

PLANTING

Mustard is a cool-season crop; it's hardy, but the seeds will not germinate well if you sow them too early. Mustard is grown like lettuce; it is more heat-tolerant than lettuce, but long hot summer days will force the plants to bolt and go to seed. Mustard has a very short growing season.

HOW TO PLANT

Mustard tolerates partial shade and needs well-worked soil, high in organic matter, with good drainage and moisture retention.

When preparing the soil, dig in a complete, well-balanced fertilizer at the rate of 1lb per 95sq feet (450g per 9sq m). Sow the seeds ⅓ inch (1cm) deep in rows 12–24 inches (30–60cm) apart, and when the seedlings are large enough to handle, thin them to stand 6–12 inches (15–30cm) apart. Transplant the thinned seedlings, or eat them in soups or as greens. For a continuous harvest, plant a few seeds at intervals, rather than an entire row at one time. As soon as the plants start to go to seed, pull them up or they will produce a great number of seeds and sow themselves all over the garden. Plant mustard again when the weather begins to cool off.

FERTILIZING AND WATERING

Fertilize before planting and again at midseason, at the same rate as the rest of the garden.

Water mustard before the soil dries out to keep the leaves growing quickly.

PESTS

Mustard is almost always attacked by some pest or other and is more susceptible than other crops to attack by beetles and aphids. Handpick or hose these pests off the plant, or pinch out aphid-infested foliage. Or use a chemical spray of Malathion or Diazinon. Because of its pest problems, mustard is not the ideal crop for the organic gardener.

DISEASES

Mustard has no serious disease problems.

HARVESTING

Pick off individual leaves as they grow, or cut the entire plant. Harvest when the leaves are young and tender; in summer the leaf texture may become tough and the flavor strong. Harvest the whole crop when some of the plants start to go to seed.

STORING AND PRESERVING

You can store mustard in the refrigerator for up to one week, or you can freeze, bottle or dry your excess crop; use the recipes for greens. You can also sprout mustard seeds.

Freezing
1. Choose young, tender leaves.
2. Wash well in several changes of water.
3. Remove tough stems or bruised leaves.
4. Blanch each pound (450g) of greens in 2½ gallons (9 liters) boiling water for 2 minutes; collard greens, 3 minutes. Stir to keep greens from sticking together. Cool, drain well.
5. Pack into containers, leaving ⅛

in. (0.5cm) head space. Seal, label and freeze.

6. Cook frozen greens 8 to 15 minutes.

Drying

1. Choose very fresh, perfect leaves.

2. Wash leaves well; shake dry. Remove any large, tough stalks.

3. Blanch in boiling water about 1½ minutes; or in steam about 2½ minutes, until completely wilted. Drain very well, chill and pat dry with paper towels.

4. Arrange leaves in a single layer on baking sheets or racks.

5. Dry until brittle, 2½ to 8 hours or more.

6. Put the dried vegetables into a deep container, cover lightly with cheesecloth and condition, stirring once a day for a week to 10 days.

7. Pack into vapor/moistureproof, airtight containers or double plastic bags and store in a cool, dark, dry place for up to 12 months.

8. Rehydrate in 1 cup of boiling water for each cup of greens, about ½ hour.

SERVING SUGGESTIONS

Use young, tender leaves of mustard in a salad, alone or mixed with other greens. Boil the older leaves quickly in just the water that clings to them after washing; dress them with a little olive oil and vinegar, or add some crumbled bacon. Substitute mustard greens for spinach in an omelet.

New Zealand Spinach

See Spinach

Okra

Common names: okra, lady's fingers, gumbo

Botanic name: *Hibiscus esculentus*

Origin: Africa

Okra, a member of the cotton and hibiscus family, is an erect, tender annual with hairy stems and large maple-like leaves. It grows 3–6½ feet (1–2m) tall, and has large flowers that look like yellow hibiscus blossoms with red or purplish centers. When mature, the pods are 6–10 inches (15–25cm) long and filled with buckshot-like seeds.

PLANTING

Okra is very sensitive to cold; the yield decreases with temperatures under 72°F (22°C). Sow seed direct when soil has warmed up. Okra does not grow well in containers. S.T.- autumn to spring. T&C-spring and summer.

HOW TO PLANT

Okra will grow in almost any warm, well-drained soil and needs a place in full sun. When preparing the soil, dig in a complete, well-balanced fertilizer at the rate of 1lb per 95sq feet (450g per 9sq m). Sow seeds ⅓–1 inch (1–2.5cm) deep in rows 24–35 inches (60–90cm) apart, and when the seedlings are growing strongly, thin them to 12–18 inches (30–45cm) apart.

FERTILIZING AND WATERING

Fertilize before planting and again at midseason, at the same rate as the rest of the garden.

Keep the plants on the dry side. The stems rot easily in wet or cold conditions.

SPECIAL HANDLING

Don't work with okra plants when they're wet. You may get an allergic reaction.

PESTS

Cutworms, corn earworms, cabbage loopers, stinkbugs and aphids. Use collars around transplanted seedlings to protect against cutworms. Pick off corn earworms, cabbage loopers and stinkbugs. Pinch out aphid-infested vegetation, control the aphids chemically with Malathion or Diazinon.

DISEASES

Okra may be attacked by verticillium or fusarium wilt. Okra varieties are not resistant to these diseases, but maintaining the general cleanliness and health of your garden will help cut down the incidence of disease. If a plant does become infected, remove it before it can spread disease to healthy plants. Rotate crops to prevent the buildup of diseases in the soil.

HARVESTING

Time from planting to harvest is 4–5 months and a 30-foot (9m) row will yield about 4½lbs (2kg) of pods. When the plants begin to set their pods, harvest them at least every other day. Pods grow quickly, and unless the older ones are cut off, the plant will stop producing new ones. Okra will grow for a year if not killed by frost and if old pods are not left on the plant. Keep picking the pods while they are quite small; when they're only about 2 inches (5cm) long they are less gluey. If you let the pods mature you can use them in winter flower arrangements; the pods and the stalks are quite dramatic.

VARIETIES

Clemson Spineless, Clemson 80, Emerald, Annie Oakley, Dwarf Green Long Pod, Blond, Red Okra, White Velvet, Baby Bubba, Louisiana Green Velvet, North & South.

STORING AND PRESERVING

Pods will store in the refrigerator for seven to 10 days. You can also freeze, bottle or dry them.

Freezing
1. Choose young, tender, green pods.
2. Wash well. Cut off the stems, but don't cut open the seed cells. Sort by size.
3. Blanch small pods 3 minutes;

large pods 4 minutes. Cool; drain well.
4. Slice crosswise in ½ inch (1–2cm) slices, or leave whole.
5. Tray freeze or pack into containers, leaving ⅛ inch (0.5cm) head space. Seal, label and freeze.
6. Cook frozen okra about 5 minutes.

Drying

Okra doesn't require blanching.
1. Select fresh, perfect pods.
2. Wash well, then trim off tops and tips. Cut cross-wise into thin slices.
3. Arrange slices in a single, even layer on baking sheets or racks.
4. Dry until very brittle, 4 to 10 hours.
5. Put the dried vegetables into a deep container, cover lightly with cheesecloth and condition, stirring once a day for a week to 10 days.
6. Pack into vapor/moistureproof, airtight containers or double plastic bags and store in a cool, dark, dry place for up to 12 months.
7. Rehydrate in 3 cups boiling water for each cup of okra, about ½ hour.

SERVING SUGGESTIONS

Many people are disappointed because their first mouthful often tastes like buckshot in mucilage.

A taste of okra is perhaps an acquired one. Try it in gumbo, mixed with tomatoes, or sautéed.

Onion

Common name: onion
Botanic name: *Allium cepa*
Origin: South West Asia

Onions are hardy biennial vegetables usually grown as annuals. They have hollow leaves, the bases of which enlarge to form a bulb. The flower stalk is also hollow, taller than the leaves and topped with a cluster of white or lavender flowers. The bulbs vary in color from white through yellow to red. All varieties can be eaten as green onions, though spring onions, bunching onions, scallions and green onions are grown especially for their tops. Green onions take the least time to grow.

PLANTING

Onions are sensitive to temperature, generally requiring cool weather to produce their tops and warm weather to produce their bulbs. They're frost-hardy.

HOW TO PLANT

Onions are available in three forms—seeds, seedlings and sets. Sets are onions with a case of arrested development—their growth was stopped when they were quite small. The smaller the sets are, the better; any sets larger

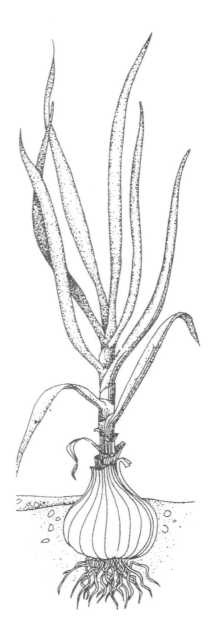

than the nail of your little finger are unlikely to produce good bulbs. Sets are the easiest to plant and the quickest to produce a green onion, but they are available in the least number of varieties, and are not the most reliable for bulb production—sometimes they'll shoot right on to the flowering stage without producing a bulb. Seedlings are available in more varieties than sets and are usually more reliable about producing bulbs. Seeds are the least expensive and are available in the greatest variety, but they have disease problems that sets don't have and take such a long time to grow that the forces of nature often kill them before they produce anything.

In limited space you can grow onions between other vegetables, such as tomatoes or cabbages, or tuck them in among flowers—they don't take much room. They can also be grown in containers. An 8-inch (20cm) flowerpot can hold 8 to 10 green onions.

Onions appreciate a well-made, well-worked bed with all the lumps removed to a depth of at least 6 inches (15cm). The soil should be fertile and rich in organic matter. Locate most bulbs in full sun—green onions can be placed in a partially shaded spot. When preparing the soil, dig in a complete, well-balanced fertilizer at the rate of 1lb per 95sq feet (450g per 9sq m).

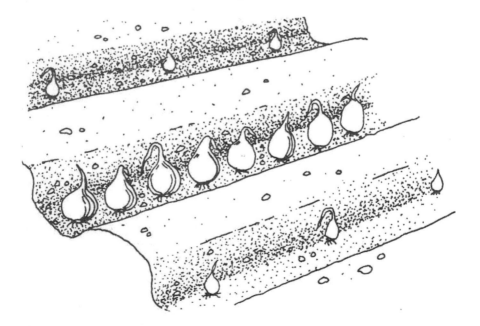

Plant large sets close together for green onions, and small sets farther apart for dry onions.

When you plant seedlings and sets, remember that large seedlings and large sets (over 1 inch/2cm in diameter) will often go directly to seed and should be grown only for green or pulling onions. Grow smaller seedlings or sets for bulbs. Plant seedlings or sets 1–2 inches (2.5–5cm) deep and 2–3 inches (5–7.5cm) apart in rows 12–18 inches (30–45cm) apart. The final size of the onion will depend on how much growing space it has. The accompanying illustration shows how to plant onion seedlings or sets. Sow the seeds ⅕ inch (0.5cm) deep in rows 12–18 inches (30–45cm) apart, and thin to 1–2 inches (2.5–5cm) apart.

FERTILIZING AND WATERING

Fertilize before planting and again at midseason, at the same rate as the rest of the garden.

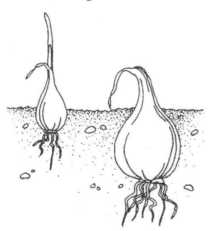

Plant large onion sets deeper than small sets.

The soil should not be allowed to dry out until the plants have started to mature—at this stage the leaves start to get yellow and brown and to droop over. Then let the soil get as dry as possible.

SPECIAL HANDLING

Onions are not good fighters; keep the weeds from crowding in and taking all their food and water. Keep the weeds cut off from the very beginning since they are hard to remove when they snuggle up to the onion. Thin conscientiously; in a crowded bed onions will mature when very small without growing a bulb.

PESTS

Onion thrips and maggots are the pests to watch for. Discourage thrips by hosing them off the plants or control them chemically with Malathion or Diazinon. Prevention is the best non-chemical control for maggots—put a 3–4 inches (7.5–10cm) square of plastic around the plants to discourage flies from laying their eggs near the plants. To control maggots chemically, drench the soil around the plants with Diazinon at the first sign of damage.

DISEASES

In areas that produce onions commercially, onions are susceptible to bulb and root rots, smut and

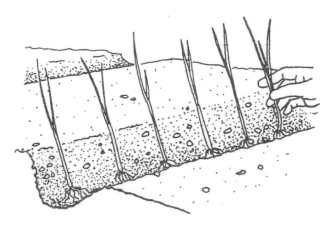

Space onion seedlings to allow room for growth.

downy mildew. Planting disease-resistant varieties when possible and maintaining the general cleanliness and health of your garden will help cut down the incidence of disease. If a plant does become infected, remove it before it can spread disease to healthy plants.

HARVESTING

Harvest some leaves for flavoring throughout the season and harvest the green onions when the bulb is full but not much larger in diameter than the leaves. Harvest dry onion bulbs after the leaves have dried.

Lift them completely out of the soil; if the roots touch the soil they may start growing again and get soft and watery.

VARIETIES

Soil and growing conditions affect the flavor of an onion as much as the variety. These are early, mid-season and late maturing types, strong- or mild-flavored types.

Good storing varieties: Yellow Globe, Early Yellow Globe, White Portugal, Sweet Spanish. Good red varieties: Granex, Southport Red Globe, Red Wethersfield. Large sweet varieties: Sweet sandwich, Giant Red, White Bermuda, Yellow Bermuda. Good pickling varieties: White Portugal, Crystal Wax Pickling. Scallion (Green Onion) varieties: White Bunching, Beltsville Bunching, Japanese Bunching, Evergreen White, Southport White Bunching, He-Shi-Ko.

STORING AND PRESERVING

Store green onions in the refrigerator for up to one week. Let mature bulbs air-dry for about a week outside then store them in a cold, dry place for up to six or seven months. Do not refrigerate mature onions. You can also freeze, dry or pickle onions.

Freezing

1. Choose the highest-quality, fully mature onions. Freeze only chopped or sliced onions. Store whole onions in a cool, dry place.

2. Peel, wash and chop or slice.

3. Package onions in recipe-size amounts. Or tray freeze them and then pack or bag the onions in recipe-size amounts so you can pour out what you need. Onions don't need to be blanched, but they shouldn't be stored in the freezer longer than 3 to 6 months at 0°F (-18°C).

Drying

Onions require neither blanching nor rehydrating as long as the pieces are small and you're adding them to other foods that have some moisture.

1. Choose large, flavorful, perfect onions.

2. Cut off the stems and bottoms, and remove the peels.

3. Slice the onions very thin or chop finely. Separate the slices into rings.

4. Arrange the pieces or rings in a single, even layer on baking sheets or racks.

5. Dry until very crisp and brittle, 3 to 12 hours.

6. Put the dried vegetables into a deep container, cover lightly with cheesecloth and condition, stirring once a day for a week to 10 days.

7. Pack into vapor/moistureproof, airtight containers or double plastic bags and store in a cool, dark, dry place for up to 12 months.

8. If desired, rehydrate in 2 cups boiling water for each cup of dried onions.

SERVING SUGGESTIONS

Onions are probably the cook's most indispensable vegetable. They add flavor to a huge variety of cooked dishes, and a meat stew or casserole without onions would be a sad thing indeed. Serve small onions parboiled with a cream sauce, or stuff large ones for baking. Serve onion slices baked like scalloped potatoes. Perk up a salad with thin onion rings, or dip thick rings in batter and deep-fry them. Serve onions as one of the vegetables for a tempura. Add chopped, sautéed onion to a cream sauce for vegetables, or fry a big panful of slices to top liver or hamburgers. Serve pickled onions with cheese and crusty bread for a "farmer's lunch." It's virtually impossible to run out of culinary uses for your onion crop.

Parsnip

Common name: parsnip

Botanic name: *Pastinaca sativa*

Origin: Europe

Parsnips are biennials grown as annuals and belong to the same family as celery, carrots and parsley. A rosette of celery-like leaves grows from the top of the whitish, fleshy root. Parsnips taste like sweet celery hearts. Roman Emperor Tiberius demanded annual supplies of parsnips from Germany. Parsnips were the potato of medieval and Renaissance Europe.

PLANTING

Parsnips need a long, cool growing season. They will tolerate cold at both the start and the end of their growing season and they can withstand freezing temperatures. S.T.- autumn; T- spring to early autumn; C- spring to late summer.

HOW TO PLANT

Parsnips prefer full sun but will tolerate partial shade. Before planting, work a 5-10-10 fertilizer into the soil at the rate of 4oz per 95 sq feet (115g per 9 sq m). Turn the soil thoroughly to a depth of 10–12 inches (25–30cm) and remove all lumps and rocks. This initial soil preparation is essential for a healthy crop; soil lumps, rocks or other obstructions in the soil will cause the roots to split, fork or become deformed. Don't use manure in the soil bed for root crops unless it is very well rotted; it may also cause forking. Sow seeds ⅓ inch (1cm) deep in wide rows 18–24 inches (45–60cm) apart. When the seedlings develop two true leaves, thin them to 2–4 inches (5–10cm) apart. Thinning is very important; parsnips must have adequate space for root development. Do not pull out the thinned seedlings; cut them off at ground level to avoid disturbing the remaining seedlings.

FERTILIZING AND WATERING

Fertilize before planting and again at midseason, at the same rate as the rest of the garden.

To keep parsnips growing quickly, give them plenty of water. As they approach maturity, water less; too much moisture at this stage may cause the roots to crack.

SPECIAL HANDLING

In areas with high soil temperature, roots will grow short unless you mulch to regulate the soil temperature. Control weeds, especially during the first few weeks, but cultivate shallowly to avoid damaging the young roots.

PESTS

Parsnips have few enemies, but root maggots may be troublesome. Discourage flies from laying eggs near the plants by putting a 3–4 inches (7.5–10cm) square of plastic around each plant. Control maggots chemically by drenching the soil around the plant with Diazinon. Carrot weevil may also become a problem, so clean up garden debris in autumn. Beneficial nematodes are available. Apply as directed on label. Also, watch for leafhoppers that can spread disease.

DISEASES

Parsnips have no serious disease problems.

HARVESTING

Leave the parsnips in the soil as long as possible or until you need them. The roots are not harmed by frost. In fact, some people think it makes them taste better. The low temperatures convert the roots' starch to sugar. Dig them up before the ground becomes unworkable.

VARIETIES

Harris Model, Hollow Crown, All American.

STORING AND PRESERVING

Store parsnips in the refrigerator for one to three weeks, or in a cold, moist place for two to six months. You can also freeze them.

Freezing

1. Choose small to medium, tender, not woody, parsnips.
2. Remove tops, wash, pare and cut in ½ inch (1cm) cubes or slices.
3. Blanch 3 minutes. Cool; drain well.
4. Pack in containers, leaving ⅛ inch (0.5cm) head space. Seal, label and freeze.

5. Cook frozen parsnips about 10 to 12 minutes.

SERVING SUGGESTIONS

Parsnips can be cooked like carrots. If the roots are very large, remove the tough core after cooking. Put parsnips around a beef roast so that they cook in the meat juices, or puree them and add butter and seasonings.

Pea

Common names: pea, sweet pea, garden pea, sugar pea, English pea

Botanic name: *Pisum sativum*

Origin: Europe, Near East

Peas are hardy, weak-stemmed, climbing annuals that have leaf-like stipules, leaves with one to three pairs of leaflets, and tendrils that they use for climbing. The flowers are white, streaked, or colored. The fruit is a pod containing 4 to 10 seeds, either smooth or wrinkled depending on the variety. Custom has it that you can make a wish if you find a pea pod with nine or more peas in it.

Edible-pod peas are a fairly recent development. Grow them the same way as sweet peas, but harvest the immature pod before the peas have developed to full size. Peas have traditionally been a difficult crop for the home gardener to grow, with yields so low that it was hardly worth planting them. The introduction of the new easy-to-grow varieties of edible-pod peas has made growing peas a manageable undertaking for the home gardener, and no garden should be without them. All you need to grow peas is cool weather and a 7-foot (2m) support trellis.

PLANTING

Peas are a cool-season crop that must mature before the weather gets hot. Ideal growing weather for peas is moist and between 59–63°F (15–17°C). Sow — S.T.- September January; T- August-February; C- December-early April.

Frost will damage the plant badly so do not plant so that the

peas are in flower during likely frost periods.

HOW TO PLANT

Peas tolerate partial shade and need good drainage in soil that is high in organic material. They produce earlier in sandy soil, but yield a heavier, later crop if grown in clay soil. Although soaking seeds can speed germination, they can be ruined by oversoaking and peas are harder to plant when wet, because the seeds tend to break. Before planting, work a complete well-balanced fertilizer into the soil at the rate of 1lb per 95sq feet (450g per 9sq m). Plant the peas 2 inches (5cm) deep, 1–2 inches (2.5–5cm) apart, in rows 18–24 inches (45–60cm) apart.

FERTILIZING AND WATERING

Fertilize before planting and again at midseason, at the same rate as the rest of the garden.

Peas need ample moisture; don't let the soil dry out. When the vines are flowering, avoid getting water on the plants; it may damage the flowers and reduce the crop.

Provide trellises to support the pea vines. Cultivate very gently to avoid harming the fragile roots.

PESTS

Aphids, pea weevils, birds and people are attracted to pea vines.

Control aphids by pinching out infested foliage or by hosing them off the vines. For pea weevils, dust your crop with lime, or use rotenone. Discourage birds with a scarecrow or cover the rows with netting. Stern words may do the trick with human trespassers. Despite this competition, peas are an excellent crop for any garden.

DISEASES

Peas are susceptible to rot, wilt, blight, mosaic and mildew. New, highly disease-resistant varieties are available; use them to cut down on disease problems in your garden. You will also lessen the incidence of disease if you avoid handling the vines when they're wet, and if you maintain the general health and cleanliness of the garden. If a plant does become diseased, remove and destroy it before it can spread disease to healthy plants.

HARVESTING

Early varieties take 2–2½ months from planting to harvest; late take 3–4 months. A 10-foot (3m) row may give you about 3lbs 5oz (1½kg) of pods. Pick shelling peas when the pods are full and green, before the peas start to harden. Overmature peas are nowhere near as tasty as young ones; as peas increase in size, the sugar content goes up. Sugar will also begin converting to starch as soon as peas are picked. To slow this process, chill the peas in their pods as they are picked and shell them immediately before cooking.

Harvest edible-pod peas before the peas mature. Pods should be plump, but the individual peas should not be completely showing through the pod.

VARIETIES

Freezonian, Little Marvel, Alderman, Lincoln, Wando, Dwarf Grey Sugar, Sugar Daddy, Sugar Snap, Sugar Ann, Oregon Sugar Pod II, Little Sweetie, Mammoth Melting Sugar.

STORING AND PRESERVING

Storing fresh shelling peas is seldom an issue for home gardeners; there are seldom any left to store but they can be stored in the refrigerator, unshelled, up to one week. You can sprout, freeze, bottle or dry peas. Dried peas can be stored in a cool, dry place for 10 to 12 months. Edible-pod peas are also so good raw that you may not even get them as far as the kitchen. If you do have any to spare, you can store them in a plastic bag in the refrigerator for 7 to 10 days. Edible-pod peas also freeze well and, unlike shelling peas, lose little of their flavor when frozen.

Freezing
Edible Pod:
1. Choose very fresh, tender pods of the same size.

2. Wash well, then snip off the ends, if you wish.
3. Blanch 1½ minutes. Cool; drain well.
4. Tray freeze or pack into containers. Seal, label and freeze.
5. Cook edible-pod peas just until heated through and crisp-tender, about 2 to 3 minutes.
Shelling Peas:
1. Choose young pods containing tender peas.
2. Wash, shell and wash again.
3. Blanch 2 minutes in boiling water or steam blanch 3 minutes. Cool; drain well.
4. Tray freeze or pack into containers. Seal, label and freeze.
5. Cook frozen peas 3 to 5 minutes until heated through.

Drying
Shelling Peas:
1. Choose young, tender peas.
2. Shell peas; then wash and drain.
3. Blanch in boiling water about 2 minutes; or in steam 3 minutes. Drain well, chill and pat dry with paper towels.
4. Arrange peas in a single, even layer on baking sheets or racks.
5. Dry until very crisp, 3 to 12 hours or more. Tap a single pea with a hammer. When done, it will shatter easily.
6. Put the dried vegetables into a deep container, cover lightly with cheesecloth and condition, stirring once a day for a week to 10 days.
7. Pack into vapor/moistureproof, airtight containers or double plastic

bags and store in a cool, dark, dry place for up to 12 months.

8. Rehydrate in 2½ cups water for each cup of peas, about ½ hour.

SERVING SUGGESTIONS

Freshly shelled peas are a luxury seldom enjoyed by most people. Cook them quickly in a little water and serve them with butter and chopped mint. Or add a sprig of mint during cooking. Fresh peas and boiled new potatoes are the perfect accompaniment for a lamb roast. Toss cold, cooked peas into a salad or add them to potato salad—throw in diced, cooked carrots as well, and you've got a Russian salad. Simmer peas in butter with a handful of lettuce tossed in at the end of the cooking time. Or try lining the pot with lettuce leaves and cooking the peas briefly over low heat. Add a few sautéed mushrooms or onions for a sophisticated vegetable dish. Add edible pod peas to a stir-fry dish—the rapid cooking preserves their crisp texture and delicate flavor. Eat them raw, or use them alone, lightly steamed, as a side dish.

Pea, Black-eyed

Common names: pea, black-eyed pea, cowpea, chowder pea, southern pea, black-eyed bean, China bean

Botanic name: *Gigna sinensis*

Origin: Asia

Black-eyed peas are tender annuals that can be either bushy or climbing plants, depending on the variety. The seeds of the dwarf varieties are usually white with a dark spot (black eye) where they're attached to the pod; sometimes the spots are brown or purple. Black-eyed peas originated in Asia. Slave traders brought them to Jamaica, where they became a staple of the West Indians' diet.

PLANTING

Unlike sweet peas, black-eyed peas tolerate high temperatures but are very sensitive to cold—the slightest frost will harm them. If your area has a long enough warm season, plant black-eyed peas from seed when the soil has warmed up.

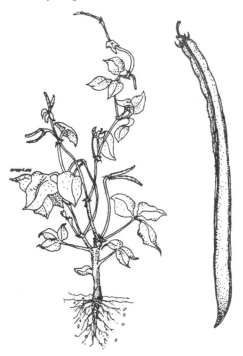

HOW TO PLANT

Black-eyed peas will tolerate partial shade and will grow in very poor soil. In fact, like other legumes, they're often grown to improve the soil. Well-drained, well-worked soil high in organic matter increases their productivity. When preparing the soil for planting, work in a complete, well-balanced fertilizer at the rate of 1lb per 95sq feet (450g per 9sq m). Sow seeds ⅓ inch (1cm) deep and about 2 inches (5cm) apart in rows 1½–3 feet (0.5–1m) apart; when the seedlings are large enough to handle, thin them to 3–4 inches (7.5–10cm) apart.

FERTILIZING AND WATERING

Fertilize before planting and again at midseason, at the same rate as the rest of the garden.

Don't let the soil dry out, but try to keep water off the flowers; it may cause them to fall off, and this will reduce the yield.

PESTS

Beetles, aphids, spider mites and leafhoppers attack black-eyed peas. Control aphids and beetles physically by handpicking or hosing them off the plants, pinch out aphid-infested vegetation, or using a chemical spray of Diazinon or Malathion. Hose leafhoppers off the plants or spray with Carbaryl. Spider mites are difficult to control even with the proper chemicals; remove the affected plants before the spider mites spread, or spray the underside of the foliage with Diazinon.

DISEASES

Black-eyed peas are susceptible to anthracnose, rust, mildew, mosaic, and wilt. Planting disease-resistant varieties when possible and maintaining the general cleanliness and health of your garden will help cut down the incidence of disease. To avoid spreading disease, don't work with the plants when they're wet. If a plant does become infected, remove it before it can spread disease to healthy plants.

HARVESTING

Time from planting to harvest is 2½–3½ months. You can eat either the green pods or the dried peas. Pick pods at whatever stage of maturity you desire—either young and tender or fully matured to use dried.

STORING AND PRESERVING

Unshelled black-eyed peas can be kept up to one week in the refrigerator. Young black-eyed peas can be frozen, pod and all; the mature seeds can be dried, bottled or frozen. Dried shelled black-eyed peas can be stored in a cool, dry place for 10 to 12 months.

Freezing

1. Choose pods with tender and barely grown seeds.
2. Wash, shell and pick over peas. Discard too mature or insect-damaged peas. Wash again.
3. Blanch small peas 1 minute; larger peas 2 minutes. Cool; drain well.
4. Tray freeze or pack peas in containers, leaving ⅛ inch (0.5cm) head space. Seal, label and freeze.
5. Cook frozen peas 15 to 20 minutes.

Drying

1. Choose fresh, just-mature peas.
2. Shell the peas; wash and drain.
3. Blanch in boiling water 15 minutes. Drain well, chill and pat dry with paper towels.
4. Arrange peas in a single, even layer on racks.
5. Dry until brittle, 4 to 12 hours.
6. Put the dried vegetables into a deep container, cover lightly with cheesecloth and condition, stirring once a day for a week to 10 days.
7. Pack into vapor/moistureproof, airtight containers or double plastic bags and store in a cool, dark, dry place for up to 12 months.
8. Rehydrate in 2½ cups of boiling water for each cup of black-eyed peas, about 1½ hours.

SERVING SUGGESTIONS

Eat young black-eyed peas in the pod like green beans; dry the shelled peas for use in casseroles and soups. Combine cooked black-eyed peas and rice, season with red pepper sauce and bake until hot; or simmer the peas with pork or bacon for a classic Southern dish.

Peanut

Common name: peanut

Botanic name: *Arachis hypogaea*

Origin: South America

The peanut is a tender annual belonging to the pea family. It grows 6–18 inches (15–45cm) tall, depending on whether it's the bunch type, which grows upright, or the runner type, which spreads out over the ground. Small clusters of yellow, sweet-pea-like flowers grow on stems called pegs. The pegs grow down and push into the soil, and the nuts develop from them 1–3 inches (2.5–7.5cm) underground. You can grow a peanut plant indoors if you give it lots of sunlight; it's a novel and entertaining houseplant.

Peanuts are 30 percent protein and 40 to 50 percent oil.

PLANTING

Peanuts need a frost-free growing season four to five months long. If your growing season is short, start

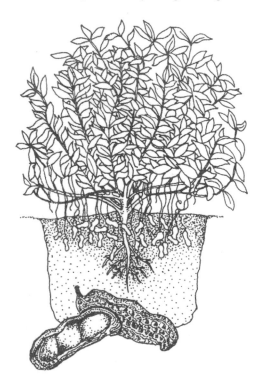

the peanuts in pots inside and then transplant them outdoors when the weather warms up.

HOW TO PLANT

Peanuts like well-worked sandy soil high in organic matter. The pegs have difficulty penetrating a heavy clay soil. When preparing the soil for planting, work in a complete, well-balanced fertilizer at the rate of 1lb per 95sq feet (450g per 9sq m). Plant either shelled raw peanuts or seedlings 6–8 inches (15–20cm) apart, in rows 14–16 inches (30–45cm) apart. If growing from seed, plant the seeds 1–3 inches (2.5–7.5cm) deep. Grow them in double rows to save space.

FERTILIZING AND WATERING

Fertilize before planting and again at midseason, at the same rate as the rest of the garden.

Peanut seedling

Keep soil moisture even until the plants start to flower, then water less. Blind (empty) pods are the result of too much rain or humidity at flowering time.

SPECIAL HANDLING

Use a heavy mulch to keep the soil surface from becoming hard—the peanut pegs will not have to work so hard to become established in the soil. Mulching will also make harvesting easier.

PESTS

Local rodents will be delighted that you've become a peanut farmer. Discourage them by removing their hiding places and fencing them out of your garden. Peanuts have no other serious pest problems. In warm climates they are a good crop for the organic gardener.

DISEASES

Peanuts have no serious disease problems.

HARVESTING

Time from planting to harvest is 4–5 months. Your yield depends on the variety of peanut and the weather at the time of flowering, but usually there are not as many peanuts as you might imagine. Start harvesting when the plants begin to suffer from frost. Pull up the whole plant and let the pods dry on the vine.

STORING AND PRESERVING

Shelled peanuts can be sprouted, frozen or used for peanut butter, or roasted for snacks. Dried shelled peanuts can be stored in a cool, dry place for 10 to 12 months.

Freezing
1. Select fully mature peanuts.
2. Wash, drain, shell and wash again. Sort by size.
3. Blanch small peanuts 1 minute; medium peanuts 2 minutes; large peanuts 3 minutes. Cool, drain well.
4. Tray freeze or pack into containers. Seal, label and freeze.
5. Cook peanuts in water to cover until very tender, about 2 hours.

Drying
Peanuts should be air-dried slowly, without the blanching and heating used for other foods. Use raw, dried peanuts for sprouting or baking; roast the dried nuts for snacks and peanut butter.
1. Leave peanuts in the soil until the leaves have turned yellow.
2. Harvest peanuts by digging up the entire plant, before the first killing frost. Shake loose dirt from the roots.

3. Tie the plants in bundles and hang them to dry in a warm, dark, dry place; or stack them on the floor in a warm, dark, dry room.
4. Let dry for 1 week, until the plants are dry and brittle. Shake off any remaining soil.
5. Pull the peanuts off the plants and spread them on clean newspaper on the floor in a warm, dry room. Let dry 1 to 2 weeks, until the peanuts are completely dry.
6. When peanuts are completely dry, shell them and discard the pods.
7. Pack into vapor/moistureproof, airtight containers or double plastic bags and store in a cool, dark, dry place for up to 12 months.
8. Use for sprouting or for planting the following year.
9. To roast shelled nuts, spread in a shallow pan. Roast in a conventional oven at 355°F (180°C) for 20 minutes.

SERVING SUGGESTIONS

You probably won't be able to resist eating your peanuts as snacks, but if you've got lots, make peanut butter. Run the nuts through a meat grinder for crunchy peanut butter; for the smooth kind put them in the blender. Add peanuts and candied orange peel to a fudge recipe—it makes a delicious crunchy candy.

Pepper

Common names: pepper, bell pepper, sweet pepper, hot pepper, wax pepper, chili pepper, pimento

Botanic names: *Capsicum frutescens* (hot pepper), *Capsicum annuum* (sweet and hot peppers)

Origin: New World tropics

Peppers are tender erect perennials that are grown as annuals. They have several flowers growing in the angle between the leaf and stem. Sweet peppers are erect annuals that have only a single flower growing from the space between the leaf and the stem.

When Columbus was looking for the black pepper—the dried berries of the Piper nigrum vine—he found the fruit of the bell peppers; it wasn't related in any way to the peppers he'd started out to find, but that did not stop him from using the name.

Bell pepper

Peppers are members of the solanaceous family, which includes tomatoes, potatoes, eggplants and tobacco. Peppers range in size from the large sweet types to the tiny, fiery ones. Peppers also grow in many shapes: round, long, flat and twisted. Some like them hot, some like them sweet. The large sweet ones are used raw, cooked or pickled and the hot ones are used as an unmistakable flavoring or relish. In Jamaica, there are some peppers so hot that people claim a single drop of sauce will burn a hole in the tablecloth. Choose peppers carefully when you make a selection to be sure the variety you're growing suits your palate.

PLANTING

Peppers prefer a soil temperature above 64°F (18°C). They don't produce well when the day temperature gets above 90°F (32°C), although hot peppers tolerate hot weather better than sweet peppers. The ideal climate for peppers is a daytime temperature around 77°F (25°C) and a nighttime temperature around 59°F (15°C).

The easiest way to grow peppers is from seedlings. You can also grow them from seed, starting 7 to 10 weeks before your outdoor planting date. And if you have a very long growing season, you can seed peppers directly in the garden. S.T.- spring to autumn; T&C- spring.

Try growing peppers in a large pot or container indoors or on the patio. A single chili (hot pepper) plant is very decorative and can fill many people's hot pepper requirements for a whole year.

HOW TO PLANT

Peppers do best in a soil high in organic matter and that holds water but drains well. When preparing the soil for planting, work in a complete, well-balanced fertilizer at the rate of 1lb per 95sq feet (450g per 9sq m). Plant the pepper seedlings in full sun, 18–24 inches (45–60cm) apart in rows 24–35 inches (60–90cm) apart.

FERTILIZING AND WATERING

Fertilize before planting and again at midseason, at the same rate as the rest of the garden. Do not overfertilize peppers; too much nitrogen will cause the plants to grow large but to produce few peppers.

Keep the soil evenly moist but not wet.

SPECIAL HANDLING

Peppers are shallow-rooted, so cultivate them gently to eliminate weeds. Use a mulch to keep soil temperature and moisture even.

PESTS

Peppers are almost always attacked by some pest and may not be a good choice for the organic gardener. Aphids, cutworms, fruit fly and borers will attack peppers. Discourage cutworms by placing a collar around each seedling at the time of planting. Hose aphids off the plants and pinch out aphid-infested foliage. Chemically control aphids with Malathion or Diazinon. Carbaryl can also be used to control cutworms; apply it to the base of the plants. Spray with Rogor to deter fruit fly. This pest is most serious near the coast. Remove borers by hand and destroy infested plants.

DISEASES

Pepper plants are susceptible to rot, blossom end rot, anthracnose, tobacco mosaic virus, bacterial spot and mildew. Planting disease-

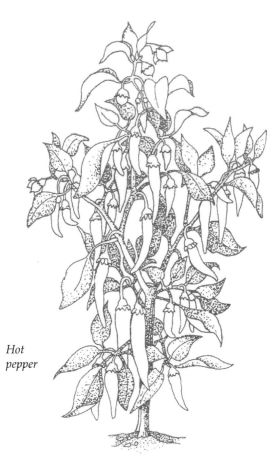

Hot pepper

resistant varieties and maintaining the general cleanliness and health of your garden will help cut down the incidence of disease. If a plant does become infected, remove it before it can spread disease to healthy plants. If you smoke, wash your hands before working with the plants to avoid spreading tobacco mosaic virus.

HARVESTING

If you want sweet red peppers, leave your sweet green peppers on the vine until they ripen and turn red. Cut the peppers off the vine; if you pull them off, half the plant may come up with the fruit. Hot peppers can irritate skin, so wear gloves when you pick them.

VARIETIES

Peppers come in bell (sweet) or hot varieties. The bell peppers are the most familiar; most are sweet, but there are a few hot varieties. They're usually harvested when green, but will turn red (or occasionally yellow) if left on the plant. Hot peppers—sometimes called chili peppers—are intensely flavored, and there are more than a hundred varieties.

Bell varieties: Yolo Wonder, California Wonder, Early Calwonder, Bell Boy, Golden Bell, Golden Summer, Sweet Banana, Gypsy, Quadrato D'Oro, Cubanelle. Hot varieties: Hungarian Yellow Wax, Red Chili, Tam Nild Jalapeno, Serrano Chili, Large Hot Red Cherry, Jalapeno.

STORING AND PRESERVING

Peppers will keep up to one week in the refrigerator or for two to three weeks in a cool, moist place. Sweet or hot peppers can be pickled whole or in pieces, or they can be chopped and frozen or dried. Whole peppers can be strung up to dry—a wreath of hot peppers makes a great kitchen decoration.

Freezing
1. Choose shapely, firm, evenly colored peppers.
2. Cut out the stems; remove seeds of sweet peppers.
3. Leave whole, cut in half, slice or dice. It's not necessary to blanch peppers.
4. Tray freeze or pack into containers. Seal, label and freeze.
5. Add frozen chopped pepper to uncooked or cooked dishes, or cook about 5 minutes.

Drying
Peppers don't need to be blanched or rehydrated. Dried sweet peppers are handy to toss into soups, stews and casseroles.
1. Choose tender, ready-to-eat, sweet or hot peppers.
2. Cut out the stems and seeds.
3. Chop in ⅛ inch (0.5cm) pieces.
4. Arrange pieces in a single, even layer on baking sheets or racks.

5. Dry until brittle, 3 to 12 hours.

6. Put the dried vegetables into a deep container, cover lightly with cheesecloth and condition, stirring once a day for a week to 10 days.

7. Pack into vapor/moistureproof, airtight containers or double plastic bags and store in a cool, dark, dry place for up to 12 months.

8. If desired, rehydrate in 2 cups boiling water for each cup dried peppers, about 1 hour.

SERVING SUGGESTIONS

Stuffed, raw, pickled or roasted, sweet and hot peppers add lively flavor to any meal. Stuff sweet peppers with tuna, chicken, a rice and meat mixture, or chili con carne. For a vegetarian dish, stuff them with rice and chopped vegetables, a cheese mixture, or seasoned breadcrumbs. Stuff raw peppers with cream cheese, slice into rings and serve in a salad. Use thick rings in a dish of vegetables for tempura. French-fry peppers, or fry them Italian-style in oil and garlic. Use chopped peppers in chili and spaghetti sauce recipes and add a spoonful of chopped hot pepper to a cream corn soup for an interesting flavor contrast.

When preparing raw hot peppers, cut and wash them under running water and wash your hands well afterwards. Avoid rubbing your eyes while handling hot peppers. Milk is more soothing than water for washing the hot pepper's sting from your skin.

Potato

Common names: potato, white potato, Irish potato

Botanic name: *Solanum tuberosum*

Origin: Chili, Peru, Mexico

The potato is a perennial grown as an annual. It's a weak-stemmed plant with hairy, dark green compound leaves that look a little like tomato leaves, and it produces underground stem tubers when mature. The potato is a member of the solanaceous family, and is related to the tomato, the eggplant and the pepper; it originated at high altitudes and still prefers cool nights.

Potatoes haven't always been as commonplace as they are now. They grew in temperate regions

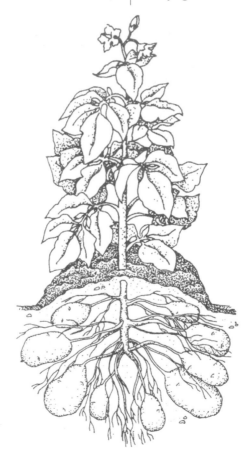

along the Andes for a couple of thousand years before Spanish explorers introduced them to Europe in the 16th century. To encourage the growing of potatoes, Louis XVI of France wore potato flowers in his buttonhole and Marie Antoinette wore a wreath of potato flowers in her hair to a ball. But the people didn't become interested in potatoes until an armed guard was assigned to watch the royal potato patch.

PLANTING

Potatoes need a frost-free growing season of 4–5 months. S.T.- grow from July-February to avoid the rainy season. Warm to temperate—spring and autumn. Cold districts—February-June. Never expose potatoes to frost or cold soil.

HOW TO PLANT

Potatoes are grown from whole potatoes or pieces of potatoes—these are called seed pieces; each piece must have at least one eye. Always plant certified disease-free seed pieces, and don't try to use supermarket potatoes, which have been chemically treated to prevent sprouting. Some suppliers are experimenting with potatoes grown from actual seed, but these have yet to prove themselves, and the use of potato seed is not recommended at this stage.

Potatoes need well-drained fertile soil, high in organic matter, with pH of 5.0 to 5.5. Adding lime to improve the soil and reduce acidity usually increases the size of the crop, but it also increases the incidence of scab—a condition that affects the skin of the potato but not the eating quality. When you're preparing the soil for planting, work in a complete, well-balanced fertilizer at the rate of 1lb per 95sq feet (450g per 9sq m). Plant potatoes or potato pieces in full sun, 4 inches (10cm) deep, 14–16 inches (30–45cm) apart in rows 24–35 inches (60–90cm) apart. You can also plant in a trench or on top of the ground and cover them with a thick mulch, such as 12-inch (30cm) straw or hay. For a very compact plant, you can grow potatoes in barrels, old tires or large bags—as the plant grows you add layers of soil to cover the leaves and stems. This encourages the plant to produce new tubers.

FERTILIZING AND WATERING

Fertilize before planting and again at midseason, at the same rate as the rest of the garden.

For the best production, try to maintain even soil moisture; watering before the soil dries out. A thick mulch will conserve soil moisture, keep down weeds and keep the soil from getting too warm.

PESTS

Colorado potato beetles, aphids, flea beetles, leaf hoppers, tuber moth caterpillars, slugs, snails, wireworms. Spray aphids with Malathion. Potatoes have so many pest problems they may not be a good choice for the organic gardener. For Colorado potato beetles, handpick beetles, eggs and larvae. A hard stream of water can be used to remove aphids from plants. Wash off with water occasionally as needed early in the day. Check for evidence of natural enemies such as gray-brown or bloated parasitized aphids and the presence of alligator-like larvae of lady beetles and lacewings. For flea beetles, use row covers to help protect plants from early damage. Put in place at planting and remove before temperatures get too hot. Control weeds. For leaf hoppers, wash small nymphs off with a hard stream of water.

DISEASES

Potatoes are susceptible to blight and to scab, which causes a curly roughness of the skin but does not affect the eating quality of the potato. Plant resistant varieties for the best results, especially for large plantings, and use seed certified as true to type and free of disease.

Maintaining the general health and cleanliness of your garden will also lessen the incidence of disease. If a plant does become infected, remove and destroy it to avoid spreading disease to healthy plants.

HARVESTING

Time from planting to harvest is 4–5 months and a 10-foot (3m) row will give you 6½–9lbs (3–4kg) of potatoes. Each plant will probably produce three to six regular-size potatoes and a number of small ones. Potatoes are fun to grow, and the young new potatoes are delicious. Dig up new potatoes after the plant blooms, or if it doesn't bloom, after the leaves start to yellow. For potatoes that taste like store-bought ones, dig up the tubers two weeks after the vine dies in autumn. Use a spading fork to dig the potatoes and be as gentle as possible to avoid bruising or damaging the skins.

VARIETIES

Red Pontiac, Red La Soda, Red Norland, Irish Cobbler, Dennebec, Katahdin, Russet Burbank, Sebago, Viking, Norgold Russet, Crystal, Fingerling, Lady Finger.

STORING AND PRESERVING

Cure potatoes in a dark, humid place for 10 days at 50–59°F (10–15°C); then store them in a cold, moderately moist place for four to six months. Be careful not to let them get wet, or they'll rot. Do not refrigerate them. Prepared or new potatoes freeze well and potatoes can also be dried.

Freezing

Baked:

1. Bake potatoes, then let cool. Scoop out potatoes and mash. Season and stuff mashed potato back into shells, if desired.
2. Tray freeze, then wrap shells individually. Seal, label and freeze.
3. Cook by unwrapping and reheating in a 390°F (200°C) oven until hot, about 30 minutes.
4. Freeze leftover baked potatoes unstuffed, then thaw and slice or cube them for creamed or scalloped potatoes, potato salad, or American fries.

French-fried:

1. Choose large, mature potatoes.
2. Wash, pare and cut them in sticks about ½ inch (1cm) thick.
3. Rinse well in cold water; drain. Pat dry.
4. Fry small amounts at a time in deep fat 355°F (180°C) for 5 minutes or until tender but not brown.
5. Drain well on paper towels. Cool.
6. Pack into containers. No head space is necessary. Seal, label and freeze.
7. Cook frozen French fries in deep fat 375°F (190°C) until browned. Or spread them in single layer on biscuit sheet and heat in 450°F (230°C) oven, 5 to 10 minutes or until browned.

New Potatoes:

1. Choose smooth, tiny new potatoes.
2. Scrub well.
3. Blanch 3 to 5 minutes, depending on size. Cool; drain well.
4. Pack in containers. Seal, label and freeze.
5. Cook frozen new potatoes just until tender.

Drying

1. Select fresh dug, perfect potatoes.
2. Scrub well and then peel. Cut julienne or shoe-string, about ⅛ inch (0.5cm) thick.
3. Blanch in boiling water 5 to 6 minutes; or in steam 6 to 8 minutes. Drain well, chill and pat dry with paper towels.
4. Spread in a single, even layer on baking sheets or racks.
5. Dry until brittle, about 4 to 12 hours.
6. Put the dried vegetables into a deep container, cover lightly with cheesecloth and condition, stirring once a day for a week to 10 days.
7. Pack into vapor/moistureproof, airtight containers or double plastic bags and store in a cool, dark, dry place for up to 12 months.
8. Rehydrate in 1½ to 2 cups of boiling water for each cup of potatoes, about ½ hour.

SERVING SUGGESTIONS

Potatoes are wonderfully versatile in the kitchen—you can boil, bake, roast, fry, puree, sauté and stuff them. The enterprising cook can serve a different potato dish every day for a month. Small new potatoes are delicious boiled and tossed in butter and parsley or mint; don't peel them. Stuff potatoes with tuna and spinach for a nourishing all-in-one dish. Enjoy low-calorie fries by brushing the chipped potatoes all over with oil and baking them in a single layer on a baking sheet. Pipe pureed potatoes around the edge of a dish for an elegant garnish. Add cubed, cooked potatoes with other vegetables to an omelet. Don't throw away potato skins—they're full of goodness. Deep fry them or simmer them to make stock. When mashing potatoes use hot milk, not cold—they'll be lighter and fluffier; a teaspoon of baking powder will have the same effect.

A non-edible use for potatoes: Cut a potato in half, and carve a picture or design on the cut surface; ink it, and press on paper for an instant block print. It's a splendid way of keeping the children busy on a wet afternoon.

Potato, Sweet

See Sweet Potato

Pumpkin

Common name: pumpkin

Botanic names: *Cucurbita maxima,
Cucurbita moschata, Cucurbita pepo*

Origin: Tropical America

Pumpkins are tender annuals with large leaves on branching vines that can grow to 6m long. The male and female flowers—sometimes as large as 4 inches (10cm) in diameter—grow on the same vine, and the fruit can weigh as much as 100lbs (45kg).

In other countries, the name pumpkin is also given to a number of other squashes and gourds—anything that's orange and hard.

PLANTING

Pumpkins need a long growing season; in cooler areas you'll do better with a smaller variety. Pumpkins are sensitive to cold soil and frost. Pumpkins are relatively easy to grow so long as you have space to accommodate them. They're not the vegetable to grow in a small home garden, although you can train them on a fence or trellis, and the bush type requires less space than the vining varieties.

HOW TO PLANT

Pumpkins can tolerate partial shade and prefer well-drained

soil, high in organic matter. Too much fertilizer tends to encourage the growth of the vines rather than the production of pumpkins. When preparing the soil for planting, work in a complete, well-balanced fertilizer at the rate of 1lb per 95sq feet (450g per 9sq m). Plant pumpkins in inverted hills, made by removing 1 inch (2.5cm) soil from a circle 12 inches (30cm) in diameter and using the soil to build up a rim around the circle; leave approximately 6½ feet (2m) between hills. Sow six to eight seeds in each hill, and thin to two or three when the seedlings appear. When the seedlings have four to six true leaves, thin to only one plant in each hill. Cut off the thinned seedlings at soil level to avoid disturbing the roots of the chosen survivor. One early fruit can suppress the production of any more pumpkins. Some people suggest removing this first pumpkin, but this is a gamble because there's no guarantee that others will set. If you remove it, eat it like squash.

Single Bush Pumpkin plants can be grown in a large tub. When grown in the garden give them 39 inches (100cm) of space all around.

FERTILIZING AND WATERING

Fertilize before planting and again at midseason, at the same rate as the rest of the garden. Be generous with water; pumpkins need plenty of water to keep the vines and fruit growing steadily.

PESTS

Squash vine borers attack pumpkins, and if the plant is wilting it may be that borers are to blame. Prevention is better than cure, because once the pest is inside the plant, chemical controls won't help. If you suspect borers are at work, apply Carbaryl to the crown of the plant weekly. If the vine wilts from a definite point onwards, look for a very thin wall or hole near the point where the wilting starts. The culprit may still be there, but you may still be able to save the plant. Slit the stem, remove the borer, and then cover the stem with soil to encourage rooting at that point.

A hard stream of water can be used to remove aphids from plants. Wash off with water occasionally as needed early in the day. Check for evidence of natural enemies such as gray-brown or bloated parasitized aphids and the presence of alligator-like larvae of lady beetles and lacewings. For squash bugs, handpick and destroy. Bury or compost plant residues after harvest. To remove spider mites, wash off with water occasionally as needed early in the day. A hard stream of water can be used to remove many mites from plants. To get rid of striped cucumber beetles, construct tents of fine netting or cheesecloth or use floating row cover over young transplants and seedlings. Put in place at planting and remove before temperatures get too hot in midsummer. Control of beetles will help to prevent bacterial wilt.

DISEASES

Pumpkins are susceptible to mildew, anthracnose, scab and bacterial wilt. Planting disease-resistant varieties when possible, maintaining the general cleanliness and health of your garden and not handling the vines when wet will help cut down the incidence of disease. If a plant does become infected, remove it before it can spread disease to healthy plants.

HARVESTING

Time from planting to harvest is 4–5½ months. A 10-foot (3m) row may give you one to three pumpkins. Leave the pumpkins on the vine as long as possible before a frost, but not too long— they become very soft when they freeze. Cut off the pumpkin with about 2 inches (5cm) of stem.

VARIETIES

Small pumpkins are grown primarily for cooking; intermediate and large sizes for cooking and the very large jumbo ones mainly for exhibition. The bush and semi-vining varieties are best suited to small home gardens. Large: Connecticut Field, Big Moon, Bix Max, Atlantic Giant, Prize-winner; Small: Jack-O'-Lantern, Spookie; Bush pumpkins: Small Sugar, Spirit, Lady Godiva (tasty seeds); Miniature: Jack Be Little, Muchkin, Baby Boo. Sow — S.T.-spring and summer; T&C- spring to early summer.

STORING AND PRESERVING

Cure pumpkins in a dark, humid place for 10 days at 86°F (30°C) then store them at 50–54°F (10–12°C), in a dry place for three to six months. Do not refrigerate. Stored pumpkins will shrink as much as 20 percent in weight; they'll still make good pies, but they look sad if kept too long. You can dry or pickle pumpkin, or freeze or bottle the cooked pulp. You can also sprout pumpkin seeds.

Freezing

1. Choose finely textured, ripe and beautifully colored pumpkins.
2. Wash, cut in quarters or small pieces and remove seeds.
3. Cook in boiling water, steam, pressure-cook, or oven-cook until tender.
4. Scoop the pulp from the skin. Mash in a saucepan, or press through a sieve or food mill into a saucepan.
5. Cool by putting the saucepan in ice water and stirring the pumpkin occasionally until cold.
6. Pack into containers, leaving a ⅛ inch (0.5cm) head space for 2 cups

(½ liter), ½ inch (1cm) for 4 cups (1 liter). Seal, label and freeze.

7. Cook frozen pumpkin just until heated through.

Pumpkin Pie Filling:

1. Prepare the pumpkin as above.

2. Combine measured amounts of mashed pumpkin with the remaining ingredients in your favorite pumpkin pie filling recipe (omit cloves, if used, and add after thawing, because freezing will change the flavor).

3. Pour the pumpkin into containers in single pie amounts. Seal, label and freeze.

4. Thaw, add cloves, turn into a pastry shell, and bake as your recipe directs.

Drying

1. Choose, mature, firm pumpkins.

2. Cut into chunks, scrape out the seeds and string. Cut in 1-inch (2.5cm) wide slices. Peel.

3. Slice 1-inch (2.5cm) strips crosswise into thin slices.

4. Blanch in boiling water about 1 minute; or in steam 2½ to 3 minutes. Drain well, chill and pat dry with paper towels.

5. Arrange in a single, even layer on baking sheets or racks.

6. Dry until tough, 4 to 12 hours or longer. Thinner slices may be brittle.

7. Put the dried vegetables into a deep container, cover lightly with cheesecloth and condition, stirring once a day for a week to 10 days.

8. Pack into vapor/moistureproof, airtight containers or double plastic bags and store in a cool, dark, dry place for up to 12 months.

9. Rehydrate in 3 cups boiling water for each cup of pumpkin, about 1 hour.

Pumpkin Seeds:

Use this procedure for drying winter squash seeds.

1. Wash seeds thoroughly in cold water to remove all pulp and strings; be careful not to damage the seed coating.

2. Rinse well, drain thoroughly and pat dry.

3. Spread seeds in a single, even layer on paper towels resting on baking racks.

4. Let dry in a warm, dry place until completely dry, 12 to 24 hours.

5. Pack into vapor/moistureproof, airtight containers or double plastic bags and store in a cool, dark, dry place for up to 12 months.

6. Use for sprouting or for planting the next year.

7. To roast for snacks, dry completely as above, or oven roast after washing. Spread in a shallow pan and roast at 355°F (180°C), 20 minutes, or until crisp and light brown.

SERVING SUGGESTIONS

Spice up the cooked pumpkin flesh for pie fillings, breads or muffins; or use it in custards, or as a stuffing for meats or vegetables. Roast the seeds for a nutritious snack.

Radish

Common name: radish

Botanic names: *Raphanus sativus* (spring radish), *Raphanus sativus longipinnatus* (winter radish)

Origin: temperate Asia

Radishes are hardy annuals or biennials that produce white, red or black roots and stems under a rosette of lobed leaves. They're fun to grow and youngsters get hooked on gardening after growing radishes more than any other vegetable. A bunch of radishes, well washed, makes a great posy to give away.

Radishes are distant relatives to horseradish.

PLANTING

Radishes can be sown almost yearlong in all districts. They mature in such a short time that you can get two to three crops in spring alone. Start planting them from seed in the garden in early spring. Radishes germinate quickly and are often used with slower-growing seeds to mark the rows. Spring radishes produce a crop so fast that in the excitement

very few people ask about the quality of the crop. Radishes can also be grown in 6 inch (15cm) pots in a bright, cool window. They will grow in sand if watered with liquid, all-purpose fertilizer diluted to quarter strength.

HOW TO PLANT

Radishes tolerate partial shade and like well-worked, well-drained soil. When preparing the soil for planting, work in a complete, well-balanced fertilizer at the rate of 1lb per 95sq feet (450g per 9sq m). If planting winter radishes, be sure to loosen the soil well and remove soil lumps or rocks that might cause the roots to become deformed. Plant seeds ⅓ inch (1cm) deep in rows or wide rows 12–18 inches (30–45cm) apart. When the seedlings are large enough to handle, thin them according to the variety; thin small spring varieties 1–3 inches (2.5–7.5cm) apart, and give winter varieties a little more space.

FERTILIZING AND WATERING

Fertilize before planting and again at midseason, at the same rate as the rest of the garden.

Give radishes enough water to keep the roots growing quickly. If the water supply is low, radishes become woody.

SPECIAL HANDLING

Radishes sometimes bolt, or go to seed, in the summer, but this is more often a question of day length than of temperature. Cover the plants in midsummer so they only get an eight-hour day; a 12-hour day produces flowers and seeds but no radishes.

PESTS

Aphids and root maggots occasionally attack radishes, but you harvest radishes so quickly that pests are not a serious problem. You can pinch out aphid-infested foliage and drench the soil around the plants with Diazinon to control root maggots.

DISEASES

If radishes become infected with clubroot, locate new plants in part of garden different from previous year's location. If that is not possible, remove infested soil and replace with fresh soil. Remove and destroy entire infested plant along with immediately surrounding soil and soil clinging to roots. If soil is infested, add lime to raise soil pH to 7.2.

HARVESTING

Time from planting to harvest is 20 to 30 days for spring radishes, 1½–2 months for winter radishes. Pull up the whole plant when the

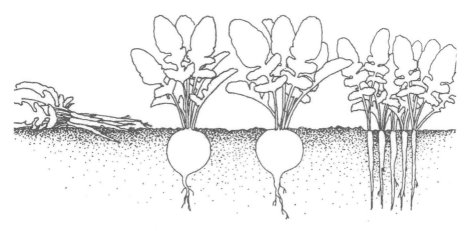

Overcrowding can ruin your root vegetable crops; thin radishes so that the roots have room to develop.

radishes are the right size. Test-pull a few or push the soil aside gently to judge the size and remember that the biggest radishes aren't necessarily the best. If you wait too long to harvest, the centers of spring radishes become pithy.

VARIETIES

Cherry Belle, French Breakfast, Scarlet Globe, Sparkler, Champion, All Seasons, Scarlet Knight, Crimson Giant, White Icicle, Easter Egg, White Chinese, China Rose, Round Black Spanish, Sakurajima, Daikon. Spring varieties are usually small and round. Winter varieties are larger, more oval and can grow to 8 inches (20cm) long.

STORING AND PRESERVING

Radishes will store for one to two weeks in the refrigerator. You can also sprout radish seeds.

SERVING SUGGESTIONS

Radishes can be sculptured into rosettes or just sliced into a salad. They are low in calories and make good cookie substitutes when you have to nibble. Put radishes on a relish tray, or on a platter of vegetables for dipping. Try "pickling" the excess crop by mincing them and marinating in vinegar.

Rhubarb

Common names: rhubarb, pie plant

Botanic name: *Rheum rhaponticum*

Origin: Southern Siberia

A hardy perennial, rhubarb grows 3–6½ feet (1–2m) tall, with large, attractive leaves on strong stalks. The leaf stalks are red or green and grow up from a rhizome or underground stem, and the flowers are small and grow on top of a flower stalk. Don't allow the plant to reach the flowering stage; remove the flower stalk when it first appears. You eat only the rhubarb stalks, the leaves contain a toxic substance and are not for eating.

PLANTING

Rhubarb is very hardy and prefers cool weather. In areas where the weather is warm or hot, the leaf stalks are thin and spindly. Rhubarb can be grown from seed, but the plants will not grow "true"—which means they won't be the same variety as the parent plant. Grow from the divisions that grow up from the parent stems for a close or exact copy of the parent plant. Buy divisions or divide your own plants in spring when the soil has warmed up. The timing is not crucial, because you won't harvest rhubarb the first year.

HOW TO PLANT

Rhubarb likes rich, well-worked soil that is high in organic matter and drains well. Give it a place in full sun or light shade. When preparing the soil for planting, work in a complete, well-balanced fertilizer at the rate of 1lb per 95sq feet (450g per 9sq m). Plant the divisions about 3 feet (1m) apart in rows 3–5 feet (1–1.5m) apart, with the growing tips slightly below the soil surface.

FERTILIZING AND WATERING

Fertilize before planting and again at midseason, at the same rate as the rest of the garden.

Rhubarb does best with even soil moisture. Water it thoroughly before the soil dries out, but don't let the soil get soggy.

SPECIAL HANDLING

Keep grass and other competitors away from rhubarb and mulch it, especially in winter. To get earlier and longer leaf stalks, cover the plants with bottomless boxes in the early spring. Remove the flower stalks when they appear in order to keep the leaf stalks growing strongly; divide the plant every three to four years. Rhubarb can be forced or made to produce before its natural maturity. To do this dig up roots at least two years old and pile them on the ground so they will be frozen with the first hard frost. After the freeze, put them into pots or boxes filled with sand and surround the containers with sand to keep the roots moist. Store the containers in a cold place but not where the temperature could fall more than a couple of degrees below freezing. When you move the roots to a dark, cool place about 59°F (15°C), the stalks will grow tall with very small, pale, folded-up leaves. Rhubarb can also be forced in a cold frame later in the year; these stalks will be greener and more nutritious, and the leaves will be almost normal size.

PESTS

Rhubarb has no serious pest problems. It's a trouble-free crop for any garden.

DISEASES

Rhubarb has no serious disease problems. Some old clumps may develop crown rot, but this can be avoided by dividing the clumps before they get too large. And as fungal leaf spot may also be a possible disease, avoid wetting foliage if possible. Water early in the day so aboveground plant parts will dry as quickly as possible. Avoid crowding plants. Space apart to allow air circulation. Eliminate weeds around plants and garden area to improve air circulation. Practice plant sanitation. When plants are not wet, carefully remove and destroy or discard affected plant parts. In autumn, rake and dispose of all fallen or diseased leaves and stalks.

HARVESTING

Don't expect quick results from your rhubarb crop; you'll have to wait two to three years from the time of planting while the roots establish themselves. You can sneak a single-leaf stalk the first year, if the plant has four or more leaves. A 10-foot (3m) row of rhubarb should give you 9–10lbs (4–4.5kg) of mature stems. To harvest, twist off the leaf stalk at the soil line. To keep the plant going strong, do not cut more than a third of the leaves in any year.

VARIETIES

Victoria, Ruby, Valentine, Cherry, Giant Cherry, Canada Red, MacDonald Crimson.

STORING AND PRESERVING

Rhubarb can be stored in the refrigerator for up to two weeks; cut off the leaves first. Freeze or make preserves from any extra rhubarb. It can also be bottled or dried.

Freezing

This spring fruit will probably be the garden's first contribution to your freezer.
1. Select colorful, firm but tender stalks with few fibers.
2. Wash and trim off leaves and woody ends.
3. Cut in 1 or 2 inch (2.5 or 5cm) lengths.
4. Blanch 1 minute. Cool quickly in cold water to save color and flavor; drain well.
5. Unsweetened pack: Pack rhubarb pieces tightly in containers. Seal, label and freeze. Syrup pack: *Pack rhubarb pieces tightly in containers. Cover with cold 40 percent syrup, leaving ⅛ inch (0.5cm) head space for 2 cups (½ liter), ½ inch (1cm) for 4 cups (1 liter). Crumple a small piece of plastic wrap, waxed paper or freezer paper and put in on top of rhubarb in each container. Seal, label and freeze.

*For 40 percent syrup, mix 3 cups sugar with 4 cups water until sugar dissolves. Chill in refrigerator until ready to use. This makes 5½ cups. You'll need about ½ cup of syrup for each 2 cups (½ liter) of rhubarb.

Drying

1. Choose young, tender, perfect rhubarb. Trim off leaves and root ends; wash well.
2. Slice about ⅛ inch (0.5cm) thick.
3. Blanch in boiling water 2 minutes; or in steam 2 minutes. Drain well, chill and pat dry.
4. Spread the slices in a single, even layer on baking sheets or racks.
5. Dry until hard, about 8 to 16 hours.
6. Put the dried vegetables into a deep container, cover lightly with cheesecloth and condition, stirring once a day for a week to 10 days.
7. Pack into vapor/moistureproof, airtight containers or double plastic bags and store in a cool, dark, dry place for up to 12 months.
8. Rehydrate rhubarb in 1 1/4 cups of boiling water for each cup of rhubarb, 2 to 3 hours or overnight.

SERVING SUGGESTIONS

Botanically, rhubarb is a vegetable, but for culinary purposes it is a fruit. It's good in pies, jams and jellies, and can be eaten baked or stewed as a topping for a cooked breakfast cereal. It has a tart taste and needs added sugar. The sweetened juice makes a refreshing cold drink. Add finely chopped rhubarb to any nut bread recipe.

Rutabaga

Common names: Swedish turnip,
swede, Russian turnip, yellow turnip

Botanic name: *Brassica napobrassica*

Origin: Northern Europe

The rutabaga is a hardy biennial grown as an annual. It has a rosette of smooth, grayish-green leaves that grow from the swollen stem, and it has a root that can be yellow, purple, or white. The rutabaga can be distinguished from the turnip by the leaf scars on its top, and the leaves are more deeply lobed than the turnip's. As vegetables go, rutabagas are a fairly modern invention. They were created less than 200 years ago by crossing a cabbage with a turnip (probably Swedish).

PLANTING

Rutabagas are very hardy and grow better in cool weather. They like a definite difference between day and night temperatures. In hot weather they produce lots of leaves, but small stringy roots. S.T.-autumn; T- summer to autumn; C-summer to early autumn.

HOW TO PLANT

Rutabagas do best in well-drained soil high in organic matter.

Although less likely to fork or split than carrots they need well-worked soil with all the rocks and soil lumps removed. When preparing the soil for planting, work in a complete, well-balanced fertilizer at the rate of 1lb per 95sq feet

(450g per 9sq m). Plant the seeds ⅓ inch (1cm) deep in rows 18–24 inches (45–60cm) apart and when the seedlings are large enough to handle, thin them to 6–8 inches (15–20cm) apart. Thinning is important; like all root crops, rutabagas must have room to develop.

FERTILIZING AND WATERING

Fertilize before planting and again at midseason, at the same rate as the rest of the garden.

Water thoroughly before the roots dry out, and water often enough to keep the rutabagas growing steadily. If their growth slows down, the roots will be tough.

PESTS

Aphids attack rutabagas and can be persistent. Try to control them physically by pinching out infested foliage or hosing the aphids off the plants. Chemically, control them with Malathion or Diazinon, being sure to spray the underside of the foliage. To prevent flea beetles, use row covers to help protect plants from early damage. Put in place at planting and remove before temperatures get too hot (midsummer). Control weeds. In the case of cabbage root maggots, use row covers.

DISEASES

Rutabagas have no serious disease problems. However, they may become infected by black leg, black rot or turnip mosaic virus.

HARVESTING

Time from planting to harvest is about 3 months and a 10-foot (3m) row may give you over 110lbs (5kg) of rutabagas if the weather has been right. To harvest, dig up the whole roots when the rutabagas are 3–5 inches (7.5–12.5cm) in diameter. In cold areas, mulch heavily to extend the harvesting period.

VARIETIES

American Purple Top, Laurentian, Long Island Improved, Macomber.

STORING AND PRESERVING

Leave the rutabagas in the ground for as long as possible until you're ready to use them; in very cold areas, mulch them heavily. Store rutabagas in a cold, moist place for two to four months; do not refrigerate. They can also be frozen.

SERVING SUGGESTIONS

Peel rutabagas and steam or boil until tender; then mash them for use in puddings and pancakes. They can also be served sliced or diced. Add rutabagas to vegetable soups and stews. Sauté them in butter with apples and brown sugar. Rutabagas are very good with lots of butter or sour cream; low-calorie alternatives are yogurt or low-fat cream cheese.

Salsify

Common names: salsify, oyster plant

Botanic name: *Tragopogon porrifolius*

Origin: Southern Europe

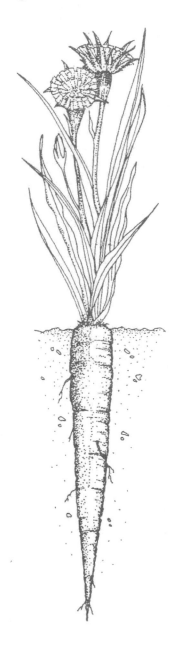

Salsify is a hardy biennial grown as an annual. It's related to dandelion and chicory, and its flowers look like lavender chicory blossoms. The edible part is the long taproot. This salsify should not be confused with black salsify (Scorzonera hispanica) or Spanish salsify (Scolymus hispanicus); both of these are related to the radish. Some people claim that salsify has a slight oyster flavor—hence the name "oyster plant." In fact, it tastes rather like artichoke hearts.

PLANTING

Salsify is hardy and tolerates cold. Like its prolific cousin, the dandelion, it's very easy to grow. It can adapt to all types of climate.

HOW TO PLANT

Sow salsify seeds in spring in full sun in rich, well-worked soil. When preparing the soil for planting, work in a complete, well-balanced fertilizer at the rate of 1lb per 95sq feet (450g per 9sq m). Work the soil thoroughly to a depth of 8–12 inches (20–30cm) and remove all stones, soil lumps or rocks that might cause the roots to fork and split. Sow the seeds ⅓ inch (1cm) deep in rows 18–24 inches (45–60cm) apart and when the seedlings are large enough to handle, thin them to 2–4 inches (5–10cm) apart.

FERTILIZING AND WATERING

Fertilize before planting and again at midseason, at the same rate as the rest of the garden. Don't over-fertilize salsify; it will cause the roots to fork and split.

Keep salsify evenly moist to prevent the roots from getting stringy.

PESTS

Salsify has no serious pest problems.

DISEASES

Salsify has no serious disease problems.

HARVESTING

Time from planting to harvest is about 4 months, and a 10-foot (3m) row should yield 20 to 40 roots. Salsify roots can take freezing, so leave them in the ground as long as possible until you want them. The longer they're out of the ground, the less they taste like oysters. To harvest, dig up the whole root.

STORING AND PRESERVING

Cut the tops off salsify and store the roots in the refrigerator for one to three weeks, or store in a cold, moist place for two to four months. For freezing, handle salsify like parsnips.

SERVING SUGGESTIONS

Salsify roots should not be peeled before cooking; they can "bleed": Scrub them clean, steam and slice them, then dip the slices in batter or breadcrumbs and fry; serve with tartar sauce. People who have never had oysters can't tell them apart. Try salsify braised with lemon and butter—the lemon helps preserve the color. Or serve it with a white sauce; add chopped parsley for color."

Shallot

Common name: shallot

Botanic name: *Allium cepa*

Origin: Asia

The shallot is a very hardy biennial grown as an annual, and is a member of the onion family. It's believed that French knights returning from the Crusades introduced them to Europe. Shallot plants grow about 8 inches (20cm) in a clump, with narrow green leaves, and look very much like small onions; they're favorites with gourmets. The roots are very shallow and fibrous, and the bulbs are about ½ inch (1cm) in diameter when mature. The small bulbs have a more delicate flavor than regular onions. Use the young outer leaves like chives.

PLANTING

Shallots are very hardy and easy to grow from cloves planted from mid to late winter.

HOW TO PLANT

Shallots can be grown in any soil but may have less flavor when they're grown in clay soils. Shallots are very shallow-rooted plants and need little soil preparation. Although they prefer full sun, they'll survive in partial shade. Shallots seldom form seed, so they're usually grown from small cloves broken from the bulbs—

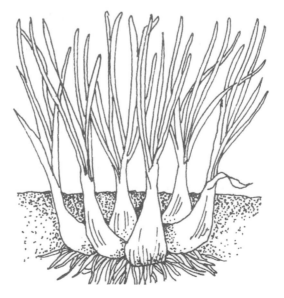

very like garlic. When preparing the soil for planting, work in a complete, well-balanced fertilizer at the rate of 1lb per 95sq feet (450g per 9sq m). Plant the cloves 6–8 inches (15–20cm) apart in rows 1 foot (30cm) apart, and set them so that the tops of the cloves are even with the soil, but no deeper. Keep them carefully cultivated when they're small; the shallow root systems don't like to compete with weeds.

FERTILIZING AND WATERING

Fertilize before planting and again at midseason, at the same rate as the rest of the garden.

Water the shallots regularly; do not allow the soil to dry out.

PESTS

Shallots have no serious pest problems. However, in the case of onion maggot, locate new plants in a part of the garden different from previous year's location. If that is not possible remove infested soil and replace with fresh soil. Use floating row covers to prevent onion maggot infestations.

DISEASES

Shallots have no serious disease problems.

HARVESTING

Cut the green shallot leaves throughout the growing season, but be careful not to cut away any new growth coming from the central stem. Dig up bulbs when the tops wither and fall over.

STORING AND PRESERVING

Store shallots in the refrigerator for up to one week or store the bulbs like onions in a cold, dry place for two to eight months.

You can also freeze or dry them like onions. The greens can be chopped and frozen like chives.

SERVING SUGGESTIONS

Shallots have a delicate flavor and are less overpowering than many onions. They're very good stirred into sour cream as a dressing for vegetables or fish, or chopped and added to an oil-and-vinegar dressing for salads. Use the small bulbs in the classic French beef stew, boeuf bourguignonne.

Silver Beet

See Swiss Chard

Sorrel

Common names: garden sorrel, herb patience or spinach dock, French sorrel, spinach rhubarb

Botanic names: *Rumex acetosa, Rumex patientia, Rumex scutatus, Rumex abyssinicus*

Origin: Europe

Several varieties of sorrel will do well in your garden. Garden sorrel (*R. acetosa*) grows about 35 inches (90cm) tall and produces leaves that are good used fresh in salads; herb patience or spinach dock (*R. patientia*) is a much taller plant, with leaves that can be used either fresh or cooked. French sorrel (*R. scutatus*) grows only 6–12 inches (15–30cm) tall; its fiddle-shaped leaves make good salad greens. Spinach rhubarb (*R. abyssinicus*) is a lofty plant—it grows up to 8 feet (2.5m). As the name suggests, you can cook the leaves like spinach and the stalks like rhubarb. Avoid other varieties—they're weeds and not good for eating.

PLANTING

All the sorrels are very hardy. Start them from seed in the early spring.

HOW TO PLANT

All the sorrels require a sunny location with well-drained, fertile soil. When you're preparing the soil, dig in a complete, well-balanced fertilizer at the rate of 1lb per 95sq feet (450g per 9sq m). Sow the seeds ⅓ inch (1cm) deep in rows 18–24 inches (45–60cm) apart and when the plants are six to eight weeks old, thin them to 12–18 inches (30–45cm) apart.

FERTILIZING AND WATERING

Fertilize before planting and again at midseason, at the same rate as the rest of the garden.

Sorrel plants should be kept moist; water them more often than the rest of the garden.

PESTS

Aphids will probably show interest in your sorrel. Control them by pinching out infested areas or hosing the aphids off the plants; or spray with Malathion or Diazinon.

DISEASES

Sorrel has no serious disease problems.

HARVESTING

Pick the fresh leaves of the sorrel throughout the growing season. Pick off the flowers before they mature to keep the plants producing new leaves long into autumn.

STORING AND PRESERVING

Use sorrel fresh, or store sorrel leaves in the refrigerator for one to two weeks. You can also freeze or dry the leaves as herbs; but you'll lose some flavor.

SERVING SUGGESTIONS

You can use sorrel leaves raw, as salad greens or very lightly steamed or boiled and tossed in butter. Sorrel soup is a classic French favorite, and the Russians use sorrel in a green borscht soup. In the time of Henry VIII, sorrel was used as a spice and to tenderize meat. The English also mashed the leaves with vinegar and sugar as a dressing for meat and fish—hence the name green sauce.

Spinach

Common name: spinach

Botanic name: *Spinacla oleracea*

Origin: Asia

There are two kinds of spinach—the regular kind which is a hardy annual, and the less well-known New Zealand spinach, which is a tender annual and is not really spinach at all. Spinach, the regular kind, is a hardy annual with a rosette of dark green leaves. The leaves may be crinkled (savoy leaf) or flat. Spinach is related to beets and swiss chard. The cartoon character Popeye made spinach famous with young children because he attributed his great strength to eating spinach—probably with some justification, because spinach has a very high iron content.

New Zealand spinach (*Tetragonia expansa*) comes—as the name indicates—from New Zealand. It's a tender annual with weak, spreading stems 1½–4 feet (0.5–1.25m) long, sometimes longer, and it's covered with dark green leaves that are 2–4 inches (5–10cm) long. New Zealand spinach is not really spinach at all, but when it's cooked the two are virtually indistinguishable. The leaves of New Zealand spinach

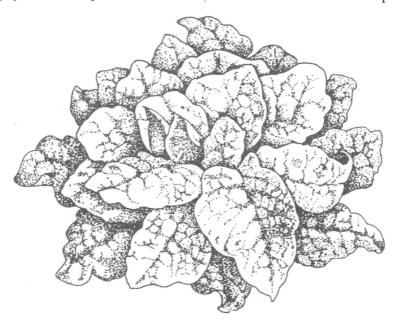

are smaller and fuzzier than those of regular spinach, and it has the advantage of being heat-tolerant and able to produce all summer. Heat makes regular spinach bolt, or go to seed, very quickly.

PLANTING

Spinach is very hardy and can tolerate cold—in fact, it thrives in cold weather. Warm weather and long days, however, will make it bolt, or go to seed. Ideal spinach weather is 50–59°F (10–15°C). S.T.-autumn; T & C- autumn to spring.

New Zealand spinach likes long warm days. It grows best at 59–77°F (15–25°C) and won't start growing until the soil warms up. It has a short season, however (55 to 65 days), so it can be grown successfully in most areas in spring. Plant New Zealand spinach to supply you with a summer harvest long after it's too hot for regular spinach.

HOW TO PLANT

Both spinach and New Zealand spinach are grown—like beets and swiss chard—from seed clusters that each produce several seedlings. This means they must be thinned when the seedlings appear. Both types tolerate partial shade and require well-drained soil rich in organic matter. Spinach does not like acid soil. When preparing the soil for planting, work in a complete, well-balanced fertilizer at the rate of 1lb per 95sq feet (450g per 9sq m). Plant spinach seed clusters ⅓ inch (1cm) deep, 2–4 inches (5–10cm) apart, in rows 12–14 inches (30–35cm) apart and when the seedlings are large enough to handle, thin them to leave the strongest seedling from each cluster.

For New Zealand spinach, plant the seed clusters ⅓ inch (1cm) deep, 12 inch (30cm) apart in rows 24–35 inches (60–90cm) apart. Thin when the seedlings are large enough to handle, leaving the strongest seedling from each cluster to grow. Cut off the others with scissors at soil level.

FERTILIZING AND WATERING

Fertilize both types before planting and again at midseason, at the same rate as the rest of the garden.

Spinach does best when the soil is kept uniformly moist. Try not to splash muddy water on the leaves—it will make the spinach difficult to clean after harvesting. Mulch to avoid getting soil on the leaves. New Zealand spinach especially needs a regular supply of water to keep it producing lots of leaves.

SPECIAL HANDLING

Spinach does not like competition from weeds. Cut weeds at ground level to avoid damaging the shallow roots of the spinach plants.

PESTS

Aphids and, occasionally, leafminers may attack spinach. Pinch out aphid-infested foliage and remove leaves on which leafminers have laid their eggs—look for the eggs on the undersides of the leaves. Control aphids chemically with Malathion or Diazinon; chemical controls are ineffective on leafminers once they're inside the leaf. New Zealand spinach has no serious pest problems and is a good crop for the organic gardener.

DISEASES

Spinach is susceptible to rust, but most varieties are rust-resistant. It is also susceptible to the mosaic virus which can be controlled by controlling the aphids or by growin resistant varieties. Planting disease-resistant varieties and maintaining the general cleanliness and health of your garden will help cut down the incidence of disease. If a plant does become infected, remove it before it can spread disease to healthy plants. New Zealand spinach has no serious disease problems.

HARVESTING

For spinach, time from planting to harvest is 2–2½ months and a 10-foot (3m) row should yield about 5½lbs (2.5kg) of spinach leaves. To harvest, either pick the outside leaves periodically, or pull up the whole plant at one time. Be sure to wash spinach thoroughly to eliminate the grit that sometimes sticks to the crinkled leaves.

For New Zealand spinach, time from planting to harvest is 2½–3 months and a 10-foot (3m) row will produce about 5½–10lbs (2.5–4.5kg) of leaves. To harvest keep cutting the tender tips off the ends of the stems; this will encourage new growth and you can harvest until the first frost.

VARIETIES

Long Standing Bloomsdale, Popeye's Choice, America, Winter Bloomsdale, Melody, Hybrid Number 7, Giant Nobel, Indian Summer, Tyee Hybrid, Space. Only a few varieties of New Zealand spinach are available.

New Zealand spinach

PRESERVING

Both types of spinach can be refrigerated for up to one week. They can also be frozen, bottled or dried. Spinach seeds can also be sprouted.

Freezing

1. Choose young, tender leaves.
2. Wash well in several changes of water.
3. Remove tough stems and bruised leaves.
4. Blanch each pound (½ kg) of spinach in 2½ gallons (9 liters) boiling water for 2 minutes. For very tender spinach, blanch only 1 ½ minutes. Stir to keep leaves from sticking together. Cool; drain well.
5. Pack into containers, leaving ⅛ inch (0.5cm) head space. Seal, label and freeze.
6. Cook frozen spinach 8 to 12 minutes.

Drying

1. Choose very fresh, perfect leaves.
2. Wash well; shake dry. Remove any large tough stalks.
3. Blanch in boiling water about 1½ minutes; or in steam about 2½ minutes, until completely wilted. Drain very well, chill and pat dry with paper towels.
4. Arrange leaves in a single, even layer on baking sheets or racks.
5. Dry until brittle, 2½ to 8 hours or more.
6. Put the dried vegetables into a deep container, cover lightly with cheesecloth and condition, stirring once a day for a week to 10 days.
7. Pack into vapor/moistureproof, airtight containers or double plastic bags and store in a cool, dark, dry place for up to 12 months.
8. Rehydrate in 1 cup of boiling water for each cup of spinach, about ½ hour.

SERVING SUGGESTIONS

Both spinach and New Zealand spinach can be used in the same ways, and the following suggestions apply to both. Fresh spinach is wonderful in salads, and its dark green leaves add color and variety to lettuce. Add orange segments and almonds to a salad of fresh spinach, and toss in a sweet-sour dressing. Or add crumbled bacon, hard-boiled eggs and croutons. Add cubes of cheese to spinach, peppers and sliced fresh mushrooms for an appealing lunchtime salad. Children who hate cooked spinach on principle often enjoy it raw. Cooked spinach is delicious creamed or in a soufflé, in crepes or topped with poached eggs. Try it with a horseradish sauce, or with melted butter and a little garlic. Spinach is an attractive ingredient for a quiche; add flaked salmon for a more substantial meal.

Sprout

See Brussels Sprout;

Squash, Summer

Common names: summer squash, crookneck, pattypan, straightneck, scallop, zucchini

Botanic name: *Cucurbita* species

Origin: American tropics

The cucumber family, to which squashes belong, probably has the greatest diversity of shapes and sizes of any vegetable family except the cabbages. It's the genus Cucurbita and includes certain gourds and pumpkins, as well as squashes. Most are trailing or climbing plants with large yellow flowers (both male and female); the mature fruits have a thick skin and a definite seed cavity. Summer squashes are eaten when they are immature; winter squashes are eaten when mature.

Squashes are hard to confine. A bush-type zucchini will grow well in a planter if kept well watered and fertilized; a vining squash can be trained up a fence. Summer squashes are weak-stemmed, tender annuals, with large, cucumber-like leaves and separate male and female flowers that appear on the same plant. Summer squash usually grows as a bush, rather than as a vine; the fruits have thin, tender skin and are generally eaten in the immature stage before the skin hardens. The most popular of the many kinds of summer squashes are crookneck, straightneck, scallop and zucchini.

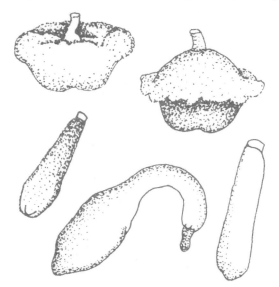

PLANTING

Squashes are warm-season crops and very sensitive to cold and frost. They like night temperatures of at least 59°F (15°C). Don't plant the seeds until the soil has warmed up in spring. Direct-seeding is best for squashes, but if you're planting a variety that requires a longer growing season than your area can provide, use seedlings from a reputable nursery or garden center, or grow your own. To grow your own seedlings, start four to five weeks before your outdoor planting date, and use individual plantable containers to lessen the risk of shock when the seedlings are transplanted. Make sure that the plantable containers are large enough for the variety of squash you're planting.

HOW TO PLANT

Squash varieties like well-worked soil with good drainage. They're heavy feeders, so the soil must be well fertilized. When preparing the soil for planting, work in a complete, well-balanced fertilizer at the rate of 1lb per 95sq feet (450g per 9sq m). When the soil is warm, plant squash in inverted hills made by removing 1 inch (2.5cm) of soil from an area about 12 inches (30cm) across and using this soil to form a ring around the circle. Make the inverted hills 3–5 feet (1–1.5m) apart and plant four or five seeds in each one. When the seedlings are large enough to handle, thin them to leave the two or three strongest young plants standing. Cut the thinned seedlings off at soil level with scissors; if you pull them out you'll disturb the roots of the remaining seedlings.

FERTILIZING AND WATERING

Fertilize before planting and again at midseason, at the same rate as the rest of the garden.

Keep the soil evenly moist; squashes need a lot of water in hot weather. The vines may wilt on hot days because the plant is using water faster than the roots can supply; if the vines ate getting a regular supply of water, don't worry about the wilting—the plants will liven up as the day gets cooler. If squash vines are wilting first thing in the morning water them immediately.

SPECIAL HANDLING

If you grow squashes indoors, or in an area where there are no insects to pollinate the female flowers, you may need to pollinate the flowers yourself. Take a soft-bristled brush and dust the inside of a male flower (the one without an immature fruit on the stem), then carefully dust the inside of the female flowers.

PESTS

Squash bugs, squash borers, and cucumber beetles are the major pests. They don't usually show up until you have a good harvest, so squash is still a good choice for the organic gardener. Squashes are prolific, so you can afford to lose a few of your crop to the bugs. Beetles can often be controlled by handpicking or hosing them off the plants. Control them chemically with Carbaryl. To control borers, apply Carbaryl to the crowns of the plants at weekly intervals. Do this as soon as there's any suspicion of damage—once the borers get inside the plants, chemical controls are ineffective. If a small hole in the stem tells you borers are already inside, you may still be able to save the plant. Slit the stem, remove the borers and dispose of them. Then cover the area with soil to encourage root development at that point.

DISEASES

Squashes are susceptible to bacterial wilt, mosaic virus, mildew and scab. Planting disease-resistant varieties when they're available and maintaining the general cleanliness and health of your garden will help lessen the incidence of disease. When watering, try to keep water off the foliage, and don't handle the plants when they're wet—this can cause powdery mildew and spread disease. If a plant does become infected, remove and destroy it before it can spread disease to healthy plants.

HARVESTING

Time from planting to harvest depends on the variety, as does the yield you can expect. Harvest summer squashes when they're young—they taste delicious when they're small, and if you leave them on the plant too long they will suppress flowering and reduce your crop. Harvest summer squashes like the zucchini and crookneck varieties when they're 6–8 inches (15–20cm) long; harvest the round types when they're 4–8 inches (10–20cm) in diameter. Break the squashes from the plant, or use a knife that you clean after cutting each one; if the knife is not perfectly clean, it can spread disease to other plants.

VARIETIES

Aristocrat, Ambassador, President Hybrid, Gourmet Globe, Gold Rush, Early Prolific Straightneck, Goldbar, Early Summer Crookneck, Seneca Prolific, Sundance, Fortune, Zucchini Elite Hybrid. Scallop varieties: Peter Pan, Early White, Bush Scallop, Sunburst, Scallopini.

STORING AND PRESERVING

Summer squashes can be stored in the refrigerator for up to one week; don't wash them until you're ready to use them. They can also be frozen, bottled, pickled or dried.

Freezing

1. Choose young, tender squash.
2. Wash, cut off the ends, and slice the squash ½ inch (1cm) thick.
3. Blanch 3 minutes. Cool; drain well.
4. Tray freeze or pack into containers. Seal, label and freeze.
5. Cook frozen summer squash about 10 minutes.

Drying

1. Choose young, tender squash with tender skins.
2. Wash well, cut off the ends, and slice about ⅛ inch (0.5cm) thick.
3. Blanch in boiling water about 1½ minutes; or in steam about 2½ to 3 minutes. Drain well, chill and pat dry with paper towels.
4. Arrange in a single, even layer on racks.
5. Dry until brittle, 4 to 12 hours.
6. Put the dried vegetables into a deep container, cover lightly with cheesecloth and condition, stirring once a day for a week to 10 days.

7. Pack into vapor/moistureproof, airtight containers or double plastic bags and store in a cool, dark, dry place for up to 12 months.
8. Rehydrate in 1 ¾ cups of boiling water for each cup of squash, about 1 hour.

SERVING SUGGESTIONS

Summer squashes lend themselves to a good variety of culinary treatments. Sauté slices of summer squash with onions and tomatoes for a robust but delicately flavored side dish. Add sliced zucchini and mushrooms to a thick tomato sauce for spaghetti. Halve summer squashes and stuff with a meat or rice mixture, or bake them with butter and Parmesan cheese. Pan-fry slices of summer squash, or simmer them with fruit juice for a new flavor. Use the popular zucchini raw on a relish tray and among vegetables for a tempura, or slice it thinly in salads. Use the larger fruits for making zucchini bread.

Squash, Winter

Common names: acorn, banana, buttercup, butternut, delicious, hubbard, spaghetti

Botanic name: *Cucurbita* species

Origin: American tropics

Thecucumber family, to which squashes belong, probably has the greatest diversity of shapes and sizes of any vegetable family, except the cabbages. It's the genus Cucurbita, and includes certain gourds and pumpkins as well as squashes. Most are trailing or climbing plants with large yellow flowers (both male and female); the mature fruits have a thick skin and a definite seed cavity. Summer squashes are eaten when they are immature; winter squashes are eaten when mature. Squashes are hard to confine. A bush-type squash will grow well in a planter if kept well watered and fertilized; a vining squash can be trained up a fence.

Gourds are a close relation of squash. They're warm-season vining crops that are grown primarily for decorative uses; you can also make cooking utensils out of them, and some of them can be eaten when immature. They have the same growing requirements as winter squash and they're harvested in autumn when the shells are hard and glossy.

Winter squashes are weak-stemmed, tender annuals, with large, cucumber-like leaves and separate male and female flowers that appear on the same plant. Most winter squashes grow as vines, although some modern

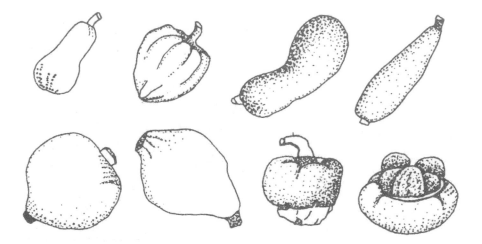

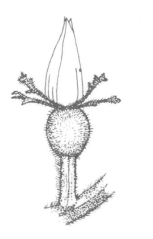

Female squash blossom

Male squash blossom

varieties have been bred to have a more compact, bushy habit of growth. Winter squash varieties have hard skins when they're harvested and eaten. Popular types of winter squash include hubbard, butternut, acorn. Spaghetti squash is technically a small pumpkin and is planted and cared for like pumpkins. Vining types of winter squash can be caged or trained to climb up a fence or trellis to save space. If growing a variety that will need support, set the support in place at the time of planting. If you do it later, you risk damaging the plants' roots.

PLANTING

Squashes are warm-season crops and very sensitive to cold and frost. They like night temperatures of at least 59°F (15°C). Don't plant the seeds until the soil has warmed

up in spring. Direct-seeding is best for squashes, but if planting a variety that requires a longer growing season that your area can provide, use seedlings from a reputable nursery or garden center, or grow your own. To grow your own seedlings, start four to five weeks before your outdoor planting date, and use individual plantable containers to lessen the risk of shock when the seedlings are transplanted. Make sure that the plantable containers are large enough for the variety of squash you're planting.

HOW TO PLANT

Squash varieties like well-worked soil with good drainage. They're heavy feeders, so the soil must be well fertilized. When preparing the soil for planting, work in a complete, well-balanced fertilizer at the rate of 1lb per 95sq feet (450g per 9sq m). When the soil is warm, plant squash in inverted hills. Make inverted hills by removing 1 inch (2.5cm) of soil from an area about 12 inches (30cm) across and using this soil to form a ring around the circle. Make the inverted hills 3–5 feet (1–1.5m) apart and plant four to five seeds in each one. When the seedlings are large enough to handle, thin them to leave the two or three strongest young plants standing. Cut the thinned seedlings off at soil level with scissors; if you pull them out you'll disturb the roots of the remaining seedlings.

FERTILIZING AND WATERING

Fertilize before planting and again at midseason, at the same rate as the rest of the garden.

Keep the soil evenly moist; squashes need a lot of water in hot weather. The vines may wilt on hot days because the plant is using water faster than the roots can supply; if the vines are getting a regular supply of water, don't worry about the wilting—the plants will liven up as the day gets cooler. If squash vines are wilting, first thing in the morning water them immediately.

SPECIAL HANDLING

If you grow squashes indoors or in an area where there are no insects to pollinate the female flowers, you may need to pollinate the flowers yourself. Take a soft-bristled brush and dust the inside of a male flower (the one without an immature fruit on the stem), then carefully dust the inside of the female flowers.

PESTS

Squash bugs, squash borers, and cucumber beetles are the major pests that squash plants attract. They don't usually show up until you have a good harvest, so squash is still a good choice for the organic gardener. Squashes are prolific, so you can afford to lose a few of your crop to the bugs. Beetles can often be controlled by handpicking or hosing them off the plants. Control them chemically with Carbaryl. To control borers, apply Carbaryl to the crowns of the plants at weekly intervals. Do this as soon as there's any suspicion of damage—once the borers get inside the plants, chemical controls are ineffective. If a small hole in the stem tells you borers are already inside, you may still be able to save the plant. Slit the stem, remove the borers, and dispose of them. Then cover the area with soil to encourage root development at that point.

DISEASES

Squashes are susceptible to bacterial wilt, mosaic virus, mildew and scab. Planting disease-resistant varieties and maintaining the general cleanliness and health of your garden will help lessen the incidence of disease. When watering, try to keep water off foliage, and don't handle the plants when they're wet—this can cause powdery mildew and spread disease. If a plant does become infected, remove and destroy it before it can spread disease to healthy plants.

HARVESTING

Leave winter squashes on the vine until the skin is so hard that it cannot be dented with your thumbnail, but harvest before the first frost.

Break it off the vine, or cut if off with a knife that you clean after cutting each one; if the knife is not perfectly clean, it can spread disease to other plants.

VARIETIES

Buttercup, Emerald, Delicata, Butternut, Early Butternut, Burpee's Butterbush, Waltham, Sweet Mama, Spaghetti Squash, Banana, Tahitian, Little Gem. Acorn varieties: Ebony Acorn, Table King, Table Ace, Jersey Golden Acorn, Sweet Dumpling. Hubbard varieties: Blue Hubbard, Green Hubbard, Golden Hubbard, Red Kuri, Blue Ballet.

STORING AND PRESERVING

Cure squashes in a dark, humid place for 10 days at 77–86°F (25–30°C); then store them at 50–59°F (10–15°C) in a moderately dry, dark place for five to six months. They can also be frozen or dried and the seeds can be sprouted.

Freezing

1. Choose firm, mature squash with hard skins.
2. Wash. Cut squash in half or in quarters. Bake, simmer or pressure-cook until tender.
3. Scoop pulp from the skin. Mash the pulp in saucepan, or press through a sieve or food mill into a medium saucepan.
4. Cool by placing the saucepan in ice water and stirring the squash occasionally until cold.
5. Pack into containers, leaving ⅛ inch (0.5cm) head space for 2 cups (½ liter), ½ inch (1cm) for 4 cups (1 liter). Seal, label and freeze.
6. Cook frozen squash just until heated through.

Drying

Peeling winter squash is not the easiest job in the world, but the storage space you save by drying squash may make it worthwhile.
1. Choose mature, well-shaped squash.
2. Cut the squash into chunks, scrape out the seeds and string. Cut into 1-inch (2.5cm) wide slices. Peel.
3. Slice 1-inch (2.5cm) strips crosswise into thin slices.
4. Blanch in boiling water about 1 minute; or in steam 2½ to 3 minutes. Drain well, chill and pat dry with paper towels.

5. Arrange in a single, even layer on racks.

6. Dry until tough, 4 to 12 hours or longer. Thinner slices may be brittle.

7. Put the dried vegetables into a deep container, cover lightly with cheesecloth and condition, stirring once a day for a week to 10 days.

8. Pack into vapor/moistureproof, airtight containers or double plastic bags and store in a cool, dark, dry place for up to 12 months.

9. Rehydrate in 3 cups of boiling water for each cup of squash, about 1 hour.

SERVING SUGGESTIONS

Winter squashes lend themselves to a good variety of culinary treatments and have the flexibility of adapting to both sweet and savory uses. Cut winter squashes into halves and bake them; serve them with honey or brown sugar and butter. Fill the halves with browned sausages, or mash the pulp and season well with salt and pepper. As a treat for the children, top mashed squash with marshmallow and brown it under the grill. Use the pulp of winter squash as a pie filling—it makes a pleasant change from pumpkin.

Swede

See Rutabaga

Sweet Corn

See Corn

Sweet Pepper

See Pepper

Sweet Potato

Common names: potato, sweet potato, yam

Botanic name: *Ipomoea batatas*

Origin: Tropical America and Caribbean

The sweet potato is a tender vining or semi-erect perennial plant related to the morning glory. It has small white, pink or red-purple flowers and swollen, fleshy tubers that range in color from creamy-yellow to deep red-orange. There are "dry" and "moist" kinds of sweet potatoes, which describe the texture when they're eaten; some dry varieties have a higher moisture content than some moist ones. The moist varieties are often called yams, but the yam is actually a different species that is found in tropical countries. Sweet potato vines are ornamental, so this vegetable is often grown as ground cover or in planters or hanging baskets. You can even grow a plant in water in your kitchen—suspend the sweet potato on toothpicks in a jar of water, and watch it grow.

PLANTING

Sweet potatoes are extremely sensitive to frost and need warm, moist growing weather. They have a long growing season—about 5 months—and in areas with a shorter growing season, tend to produce small potatoes. Don't try to hurry sweet potatoes; plant them in spring and summer in all climatic areas.

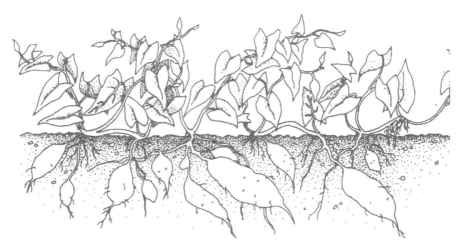

HOW TO PLANT

Sweet potatoes are planted from rooted sprouts, or slips, taken from a mature tuber. To grow your own slips, place several sweet potato roots about 1 inch (2.5cm) apart in a hotbed and cover with 2 inches (5cm) of sand or light soil. Add another 1 inch (2.5cm) of soil when the shoots appear, keep the bed at a temperature between 72°F (22°C) and 81°F (27°C), and don't let it dry out. In about six weeks you will have rooted slips that can be planted in the garden. If you don't want to go to the trouble of growing your own, buy slips from a reputable garden center or supplier.

A good, sandy soil is best for sweet potatoes. Over-rich soil produces luxuriant vines but small tubers. The soil should be moderately fertile, rich in organic matter and well worked to ensure looseness. Remove all soil lumps, rocks or other obstacles that might cause deformity of the tubers, and work in a complete, well-balanced fertilizer at the rate of 1lb per 95sq feet (450g per 9sq m). For good tuber production sweet potatoes must have full sun; in partial shade the vine will be handsome but not very productive. Set the slips on ridges made by mounding up the soil about 8 inches (20cm) high along rows 1m apart. Make the ridges about 12 inches (30cm) wide and set the slips at 12 inches (30cm) intervals.

FERTILIZING AND WATERING

Fertilize before planting and again at midseason, at the same rate as the rest of the garden.

If the soil is too wet, the roots of sweet potatoes may rot; in well-worked, loose soil this should not be a problem. Although sweet potatoes will survive dry seasons, the yield is much higher if they get 1 inch (2.5cm) of water every week until three or four weeks before harvesting. Do not water during the last three or four weeks.

PESTS

Aphids, caterpillars, cutworms, snails, slugs, wireworms.

DISEASES

Fungus diseases and rootrot may attack sweet potatoes. Planting disease-resistant varieties and maintaining the general cleanliness and health of your garden will help cut down the incidence of disease. If a plant does become infected, remove it before it can spread disease to healthy plants.

HARVESTING

The tubers are damaged by freezing or cold soils, so dig up sweet potatoes before the first frost. Be careful when you dig—these potatoes are thin-skinned and bruise easily.

VARIETIES

Porto Rico, Bunch Porto Rico, Jewel, Vardaman, White Yam, Centennial, Carolina Nugget, Hernandez.

STORING AND PRESERVING

Cure sweet potatoes in crates in a dark, humid place for 10 days at about 86°F (30°C); then store them at about 63°F (17°C) in a moderately moist place for four to six months. You can also freeze, bottle or dry them.

Freezing

1. Choose medium or large, mature potatoes that have been cured for at least a week.
2. Wash well and sort by size.
3. Simmer, bake or pressure-cook potatoes until tender. Cool.
4. Baked: Grease outside of potatoes with oil. Bake in a preheated 355°F (180°C) oven until soft. Cool, then wrap individually in moisture/ vapor proof wrapping and freeze. Heat through to serve. Candied: Cook unpeeled potatoes in water to cover at just below simmering for about 30 minutes. Pare and cut lengthwise or crosswise into ½-inch (1cm) thick slices. For each 13 ounces (375g) potato slices, prepare syrup by heating to boiling 1½ cups water, 1 cup sugar and 1 tablespoon lemon juice in saucepan. (There should be enough syrup to cover sweet potato slices.) Add sweet potato slices to boiling syrup and cook 3 minutes. Don't drain. Cool quickly by pouring slices and syrup into another pan and placing that pan in ice water. Pack tightly in containers, covering slices with syrup, and leaving ⅛ inch (½cm) head space for 2 cups (½ liter), ½ inch (1cm) for 4 cups (1 liter). Seal, label and freeze. Heat through to serve. Mashed: Simmer, bake or pressure-cook potatoes until tender. Cool, peel and put through food mill. Add ½ cup sugar, ½ cup cold water, and 1 tablespoon lemon juice for each 4½ pounds (2kg) of mashed potatoes. Pack tightly into containers, leaving ⅛ inch (0.5cm) head space for 2 cups (½ liter), ½ inch (1cm) for liters. Seal, label and freeze. Heat through to serve.

SERVING SUGGESTIONS

Sweet potatoes are very versatile; you can boil, steam, fry, or bake them, and they take well to either sweet or savory seasoning. Use pureed sweet potatoes in bread or biscuits. Candy them, or stuff them and bake them in their skins. Include slices of raw sweet potato with the vegetables for a tempura. Cinnamon, cloves, nutmeg and allspice all go well with sweet potatoes.

Swiss Chard

Common names: chard, Silver beet, sea kale, Swiss beet, sea kale beet

Botanic name: *Beta vulgaris cicla*

Origin: Europe, Mediterranean

Swiss chard is basically a beet without the bottom. It's a biennial grown as an annual for its big crinkly leaves. It is a decorative plant; with its juicy red or white leaf stems and rosette of large, dark green leaves, it can hold its own in the flower garden. It's also a rewarding crop for the home vegetable gardener—it's easy-going and very productive. If you harvest the leaves as they grow, the plant will go on producing all season. It was a popular foodstuff even before the days of the Roman Empire.

PLANTING

Swiss chard prefers cool temperatures; high temperatures slow down leaf production, but it tolerates heat better than spinach can. S.T.- autumn to spring. T- all seasons. C- spring to autumn.

HOW TO PLANT

Swiss chard tolerates partial shade and likes fertile, well-worked soil with good drainage and a high organic content; like the beet, it is not fond of acid soil. Work a complete, well-balanced fertilizer into the soil before planting, at the rate of 1lb per 95sq feet (450g per 9sq m). Sow the seed 1 inch (2cm) deep and 4–6 inches (10–15cm) apart in rows 18–24 inches (45–60cm) apart. When large enough to handle thin seedlings to stand about 10–12 inches (25–30cm) apart. They can stand crowding—they'll produce smaller leaves but more of them. A few extra plants will also give you replacements for any that bolt or go to seed in hot weather. Remove any plants that bolt, and let the others grow.

FERTILIZING AND WATERING

Fertilize before planting and again at midseason, at the same rate as the rest of the garden.

The crop needs enough water to keep the leaves growing quickly, so keep the soil moist at all times.

PESTS

Aphids and leaf miners are the major pests to contend with. You can usually control aphids by pinching out the affected area; if there are a lot of them, try hosing them off the plants. Leaf miners, wormlike insects that feed inside the leaf surfaces, can also be controlled physically; pick off the older leaves where you see that miners have laid rows of pearl-white eggs.

DISEASES

Swiss chard has no serious disease problems but leaf-spot can occur. Spray with Benlate. Swiss chard may also be infected by downy mildew.

HARVESTING

Time from planting to harvest is 2½–3 months. A 10-foot (3m) row should give you 9lbs (4kg) or more of produce. Start harvesting when the outside leaves are 2 inches (5cm) long; don't let them get much over 10 inches (25cm) long or they'll taste earthy. Some gardeners like to take off the outside leaves a few at a time; others prefer to cut the entire plant down to 2 inches (5cm) and let it grow back. Swiss chard will grow and produce steadily all summer, and if the soil is fertile and the weather doesn't get too cold, harvesting may continue into a second year.

STORING AND PRESERVING

Swiss chard can be stored for one to two weeks in the refrigerator. It can also be frozen, bottled or dried; use the recipes for greens.

Freezing

1. Choose young, tender leaves.
2. Wash well in several changes of water.
3. Remove tough stems or bruised leaves.
4. Blanch each pound (450g) of greens in 2½ gallons (9 liters) boiling water for 2 minutes; collard greens, 3 minutes. Stir to keep greens from sticking together. Cool, drain well.
5. Pack into containers, leaving ⅛ inch (0.5cm) head space. Seal, label and freeze.
6. Cook frozen greens 8 to 15 minutes.

Drying

1. Choose very fresh, perfect leaves.
2. Wash leaves well; shake dry. Remove any large, tough stalks.
3. Blanch in boiling water about 1½ minutes; or in steam about 2½ minutes, until completely wilted.

Drain very well, chill and pat dry with paper towels.
4. Arrange leaves in a single layer on baking sheets or racks.
5. Dry until brittle, 2½ to 8 hours or more.
6. Put the dried vegetables into a deep container, cover lightly with cheesecloth and condition, stirring once a day for a week to 10 days.
7. Pack into vapor/moistureproof, airtight containers or double plastic bags and store in a cool, dark, dry place for up to 12 months.
8. Rehydrate in 1 cup of boiling water for each cup of greens, about ½ hour.

SERVING SUGGESTIONS

Swiss chard is delicious steamed or cooked like spinach. The leaves have a sweet taste like spinach, and they're colorful in a salad. The stalks can be cooked like celery. Cut them into pieces about 2 inches (6cm) long and simmer until tender; serve them hot with butter or chilled with a light vinaigrette. If you're cooking the leaves and stalks together, give the stalks a five-minute head start so that both will be tender at the end of the cooking time.

Tomato

Common names: tomato, love apple

Botanic name: *Lycopersicon esculentum*

Origin: Tropical America

Tomatoes are tender perennials grown as annuals. They have weak stems and alternate lobed and toothed leaves that have a distinctive odor. The yellow flowers grow in clusters. Most tomatoes have vining growth habits and need a fair amount of space. Some are advertised as bush varieties that save space, but they'll still sprawl if you let them, and you may still have to stake or cage them. Depending on the variety, the fruit varies in size and in color—red, yellow, orange and white.

Tomatoes can be divided into two main groups, according to growth habits; determinate and indeterminate. On the determinate

Tomato plants take up a lot of space if you let them sprawl. A strong stake supports the plant and keeps the fruit clean.

tomato (bush tomato), the plant stops growing when the end buds set fruit—usually about 3 feet (1m) tall. It seldom needs staking. On the indeterminate tomato (vine tomato), the end buds do not set fruit; the plant can grow almost indefinitely if not stopped by frost. Most of the varieties that are staked or caged are indeterminate tomatoes.

Tomatoes are also classified by the size and shape of their fruit (currant, cherry, plum, pear, etc.), by their color (red, pink, orange, yellow and cream) and by their use (eating, bottling, pickling). When you're short on garden space, grow tomatoes in a large pot or container. The small-fruited tomatoes do very well in hanging baskets or window boxes. Plants growing in containers may easily exhaust the available moisture, in which case the leaves will wilt. However, the plants will revive when they're watered.

Vining tomatoes can be staked or caged to support the fruit, or can be left to sprawl on the ground. Naturally sprawling tomatoes require less work than staked or caged plants; they are less likely to develop blossom end rot and they produce more fruit per plant. In dry areas, sprawling on the ground protects the fruit from sunburn. But sprawling tomatoes are harder to cultivate than staked or caged plants and they need mulching under the fruit to keep them clean to reduce disease. Staked tomatoes give you cleaner fruit, less loss from rot, and less loss from problems that occur in warm humid areas. They require less room for each individual plant. On the negative side, they produce less fruit per plant, are much more susceptible to blossom end rot and are more work. Caged tomatoes require less work than staked tomatoes, but slightly more effort than doing nothing. Caged tomatoes conserve space, keep the fruit cleaner and are easier to work around in small areas.

PLANTING

Tomatoes grow best when the day temperature is between 59–86°F (15–30°C). They stop growing if it goes over 95°F (35°C), and if the night temperature goes above 86°F (30°C) the fruit will not turn red. The flowers will not set fruit if the temperature goes below 54°F (12°C) at night. Start tomatoes either from seed planted in the garden or from seedlings. S.T.- all seasons, T- early spring to mid-summer, C- spring to early summer.

HOW TO PLANT

Tomatoes must have full sun and need warm, well-drained, fertile soil. Although they will produce earlier in sandy soils, they will have a larger yield in clay soils. When preparing the soil for planting, work in a complete, well-balanced fertilizer at the rate of

1lb per 95sq feet (450g per 9sq m). Sow seeds ⅓ inch (1cm) deep in rows 24–47 inches (60–120cm) apart (depending on how large the variety will grow). When the seedlings are large enough to handle, thin them to 18–35 inches (45–90cm) apart.

Set the plants out on a cloudy day or in the late afternoon. If the sun is very hot, protect the plants with hats made of newspapers. Disturb the roots as little as possible when transplanting.

Tomatoes in a cage are easy to take care of.

Plants should be gently slipped out of clay and plastic pots. If they're planted in peat pots, plant the entire container. Make sure the tops of the containers are below the soil's surface or the peat will act like a wick and evaporate the soil moisture. If the plants are growing together in a seed box or tray, cut the plants apart several days before transplanting them. Put the plant in the soil so that it's deeper than it was growing before, up to the first leaves. If the stem is very long or spindly, lay it on a slant so that only the leaves are above soil level. The roots will grow from the submerged stem, making a sturdier plant. Set the seedlings 18–35 inches (45–90cm) apart in rows 24–47 inches (60–120cm) apart depending on the variety.

FERTILIZING AND WATERING

Fertilize before planting and again at midseason, at the same rate as the rest of the garden.

Tomatoes need lots of water, but they don't like to swim. Water thoroughly before the soil dries out. During the hot days of summer the leaves sometimes wilt because they use more water than their roots can supply. Don't worry about this if the tomatoes are receiving a regular supply of water. If the plants are wilting first thing in the morning, however, water them at once. Sometimes tomato plants curl their leaves in a survival tactic on hot days or during a long period of no rain. This is nothing to worry about; just water them.

SPECIAL HANDLING

To stake tomatoes use 6½ feet (2m) stakes (1 by 2 inches/2.5 by 5cm) or reinforcing rods, and set the supports at the time of transplanting. Staked tomatoes should be pruned so that they grow one straight stem. Prune by removing any suckers that appear below the first fruiting cluster—the accompanying illustration shows how to prune a staked tomato plant. The suckers are not productive, so you don't affect the yield by pruning, and pruned plants have more energy to develop fruit. Let the suckers develop two leaves above the first fruiting cluster and then pinch out the rest of the sucker; the extra leaves will provide shade for the fruit. To cage tomatoes, use 6 by 6 inches (15 by 15cm) mesh concrete reinforcing wire. A 5 feet (1.5m) width can be cut 5 feet (1.5m) long and bent into a cylinder by locking the ends. Remove the bottom strand and push the whole cage into the ground 6 inches (15cm) deep around the tomato plant. If the area is windy, drive in a supporting stake.

Tomato plants will not set fruit in rainy or very humid weather. Sometimes a plant that has plenty of water and fertilizer produces a lot of foliage but no tomatoes. As a last resort, try giving the plant a shock by pruning it back and cutting down on water; it may start producing.

PESTS

Aphids, tomato caterpillars, cutworms, fruit fly, flea beetle, colorado potato beetle and whiteflies are the major problems. Tomatoes are almost always attacked by some insect and may not be the best choice for the organic gardener; however, the fresh taste of a ripe tomato may overpower the logical choice. Collars placed around the plants at the time of transplanting help to discourage cutworms and caterpillars can be handpicked off the plants. Aphids and whiteflies can be discouraged

Staked tomatoes should be pruned to grow one straight stem.

by hosing them off the plants or pinching out infested foliage. Malathion or Diazinon chemically control aphids and whiteflies.

DISEASES

Verticillium wilt, fusarium wilt, early blight, septoria leafspot, tobacco mosaic virus and blossom end rot are diseases that can attack tomatoes. Planting disease-resistant varieties and maintaining the general cleanliness and health of your garden will help cut down the incidence of disease. Keep moisture off the leaves as far as possible and avoid handling the plants when they're wet. If you smoke, wash your hands thoroughly before working with tomato plants to avoid spreading tobacco mosaic virus. If a plant does become infected with any disease, remove it before it can spread disease to healthy plants.

HARVESTING

Time from planting to harvest is 40 to 180 days from seedlings, depending on variety, and several weeks longer from seed. Seedlings usually produce earlier than tomatoes grown from seed. A 10-foot (3m) row will give you anywhere from 10–44lbs (4.5–20kg) of tomatoes. The color when ripe depends on the variety; ripe tomatoes should feel firm—neither squashy nor too hard. When the temperature is high during the day,

the fruit may get soft but not red. Take hard green tomatoes inside at the end of the season to ripen; don't leave them on the plants.

STORING AND PRESERVING

Ripened tomatoes will keep up to one week in the refrigerator. You can also freeze, bottle or dry them whole, sliced, as juice, paste, relish or pickles. Green tomatoes harvested before a frost can be held in a cool, moist place up to one month to ripen.

Freezing

1. Choose ripe, firm, red tomatoes, free of blemishes.
2. Wash well.
3. Whole: Remove stems after washing. Wrap each tomato in plastic wrap or small plastic bag, then freeze. To use in cooked dishes, run under lukewarm water for a few seconds to loosen skin, then remove skin and blossom end. Add tomato, along with other ingredients, and cook. Stewed: Dip whole, washed tomatoes in boiling water 2 minutes to loosen skins. Peel and core. Cut in quarters or pieces; simmer 10 to 20 minutes or until tender. Cool. Pack in containers, leaving ⅛ inch (0.5cm) head space. Seal, label and freeze. Pureed: Peel tomatoes as for stewed tomatoes. Core and cut them in quarters into a blender container. For each 4 medium tomatoes, add ½ onion, chopped;

1 green pepper (seeded, stemmed and cut in quarters); 1 tablespoon salt, and 1 tablespoon sugar. Blend on low or medium speed until onion and pepper are chopped. Pack the puree in containers, leaving ⅛ inch (0.5cm) head space for 2 cups (½ liter), ½ inch (1cm) for 4 cups (1 liter). Seal, label and freeze.

Green Tomatoes:
1. Select firm, sound, green tomatoes.
2. Wash, core and slice ⅛ inch (0.5cm) thick.
3. Tray freeze, without blanching, then pack in containers or bags with layer of freezer wrap between slices. Seal, label and freeze.
4. Thaw and coat to fry.

Tomato Juice:
1. Select firm, sound, ripe tomatoes.
2. Wash well, core and cut into quarters or chunks.
3. Simmer until tender, about 5 to 10 minutes.
4. Put through a food mill or strainer. Cool.
5. Pour into containers, leaving ⅛ inch (0.5cm) head space for 2 cups (½ liter), ½ inch (1cm) for liters. Seal, label and freeze.
6. Thaw and stir to serve.

Drying
1. Choose perfect, red-ripe tomatoes.
2. Wash tomatoes. Drop into boiling water for 1 to 2 minutes to loosen the skins. Pat dry with paper towels. Peel, core and slice ⅛–½ inch (0.5–1cm) thick. Cut small or cherry tomatoes in half. Tomatoes don't require blanching.
3. Arrange in a single, even layer on baking sheets or racks.
4. Dry until leathery, 6 to 12 hours.
5. Put the dried vegetables into a deep container, cover lightly with cheesecloth and condition, stirring once a day for a week to 10 days.
6. Pack into vapor/moistureproof, airtight containers or double plastic bags and store in a cool, dark, dry place for up to 12 months.
7. Rehydrate in 2 cups of boiling water for each cup of tomatoes, about 1 hour.

Tomato Leather:
This is great just as is for a snack, added to soups or stews, or rehydrated to make tomato sauce. Use fleshy cherry tomatoes or large tomatoes. Add ingredients of your choice: green peppers, garlic, onion, lemon juice, even honey.
1. Select perfect, well–fleshed tomatoes.
2. Wash well and remove stems.
3. Puree in a blender with any added ingredients and blend until smooth.
4. Cover a baking sheet with plastic wrap, wetting the edges of the wrap to hold it in place on the sheet, or taping it in place.
5. Spread the blended tomato mixture evenly on the sheet ⅛ inch (0.5cm) thick.
6. Dry until leathery, 6 to 24 hours.
7. Peel off the plastic wrap and let the tomato leather cool. Then roll it up in a fresh piece of plastic

wrap. Seal in bags or foil. Do not rehydrate.

Tomato Paste:

1. Choose perfect, red-ripe tomatoes. Wash and quarter into a large saucepan.

2. Simmer until thick, about 1 to 2 hours; stir occasionally while the tomatoes simmer.

3. Put the tomato mixture through a food mill to remove skin and seeds.

4. Pour the mixture into a cheesecloth-lined strainer to remove the juice.

5. Spread the pulp (from the cheesecloth in the strainer) in a thin, even layer on baking sheets or racks.

6. Dry until leathery.

7. Cut into squares and pack into vapor/moistureproof, airtight containers or double plastic bags and store in a cool, dark, dry place for up to 12 months. Add to liquid mixtures without rehydrating in place of canned tomato paste.

SERVING SUGGESTIONS

Fresh tomatoes from your garden are wonderful with very little embellishment—slice them and dress them with a touch of olive oil and lemon juice and a pinch of basil; or eat them as fruit, with a little sugar. Alternate slices of fresh tomato and cooked potato for an interesting side dish—add olive oil and parsley. Add tomatoes to almost any salad, or serve them alone, sliced with bread and cheese for an instant lunch. Stuff raw tomatoes with tuna, chicken or rice, or broil them plain or topped with breadcrumbs. Serve broiled tomatoes with bacon and sausages for a hearty breakfast. Use cherry tomatoes, whole or halved, in salads or on relish trays; the green kind are delicious fried or pickled. Cooked tomatoes, whole, pureed, or as a paste, are indispensable to all sorts of dishes—spaghetti sauces, stews and casseroles—and fresh tomato sauce, seasoned with a little basil, is a delightfully simple topping for pasta. Make an unusual pie by alternating layers of sliced tomatoes with chopped chives and topping with pastry. Oregano, sage, tarragon and thyme all go beautifully with tomatoes.

Turnip

Common name: turnip

Botanic name: *Brassica rapa*

Origin: Northeastern Europe, Siberia

The turnip, a hardy biennial grown as an annual, sports a rosette of hairy, bright green leaves growing from a root—which is not really a root, but a swelling at the base of the stem. The turnip is more commonly grown for use as a root vegetable, but can also be grown for the leaves, which are used as greens. Turnips originated in the Mediterranean in prehistoric times. Englishmen have been known to refer to each other as "turniphead"; this is not a compliment, as turnips are often considered to be rather dull. In fact, they're quite versatile.

PLANTING

Turnips are a cool-weather crop. S.T.- autumn and winter; T- autumn to early spring; C- early autumn and early spring.

HOW TO PLANT

Turnips tolerate partial shade and need soil high in organic matter and well drained but able to hold moisture. Too much nitrogen in the soil encourages the plant to produce leaves and a seed stalk rather than a good-sized root, so when you're preparing the soil for planting, work in a low-nitrogen (5-10-10) fertilizer at the rate of 1lb per 95sq feet (450g per 9sq m). Sow seeds ⅓ inch (1cm) deep in rows or wide rows 12–24 inches (30–60cm)

apart. When the seedlings are large enough to handle, thin them to 3–4 inches (7.5–10cm) apart; if you're growing turnips primarily for greens, thin to 2–3 inches (5–7.5cm) apart.

FERTILIZING AND WATERING

Fertilize before planting and again at midseason, at the same rate as the rest of the garden.

Water is important to keep turnips growing as fast as possible, so water regularly, before the soil dries out. If growth is slow the roots get very strong-flavored and woody, and the plant will often send up a seed stalk.

PESTS

Aphids attack turnips. Control them by pinching out infested foliage and hosing large populations off the plants; control them chemically with Malathion or Diazinon. Flea beetles and cutworms may also become a problem. For flea beetles, use row covers to help protect plants from early damage. Put in place at planting and remove before temperatures get too hot in midsummer. Control weeds. For cutworms, control weeds. Cardboard collars around each plant give good protection.

DISEASES

Clubroot, blackroot, black leg, black rot and turnip mosaic virus are occasional problems. While susceptible to the diseases that plague other cole crops, turnip diseases usually aren't a problem if grown in well-drained soil and harvested young.

HARVESTING

Time from planting to harvest is 30 to 60 days and a 10-foot (3m) row of turnips should give you 5½lbs (2.5kg) of leaves and 10lbs (4.5kg) of roots. You can eat the tops as you thin the seedlings, or when the root is ready to be pulled. Harvest the roots when they're 1–2 inches (2.5–5cm) across.

STORING AND PRESERVING

Store turnip greens in the refrigerator up to one week, or in a cold, moist place for two to three weeks. Store the roots in a cold, moist place for four to five months; do not refrigerate. You can also freeze both the roots and the greens, and bottle or dry the greens; use the recipes for greens. Turnip seeds can also be sprouted.

Freezing
1. Choose young, tender, small to medium turnips.
2. Remove tops, wash, pare and cut in ½ inch (1cm) cubes or slices.
3. Blanch 3 minutes. Cool; drain well.
4. Pack in containers. Seal, label and freeze.

5. Cook frozen turnips about 10 to 12 minutes.

Drying

1. Choose very fresh, perfect leaves.

2. Wash leaves well; shake dry. Remove any large, tough stalks.

3. Blanch in boiling water about 1½ minutes; or in steam about 2½ minutes, until completely wilted. Drain very well, chill and pat dry with paper towels.

4. Arrange leaves in a single layer on baking sheets or racks.

5. Dry until brittle, 2½ to 8 hours or more.

6. Put the dried vegetables into a deep container, cover lightly with cheesecloth and condition, stirring once a day for a week to 10 days.

7. Pack into vapor/moistureproof, airtight containers or double plastic bags and store in a cool, dark, dry place for up to 12 months.

8. Rehydrate in 1 cup of boiling water for each cup of greens, about ½ hour.

SERVING SUGGESTIONS

When small, turnips make a great substitute for radishes. They're also easier to carve than radishes if you feel the urge to sculpture roses or daisies for decorative garnishes. Sliced raw turnips give a nice crunch to salads. Steam or boil turnips and serve them with butter or cream—add a little sugar to the cooking water to improve the flavor. They're very good in soups or stews or cooked around a roast. You can use the tops in a salad or cooked as greens.

Watercress

See Cress

Water-melon

See Melon

Yam

See Sweet Potato

Zucchini

See Squash, Summer

Herbs

Anise

Common name: anise

Botanic name: *Pimpinella anisum*

Origin: Europe

Anise is a slow-growing annual with low, spreading, bushy plants that grow 12–18 inches (30–45cm) tall and almost as wide. The flowers are yellowish-white in umbrella-shaped clusters and appear about 10 weeks after planting. The licorice-flavored seeds are most commonly used in baking, candy, or to flavor liquors. Anise used to be credited with warding off the evil eye; the Romans flavored their cakes with it on special occasions.

PLANTING

Anise needs a long growing season—at least 4 months free of frost. It also prefers a moderate and uniform rainfall, especially at harvest time.

HOW TO PLANT

Anise prefers a well-drained fertile soil. Work a complete, well-balanced fertilizer into the soil before planting at the rate of 1lb per 95sq feet (450g per 9sq m). Give anise a location in full sun, and plant it from seed in early spring. Plant the seeds ⅕ inch (0.5cm) deep in rows 18–24 inches (45–60cm) apart and when the seedlings are six weeks old, thin them to 6–12 inches (15–30cm) apart.

FERTILIZING AND WATERING

Fertilize before planting and again at midseason, at the same rate as the rest of the garden.

Anise prefers uniform moisture especially at or just before harvesting. Alternate rainy and dry periods when the seed is near maturity can cause it to turn brown, reducing quality and yield.

PESTS

Anise has no serious pest problems.

DISEASES

Anise has no serious disease problems.

HARVESTING

Harvest the anise seed heads approximately 3¼ months after planting, while they are still green and immature. Be sure to harvest before the first frost.

STORING AND PRESERVING

The dry seeds can be stored for months in airtight containers.

SERVING SUGGESTIONS

Add anise to bouillon for fish or veal stews. Sprinkle anise seeds on an apple crumble. Aniseed balls are an old-fashioned favorite children's candy.

Basil

Common name: basil

Botanic names: *Ocimum basilicum,*
Ocimum crispum, Ocimum minimum

Origin: India, Central America

These tender annuals grow 12–30 inches (30–75cm) tall, with square stems and opposite leaves. Basil may have either green or purple-red soft-textured leaves and spikes of small whitish or lavender flowers. In India basil is considered a holy herb. In Italy it is a love gift, and in Romania it is an engagement token. In Greece the connotation is less romantic; there basil is a symbol of death and hatred. Basil has the distinction of being fragrant at all stages of its development.

PLANTING

Basil prefers a climate that does not run to extremes of temperatures, but it tolerates heat better than cold. Even light frost will kill the plant. It's grown from seed or seedlings and you can plant both in spring, when the soil has warmed. Basil makes a charming houseplant—put it in a sunny window.

HOW TO PLANT

Basil needs a well-drained soil high in organic matter. It does well in soil many other plants wouldn't tolerate; and too-fertile soil is actually a disadvantage, because it encourages lush foliage but a low oil content, which affects the aromatic quality of the herb. Sow the seed ⅕ inch (0.5cm) deep in rows 18–24 inches (45–60cm) apart. When the seedlings are growing strongly, thin them to 4–6 inches (10–15cm) apart. A sunny spot is best, but basil will tolerate light shade. Basil seeds itself and will often produce good plants if the soil is not disturbed too much in the spring. Using seedlings in the spring will mean you can harvest

your basil sooner. You can also buy a healthy plant from a nursery. If you want to grow basil indoors, put it in a sunny window or under lights.

FERTILIZING AND WATERING

Do not fertilize basil; overfertilizing is a disadvantage to most aromatic herbs. If the soil is very acid, sweeten it with some lime. Otherwise, let it be.

If basil needs water the leaves will wilt—give it enough water to prevent this.

SPECIAL HANDLING

Pinch off the terminal shoots to encourage branching and slow down flower production. If you don't, the plants will get tall and leggy.

PESTS

Basil has no serious pest problems.

DISEASES

Basil has no serious disease problems.

HARVESTING

Pick the basil as you need it by cutting an inch or two (a few centimeters) off the top. This will encourage the plant to become bushy instead of going to flower.

VARIETIES

Citriodorum (lemon-scented); Dark Opal (purple-red leaves and rose-colored flowers); Minimum (dwarf variety); Spicy Globe.

STORING AND PRESERVING

Store the crushed dry leaves in an airtight container. You can also freeze the leaves.

SERVING SUGGESTIONS

Fresh basil gives a wonderful flavor to sliced tomatoes dressed with a little oil and lemon juice, and it's good in other salads, too. Fresh basil is the essential ingredient in Pesto, a luxuriously aromatic pasta dish. You can also use the leaves—fresh or dried—with fish, game and meat dishes, on eggs and in stews and sauces. Try herbed butter with basil, or make basil vinegar.

Borage

Common name: borage

Botanic name: *Borago officinalis*

Origin: Europe

Borage is a tender annual that grows 24–35 inches (60–90cm) tall. The stems and leaves are gray-green and covered with velvety hair, and the light blue flowers grow in drooping clusters. When borage is in flower it's a striking plant, especially if you set it high—on a wall, for instance—because the nodding flowers are seen to best advantage from below. The flowers are used to add color to potpourri. Borage, like thyme, is supposed to give courage. An old English jingle goes: "I, Borage, Bring Courage."

PLANTING

Borage tolerates a wide range of temperatures but will not survive a hard frost. Because of its striking coloring and unusual flowers, it makes an attractive indoor plant.

HOW TO PLANT

Borage prefers well-drained sandy soil in full sun. When preparing the soil, dig in a complete, well-balanced fertilizer at the rate of 1lb per 95sq feet (450g per 9sq m).

Sow the seeds (which germinate readily) in early spring ⅕ inch (0.5cm) deep in rows 18–24 inches (45–60cm) apart and when the plants are 6–8 inches (15–20cm) tall, thin them to stand 12 inches (30cm) apart.

FERTILIZING AND WATERING

Do not fertilize borage again at midseason.

Let borage dry out between waterings.

PESTS

Borage has no serious pest problems. Like most herbs, it's a good choice for the organic garden.

DISEASES

Borage has no serious disease problems.

HARVEST

Harvest young leaves as needed throughout the growing season, and harvest the entire plant in the autumn before frost.

STORING AND PRESERVING

Refrigerate the stems and leaves for fresh use, or freeze them.

SERVING SUGGESTIONS

Fresh borage leaves have a cucumber-like taste and can be used in salads, soups and stews, or cooked like spinach. You can peel the stems and use them in salads. Borage flowers are sometimes candied for use as a garnish in fruit drinks.

Caraway

Common name: caraway

Botanic name: *Carum carvi*

Origin: Europe

Caraway is a biennial grown for its leaves and seeds. It has fine feathery leaves that grow in a short rosette; the second year the plant produces white, dill-like flowers on fine, 24-inch (60cm) flower stalks. The finely cut foliage makes the caraway plant a charming foil to flowers in a garden border.

PLANTING

If you only want the foliage, you can grow caraway anywhere in Australia. In some colder areas, however, it may need winter protection in order to produce flowers and seeds in the second year.

HOW TO PLANT

Caraway prefers full sun but will tolerate partial shade; it grows best in a well-drained sandy soil. When preparing the soil, dig in a complete, well-balanced fertilizer at the rate of 1lb per 95sq feet (450g per 9sq m). Caraway has a taproot, which makes it difficult to transplant, so grow it from seed sown in early spring or autumn. Plant the seeds ⅕ inch (0.5cm) deep in rows 18–24 inches (45–60cm) apart and thin the plants to stand 12–18 inches (30–45cm) apart. Caraway will reseed itself in most areas, assuring you a constant supply.

FERTILIZING AND WATERING

Fertilize before planting and again at midseason, at the same rate as the rest of the garden. The second year do not fertilize at midseason.

Allow caraway plants to dry out between waterings.

PESTS

Caraway is a member of the parsley family, so you may encounter a

parsley caterpillar. Handpick it off the plant.

DISEASES

Caraway has no serious disease problems.

HARVESTING

Harvest caraway leaves as needed throughout the growing season for use in soups and salads. Harvest the seeds in the autumn of the second growing season. Harvest when they dry out and turn brown or before the first frost.

STORING AND PRESERVING

It's best to use caraway leaves fresh, but they can be stored in the refrigerator for a few weeks. The seeds can be stored for months in a sealed jar.

SERVING SUGGESTIONS

Caraway seeds have all kinds of uses—in breads, cakes and biscuits; in sauerkraut; or to flavor cheeses. They add a nice crunch, as well as a distinctive flavor.

Chervil

Common name: chervil

Botanic name: *Anthriscus cerefolium*

Origin: Europe and Asia

Chervil is a hardy annual of the parsley family, and its lacy, bright green leaves resemble those of parsley, although its flavor is more subtle. The plant grows 12–24 inches (30–60cm) and the tiny white flowers appear in umbels—umbrella-like clusters. In folk medicine, chervil was soaked in vinegar and the liquid administered as a cure for hiccups.

PLANTING

Chervil prefers a cool climate. Seed can be sown from spring to early autumn.

HOW TO PLANT

Chervil grows best in a moist and partially seeded environment. When preparing the soil, dig in a complete, well-balanced fertilizer at the rate of 1lb per 95sq feet (450g per 9sq m). Sow chervil seeds ⅓ inch (1cm) deep in rows 18–24 inches (45–60cm) apart. When the plants are six weeks old, thin them to stand 3–4 inches (7.5–10cm) apart. To encourage thicker foliage, cut the flower stems before they bloom.

FERTILIZING AND WATERING

Fertilize before planting and again at midseason, at the same rate as the rest of the garden. For best growth, keep chervil moist.

PESTS

Chervil is a member of the parsley family, so you may encounter an occasional parsley caterpillar. Handpick if off the plant.

DISEASES

Chervil has no serious disease problems.

HARVESTING

Pick fresh leaves as you need them during the growing season

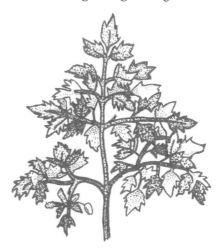

taking leaves from outside of plant. If the soft new growth in the center is picked the plant could be discouraged and die. Harvest all the stems and leaves and dry them rapidly in a shady area in autumn.

STORING AND PRESERVING

Store crushed dry leaves in a tightly sealed container. You can also freeze them.

SERVING SUGGESTIONS

Add fresh chervil leaves to salads; they make an attractive alternative to parsley as a garnish. Chervil is an especially appropriate seasoning for fish, chicken and egg dishes.

Chive

Common name: chives

Botanic name: *Allium schoenoprasum*

Origin: Europe

This hardy perennial relative of the onion has tufts of thin hollow leaves 6–8 inches (15–20cm) long. In the late spring, it produces striking flowers—rounded soft purple globes. The chive blossom appears, dried or fresh, in many Japanese dishes. Chives are perennials that will remain in your garden for years once established.

PLANTING

Chives are hardy. They do well in cool weather but can survive extremes of temperature.

HOW TO PLANT

You can grow chives from seed or divisions—small bulbs separated from clumps. The seeds take a long time to germinate and need a very cool temperature, not above 59°F (15°C); after their slow start they grow quickly. Plant either seeds or divisions in early spring, a late frost won't hurt them. Chives tolerate partial shade, and prefer sandy soil with plenty of organic matter—this is important for perennial herbs—and good drainage. When preparing the soil, dig in a low-nitrogen (5-10-10) fertilizer at the rate of 1lb per 95sq feet (450g per 9sq m). Plant seeds ⅕ inch (0.5cm) deep in rows 12 inches (30cm) apart. The plants can be fairly close together; small clumps (25 plants) can be set out 6–8 inches (15–20cm) apart in rows. They'll fill in and make an attractive array.

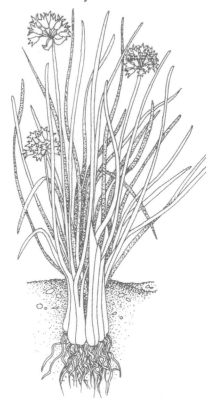

FERTILIZING AND WATERING

Don't fertilize chive plants at mid-season.

Watering is important for good growth; the plants will survive neglect, but if you let the soil dry out, the tips of the leaves—the part you want to eat—will become brown and unappetizing.

SPECIAL HANDLING

Chives will take care of themselves without much help. Separate the clumps from time to time. If you grow chives indoors, grow several pots so you can take turns clipping from them when you need chives for cooking and flavoring.

PESTS

Chives are trouble-free.

DISEASES

Chives have no serious disease problems.

HARVESTING

If you start from seed, you can start snipping chives after 90 days; from transplanted divisions, after 60 days. Either way, the plants will produce much better the second year. To harvest just snip the tops off the leaves, but if you harvest from the base you'll avoid unattractive stubble.

VARIETIES

Onion flavored, Garlic flavored. Onion chives have cylindrical leaves. Garlic chives have leaves with one flat side.

STORING AND PRESERVING

If you grow chives on the windowsill or on the border of your flowerbed, you may not need to store any—you've got a regular supply right there. However, chives can be satisfactorily freeze-dried.

SERVING SUGGESTIONS

Try a little chopped chives and parsley in an omelet. Used raw, chives add a mild onion flavor to any dish. They are often mixed with cottage cheese, sour cream or cream cheese. The blossoms can be eaten too and are best when just coming into bloom.

Coriander

Common name: coriander

Botanic name: *Coriandrum sativum*

Origin: Europe, Asia Minor and Russia

Coriander is a fast-growing annual that grows to about 12–18 inches (30–45cm) in height. It has tall slender stems with fine feathery leaves; the flowers are pale pink and grow in clusters. The seeds are used for flavoring, sweets, sauces and soups. Coriander has a strong odor and many people don't like it. It's one of the oldest known herbs and was grown in ancient Egyptian gardens and its seeds have been found in Egyptian tombs. Coriander is also mentioned as a food source in the Old Testament. The Spanish for coriander is cilantro, and the herb is sometimes known by this name.

PLANTING

Coriander grows almost anywhere temperate but is not very hardy and will not survive hard frost, so plant it in the spring after all danger of frost has passed.

HOW TO PLANT

Coriander grows best in a fertile, well-drained soil. It prefers a sunny location but will survive in a slightly shaded area. When preparing the soil, dig in a complete, well-balanced fertilizer at the rate of 1lb per 95sq feet (450g per 9sq m). Sow in growing position in warm soil, spring or autumn, seeds ⅕ inch (0.5cm) apart in rows 8–12 inches (20–30cm) apart and thin the plants to 12 inches (30cm) apart when the seedlings are growing strongly.

FERTILIZING AND WATERING

Do not fertilize coriander at mid-season.

Coriander should be kept evenly moist throughout the growing season, but when the seeds are nearing maturity too much rain can reduce the yield.

PESTS

Coriander has no serious pest problems.

DISEASES

Coriander has no serious disease problems.

HARVESTING

You can pick a few coriander leaves anytime after the plants are about 6 inches (15cm) tall—the fresh leaves are known as cilantro. Harvest the coriander seeds when they turn a light brown, two to three weeks after flowering. The seeds are small—only $\frac{1}{9}$ inch (0.3cm) in diameter—and are split in half and dried after harvesting.

STORING AND PRESERVING

The dried seeds can be stored for months in an airtight container. You can freeze or dry the leaves.

SERVING SUGGESTIONS

Add a little coriander to guacamole or to Chinese soups. The dried seeds are good in bread, biscuits, potato salad and fruit dishes.

Dill

Common name: dill

Botanic name: *Anethum graveolens*

Origin: Southeast Europe

Dill, a member of the parsley family, is a biennial grown as an annual and grows 24–47 inches (60–120cm) tall. Dill has finely cut leaves and small yellow flowers growing in a flat-topped cluster; it has a delicate feathery look and makes a good background for flowers or vegetables. Carrying a bag of dry dill over the heart is supposed to ward off the evil eye. Dill water was once used to quiet babies and get rid of wind.

PLANTING

Dill, like most herbs, can be grown pretty much anywhere, and can withstand heat or cold. Grow it from seed sown in the spring or autumn. Once established, dill will seed itself and return year after year.

HOW TO PLANT

Poor, sandy soil is an advantage—the herb will have stronger flavor—but the soil must drain well. Dill will tolerate partial shade; in light shade the plants won't get as bushy as in full sun, so they can be closer together. Sow direct or into seedling trays; in spring and early summer seeds germinate quickly. When the seedlings are growing well, thin them to 12 inches (30cm) apart. You can also thin dill to form a clump or mass rather than a row. Make sure you know where you want the plants, because dill has a taproot and is not easy to transplant. Dill is short-lived, so make successive sowings to give you a continuous crop.

FERTILIZING AND WATERING

Fertilizing is unnecessary for dill. It doesn't need too much water

and seems to do better if it's kept on the dry side.

SPECIAL HANDLING

The stems are tall and fine; you may need to stake them.

PESTS

Dill, like most herbs, is a good choice for the organic gardener. It's a member of the parsley family, so you may encounter a parsley caterpillar; handpick it off the plant.

DISEASES

Dill has no serious disease problems.

HARVESTING

Time from planting to harvest is about 2½ months for foliage, 3 months for seeds. To harvest, snip off the leaves or young flower heads for use in soups or salads. For pickling, cut whole stalks when the plant is more mature.

Gather the mature seeds for planting (although the dill will do its own planting without your help if you leave it alone) or for drying.

STORING AND PRESERVING

Dill seeds can be sprouted if they are allowed to dry naturally; store the dried seeds in an airtight jar. Crumble the dried leaves and store them the same way.

SERVING SUGGESTIONS

Dill pickles, obviously. You can also make a marvelous leek and potato soup seasoned with dill, and dill adds a new kick to rye bread. Dill is very good with fish or potatoes, and you can use it for garnish if you run out of (or are bored with) parsley.

Fennel

Common names: fennel, Florence fennel, finnochio

Botanic name: *Foeniculum vulgare dulce*

Origin: Mediterranean

Fennel is a stocky perennial grown as an annual, and looks a bit like celery with very feathery leaves. Ordinary fennel (*F. vulgare*) is also a perennial. Its leaves are picked for soups, sauces and salads. The whole herb has an anise flavor. The plant will grow 47–59 inches (120–150cm) tall, and the small, golden flowers appear in flat-topped clusters. A variant called "Copper" has charcoal-gray foliage and makes an interesting contrast to other colors in a flowerbed. In folk medicine all sorts of good results have been attributed to fennel; at one time or another it has been credited with sharpening the eyesight, stopping hiccups, promoting weight loss, freeing a person from "loathings" and acting as an aphrodisiac.

PLANTING

Fennel will grow anywhere and tolerates both heat and cold. Sow direct in spring and early summer in full sun.

HOW TO PLANT

Like most herbs, fennel needs well-drained soil high in organic matter. Sow seeds in rows 24–35 inches (60–90cm) apart. When seedlings are growing strongly, thin them to stand 12 inches (30cm) apart. Fennel is a difficult herb to transplant because of its taproot.

FERTILIZING AND WATERING

Do not fertilize fennel. Keep fennel on the dry side; it needs just enough moisture to keep it going.

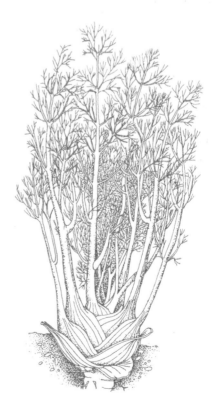

SPECIAL HANDLING

The plants grow 47–59 inches (120–150cm) tall so you may need to stake them.

PESTS

Since fennel is a member of the parsley family, the parsley caterpillar may appear. Remove it by hand. Like most herbs, fennel is a successful bet for the organic gardener.

DISEASES

Fennel has no serious disease problems.

HARVEST

You can start harvesting a few leaves as soon as the plant is well established and growing steadily; use them for flavoring. Harvest the bulbous stalk when it is 3 inches (7.5cm) or more in diameter for use as a vegetable.

STORING AND PRESERVING

The leaves of fennel can be frozen or dried. Crumble the dried leaves and store them in an airtight container. You'll probably want to eat the stalks fresh, but they can also be frozen.

SERVING SUGGESTIONS

Fennel is featured in many Italian dishes. The leaves add flavor to soups and casseroles, and fennel is a good seasoning with fish. Add the seeds to rye bread or a creamed cheese spread.

Garlic

Common name: garlic

Botanic name: *Allium sativum*

Origin: Southern Europe

Garlic is a hardy perennial plant that looks a lot like an onion, except that the bulb is segmented into cloves. The flower head looks like a tissue paper dunce cap and is filled with small flowers and bulblets. There is an old story that when the Devil walked out of the Garden of Eden after the fall of Adam and Eve, onions sprang up from his right hoof-print and garlic from his left.

PLANTING

Garlic must have cool temperatures during its early growth period, but it's not affected by heat in the later stages.

HOW TO PLANT

Garlic is grown from cloves or bulblets, which are planted plump side down. Use the plumpest cloves for cooking and plant the others. They need full sun and well-worked soil that drains well and is high in organic matter. Do not fertilize the soil. Plant the cloves in spring 1–2 inches (2.5–5cm) deep, 5–6 inches (12–15cm) apart in rows about 12 inches (30cm) apart.

FERTILIZING AND WATERING

The organic content of the soil is important, but fertilizing isn't; don't fertilize because it will decrease the flavor of the garlic bulbs.

Keep the garlic slightly dry, especially when the bulbs are near maturity; this also improves the flavor. Keep the area cultivated.

PESTS

Occasionally onion thrips may attack garlic, but they don't constitute a real problem; hose them off the plants if they do appear. Garlic is a good crop for the organic gardener.

DISEASE

Mildew may occur in a warm, moist environment, but it's not common enough to be a problem. Keep the garlic fairly dry.

HARVESTING

Harvest the bulbs when the tops start to dry—that's the sign that the bulbs are mature.

VARIETIES

Onion flavored, Garlic flavored. Onion chives have cylindrical leaves. Garlic chives have leaves with one flat side.

STORING AND PRESERVING

Store the mature bulbs under cool, dry conditions. Braid the tops of the plant together with twine and hang them to dry—very Gallic; in France you can still see rural vendors on bicycles with strings of garlic slung over their handlebars.

SERVING SUGGESTIONS

Garlic is indispensable to French cooking. If you know people who disapprove of the strong flavor of garlic, try to convert them—they'll thank you later. Spice up your next spaghetti dinner with garlic bread. Rub a salad bowl with a cut clove of garlic before tossing the salad. Add a clove of garlic to a homemade vinaigrette; let the dressing stand for a while before use if you like your salad good and garlicky. Insert slivers of garlic into small slits in a roast, or rub a cut clove over a steak before grilling.

Marjoram

Common names: marjoram, sweet marjoram

Botanic name: *Marjorana bortensis*

Origin: Mediterranean

A tender branching perennial, usually grown as an annual, marjoram grows 30–40cm tall. It has grayish opposite leaves and lavender or whitish flowers growing up most of the stem. Marjoram means "joy of the mountain." Venus was reputed to be the first to grow this herb. Its leaves and flowering heads, steeped and made into a tea, have been said to relieve indigestion and headaches.

PLANTING

Marjoram will grow in most areas but is sensitive to frost and needs winter protection to survive the winter in very cold areas.

HOW TO PLANT

Marjoram tolerates light shade and thrives in poor soil with good drainage. Don't fertilize the soil before planting; overfertile soil will produce lots of leaves, but they'll have little flavor. Sow seeds in spring and autumn ⅛ inch (0.5cm) deep in rows 12–24 inches (30–60cm) apart. Thin the seedlings to about 6 inches (15cm) apart when growing sturdily, or plant seedlings when they are 2–3 inches (5–7.5cm) tall, about 6 inches (15cm) apart. If the weather warms up quickly, mulch seedlings to protect the roots from too much heat until they're acclimatized. If you're afraid marjoram won't survive the winter, dig up the plants in autumn, let them winter as houseplants, and plant again in spring—divide the clumps before replanting.

FERTILIZING AND WATERING

Don't fertilize marjoram.

Water sparingly. The less water marjoram gets, the better the flavor will be.

SPECIAL HANDLING

About all the special attention marjoram requires is a protection of mulch to help it weather very cold winters.

PESTS

Marjoram has no serious pest problems. Like most herbs, it's a good plant for organic gardeners.

DISEASES

Marjoram has no serious disease problems.

HARVESTING

When the first blooms appear, cut the plants back a few inches (several centimeters). You can do this several times without harming the plant. Fresh leaves can be harvested at any time.

STORING AND PRESERVING

Dry leaves and flower tops quickly. Store the crumbled, dry leaves for winter use.

SERVING SUGGESTIONS

Marjoram is one of the traditional components of a bouquet garni. The leaves are good with veal and liver, in meat and egg dishes, and in poultry stuffings. Try them in soups or on roast beef sandwiches. Make herb butter with them. Add chopped marjoram leaves in melted butter to spinach just before serving.

Mint

Common name: mint

Botanic names: *Mentha piperita*
(peppermint); *Mentha spicata*
(spearmint)

Origin: Europe

A number of different varieties go by the collective name of mint; peppermint and spearmint are probably the two most popular. Both are very prolific—once you set them in a corner of the garden they'll quietly take over. Peppermint (*Mentha piperita*) is a tall, shallow-rooted, fast-spreading perennial with square stems and leaves that usually have a purple tinge. The light lavender flowers appear in terminal spikes and bloom through most of the growing season. The plant grows to about 35 inches (90cm) tall. Spearmint (*M. spicata*) is a perennial that grows 24–30 inches (60–75cm) tall, with square stems and leaves that are slightly curled and deeply veined. The flowers are light purple to white and grow in 1–2 inches (2.5–5cm) spikes that start blooming in early summer and continue well into autumn. You may also come across varieties like golden apple mint, which has a more delicate flavor than spearmint. This plant also has pale purple flowers, but the leaves are dark green streaked with gold.

Orange mint, sometimes known as bergamot mint, gets its name from its delicate scent of oranges. Orange mint has reddish-green leaves edged with purple; the flowers are lavender.

PLANTING

Both peppermint and spearmint are very hardy. Plant them from root divisions any time during the growing season.

HOW TO PLANT

Mint varieties from seed will not grow "true." So it's generally more

satisfactory to use root divisions. An innocuous little plant of mint will wander all over the garden if it gets half a chance, so plant each one in a container that will keep the roots in one place—a large coffee can with both ends removed is good. Peppermint and spearmint grow well in any soil; they prefer sun but will tolerate partial shade. For spearmint, work a complete, well-balanced fertilizer into the soil before planting at the rate of 1lb per 95sq feet (450g per 9sq m). Don't fertilize before planting peppermint—you'll get all the peppermint you can use without it. Although you can plant mints anytime during the growing season, root divisions will be established faster if planted on a cool, moist day in spring or autumn. Space plants 2–3 inches (5–7.5cm) apart in rows 18–24 inches (45–60cm) apart.

FERTILIZING AND WATERING

Don't fertilize mints in midseason; they'll never miss it.

Both peppermint and spearmint prefer moist soil, so they'll require more watering than the rest of the garden. Keep them evenly moist until root divisions are established.

PESTS

Mints have no serious pest problems.

DISEASES

Mints are susceptible to verticillium wilt and mint rust. Prevent these diseases by removing all the dead stems and leaves from the bed before winter.

HARVESTING

The more mint you pick, the better the plants will grow, and you can pick sprigs throughout the growing season. Harvest more fully as the plants begin to bloom, just as the lower leaves start to yellow. Cut the entire plant down 2–3 inches (5–7.5cm) above the soil. You'll get a second smaller harvest the same season.

VARIETIES

There are many varieties of mint, of which the best known are spearmint and peppermint. Other varieties have different flavors, like golden apple mint or orange mint, etc. Grow eau-de-cologne mint, pennyroyal cologne mint, pineapple cologne mint or the scent and flavor you like best.

STORING AND PRESERVING

Strip the mint leaves from the stem and let them dry in a warm shady area. The dried leaves can be stored in a sealed jar.

SERVING SUGGESTIONS

A sprig of fresh mint is a pretty garnish for summer drinks—and you can't have a mint julep without it. Cook peas in very little water to which you've added a couple of sprigs of mint. Toss boiled new potatoes with butter and chopped mint—a nice change from parsley. Instead of mint jelly with a lamb roast, try the traditional English mint sauce. Add a little sugar to a couple of tablespoons of chopped fresh mint leaves, add boiling water to bring out the flavor, then top off with vinegar to taste.

Oregano

Common names: oregano, wild marjoram

Botanic name: *Origanum vulgare, Origanum heracleoticum*

Origin: Mediterranean (*O. vulgare*), Cyprus (*O. heracleoticum*)

The name "oregano" is more accurately applied to a flavor than to a plant, and there are two varieties that you can grow for seasoning called oregano. *O. vulgare* is usually grown; it's hardier and easier to propagate than the alternative, *O. heracleoticum*—also known as wild marjoram. The name "oregano" itself has been traced back to an ancient Greek word translated as "delight of the mountains", which suggests that the plants once grew wild on the hillsides of Greece. Oregano (*O. vulgare*) is a very hardy perennial that may grow 30 inches (75cm) tall.

The leaves are grayish-green, slightly hairy, and oval in shape, and the flowers are pink, white, or purple. *O. heracleoticum* is a tender perennial that grows only 1 foot (30cm) high. The leaves are very hairy and oval in shape, and the plant bears small white flower clusters on tall stems. Oregano's reputed medicinal powers are varied. A tea made from the leaves and flowers was believed to relieve indigestion, headaches and nervousness. Oil extracted from the plant was used as a cure for toothache.

PLANTING

O. vulgare can be grown from root divisions or seed planted early in spring. *O. heracleoticum* can also be grown from seed or root divisions if planting is delayed until all danger of frost is past; it should be grown as an annual or given winter protection in colder areas. *O. beracleoticum* can also be grown in a container—it makes an attractive house plant.

HOW TO PLANT

Don't fertilize the planting bed for oregano—lack of nutrients even enhances the flavor. Both varieties need well-drained soil in a sunny location, although *O. vulgare* will tolerate partial shade. Plant both varieties from root divisions or seeds and space plants about 12 inches (30cm) apart. Sow seeds in spring ⅛ inch (0.5cm) deep in rows 12–18 inches (30–45cm) apart and thin to 6–12 inches (15–30cm) apart. Plant divisions 6–12 inches (15–30cm) apart in rows 12–18 inches (30–45cm) apart.

O. heracleoticum should be planted 2–3 weeks later than *O. vulgare*.

FERTILIZING AND WATERING

Don't fertilize oregano at all.

Keep the oregano plants on the dry side.

PESTS

Oregano varieties have no serious pest problems.

DISEASES

These plants have no serious disease problems.

HARVESTING

Oregano is ready to harvest when it begins to flower; cut the stems down to one or two inches (a few centimeters) above the soil. Leaves can be harvested for fresh use throughout the growing season if you cut off the flowers before they open—this encourages fuller foliage.

VARIETIES

In cold areas grow any variety of *O. vulgare*. In warmer areas grow any variety of either *O. vulgare* or *O. heracleoticum*.

STORING AND PRESERVING

Hang oregano in bunches to dry; when they're dry, remove the leaves and store them in an airtight container.

SERVING SUGGESTIONS

Oregano is essential to lots of Italian dishes. Add it to spaghetti sauce and sprinkle it on pizza. Try oregano and a touch of lemon on lamb chops or steak. Sprinkle oregano on cooked vegetables for a lively flavor.

Parsley

Common name: parsley

Botanic name: *Petroselinum crispum*

Origin: Mediterranean

Parsley is a hardy biennial treated as an annual. It has finely divided flat or curly fernlike leaves which grow in a rosette from a single tap root that in some varieties is quite large and can be eaten like parsnips.

Parsley has flat-topped clusters of greenish-yellow flowers, similar to those of dill, which belongs to the same family. The Romans wore parsley wreaths to keep from becoming intoxicated. Parsley is probably the best known of the herbs used for flavoring and for garnish.

PLANTING

Parsley will grow anywhere and can survive cold. It tolerates heat, but very hot weather will make the plant go to seed. Parsley also does well as a houseplant; some gardeners bring parsley in from the garden in autumn and let it winter in a bright window.

HOW TO PLANT

Parsley likes well-worked, well-drained soil with moderate organic content. Don't fertilize before planting. Seeds take a long time to germinate, but you can speed up the process by soaking them in warm water overnight before planting. Sow direct in spring, summer and early autumn ⅛ inch (0.5cm) deep in rows 18–24 inches (45–60cm) apart. Thin the seedlings to 12–18 inches (30–45cm) apart when they're growing strongly.

FERTILIZING AND WATERING

You don't need to fertilize the soil for parsley to grow well.

It's important to keep the soil moderately moist; parsley needs a regular supply of water to keep producing new leaves.

PESTS

The parsley caterpillar is the only pest you're likely to have to contend with. Handpick it off the plants.

DISEASES

Parsley has no serious disease problems.

HARVESTING

From planting to harvest is about 2½–3 months and a 10-foot (3m) row of parsley will keep you—and all your neighbors—well supplied. To encourage the growth of new foliage, cut off the flower stalk when it appears. The flower stalk shoots up taller than the leaves, and the leaves on it are much smaller. Harvest parsley leaves any time during the growing season; cut them off at the base of the plant. The plant will retain its rich color until early winter. Many gardeners harvest the entire parsley plant in autumn and dry it; you can also bring the whole plant inside for the winter.

VARIETIES

Crinkly parsley; Italian parsley (*P. crispum neopolitanum*)

STORING AND PRESERVING

Parsley lends itself well to freezing and drying. Store the dried leaves in an airtight container.

SERVING SUGGESTIONS

Parsley's reputation as a garnish often does it a disservice—it gets left on the side of the plate. In fact it's been known for thousands of years for its excellent flavor and versatility. Add chopped parsley to buttered potatoes and vegetables; toss a little on a sliced tomato salad along with a pinch of basil. Add it to scrambled eggs or an *omelette aux fine herbs*. Parsley is a natural breath-freshener.

Rosemary

Common name: rosemary

Botanic name: *Rosemarinus officinalis*

Origin: Mediterranean

Rosemary is a half-hardy, evergreen, perennial shrub with narrow, aromatic, gray-green leaves. It can grow 71 inches (180cm) tall and the flowers are small, light blue or white. It's a perennial, but in areas with very cold winters it's grown as an annual. Rosemary is one of the traditional strewing herbs; in the language of flowers its message is "remember." In Shakespeare's play, Ophelia gives Hamlet a sprig of rosemary "for remembrance." Keep up the old tradition of an herb of remembrance by tying a sprig of rosemary to a gift.

PLANTING

Rosemary can handle temperatures a little below freezing and tolerates cold better in a sandy, well-drained location. Less-than-ideal conditions improve its fragrance. Grow it in a cold-winter area if willing to mulch it for winter protection.

HOW TO PLANT

Like most herbs, rosemary is most fragrant and full of flavor if grown in well-drained, sandy soil high in organic matter but not over-rich. Very fertile soil will produce beautiful plants but decrease the production of the aromatic oils on which the plant's fragrance depends. Don't fertilize the soil, except if you're growing it as a perennial in a mild winter climate; in this case, work a low-nitrogen (5-10-10) fertilizer into the soil before planting at the rate of about ½lb. per 95sq feet (225g per 9sq m). Sow seeds in spring, summer or early autumn and transplant seedlings to a location in full sun 12 inches (30cm)

apart and 18–24 inches (45–60cm) between the rows. You can also grow rosemary from stem cuttings. Pot a rosemary plant from the garden in autumn and bring into the house for winter use. In the spring take stem cuttings to propagate your new crop.

FERTILIZING AND WATERING

Do not fertilize at midseason.

If the weather is dry, water regularly to keep the soil moist. Don't let the roots dry out.

PESTS

Rosemary has no serious pest problems. Like most herbs, it does well in the organic garden.

DISEASES

Rosemary has no serious disease problems.

HARVESTING

You can take some of the leaves, which look like short pine needles, and use them fresh any time you want them. Growth can be pruned back several times during a season.

VARIETIES

There are both upright and low-growing types.

STORING AND PRESERVING

Dry the leaves and store them in airtight containers.

SERVING SUGGESTIONS

Treat rosemary with respect; it can easily overpower more delicate herbs. Rosemary is traditionally used with lamb or pork; it's also excellent combined with a little lemon juice and chopped parsley and sprinkled on chicken before it's baked.

Sage

Common name: sage

Botanic name: *Salvia officinalis*

Origin: Mediterranean

Sage is a hardy, perennial shrub that grows to 24 inches (60cm) tall and gets quite woody. The leaves are oval, sometimes 5 inches (12cm) long. Gray leaves are more common but several varieties have variegated leaf color. The flowers are bluish-lavender and grow on spike-like stems. Traditionally, sage water is supposed to improve the memory and keep the hair from falling out. The purple or golden varieties make delightful ornamental houseplants. They're smaller plants than the green or gray varieties, but they're prettier, and the flavor is just as good. Most garden shops and catalogue lists offer only the gray varieties. Go to an herb specialist for the less common types.

PLANTING

Sage, like most herbs, is an accommodating plant that will grow anywhere. In cold areas, mulch to help the plants survive the winter.

HOW TO PLANT

Sage can be reproduced by layering, by division, or by using stem cuttings. You can also start it from seed. Sage thrives in poor soil as long as the drainage is good and it's not normally necessary to fertilize — if the soil is too rich the flavor will be poorer. If planting sage as a perennial, fertilize the first year only with a low-nitrogen fertilizer. When preparing the soil for planting, work a 5-10-10 fertilizer into the soil at the rate of ½lb. per 95sq feet (225g per 9sq m). Sow direct in spring, summer and early autumn with seeds ⅛ inch (0.5cm) deep in rows 18–24 inches (45–60cm) apart and thin to 12 inches (30cm) apart. Plant divisions or cuttings

12 inches (30cm) apart in rows 18–24 inches (45–60cm) apart. They should be in full sun; the plant will tolerate partial shade, but the flavor will be impaired.

FERTILIZING AND WATERING

Don't fertilize at midseason. Keep sage plants on the dry side.

PESTS

Sage has no serious pest problems. Like most herbs, it does well in the organic garden.

DISEASES

Sage has no serious disease problems. If the area is too damp or shady, rot may occur. Avoid this by planting sage in a dry, sunny location.

HARVESTING

Sage takes about 2½ months from planting to harvest, and a few plants will supply you and a lot of other people, too. At least twice during the growing season, cut 6–7 inches (15–18cm) from the top of the plants. Pick the leaves as desired as long as you don't cut back more than half the plant—if you do it will stop producing.

VARIETIES

Albilora (white flowers); Aurea (variegated leaves); Purpurea (reddish-purple upper leaves), Golden Sage, Tricolor, Pineapple sage, Clary sage.

STORING AND PRESERVING

Store dried sage leaves in an airtight container.

SERVING SUGGESTIONS

Sage and onion make a good combination and are traditionally used together in stuffings for pork, turkey or duck. Sage can overwhelm other seasonings, so handle it with care. Some people steep dried sage leaves to make an herb tea.

Savory

Common names: summer savory,
winter savory

Botanic names: *Satureja hortensis*
(summer savory); *Satureja montana*
(winter savory)

Origin: Mediterranean, Southern
Europe

B oth types of savory belong
to the mint family. Summer
savory is a bushy annual
with needle-shaped leaves and
stems that are square when
the plant is young and become
woody later. The flowers are light
purple to pink, and the plant
grows to a height of about 18
inches (45cm). Winter savory is
a bushy hardy perennial that
grows about 12 inches (30cm)
tall. The small flowers are white
or purple and, like the summer
variety, winter savory has needle-
shaped leaves and square stems
that become woody as they
develop. The winter variety has
sharper-flavored leaves than the
summer kind.

PLANTING

Seeds of both varieties can be sown
in spring and summer. The plants
can then also be increased by root
division or by taking cuttings.

HOW TO PLANT

Summer savory can be grown in
almost any soil; winter savory
prefers soil that is sandy and
well drained. Both need full sun.
Before planting, work a complete,
well-balanced fertilizer into the
ground at the rate of 1lb per 95sq
feet (450g per 9sq m). Sow seeds of
both summer and winter varieties
⅓ inch (1cm) deep in rows 12–18
inches (30–45cm) apart. When
the seedlings are four to six weeks
old thin summer savory plants to
3–4 inches (7.5–10cm) apart. Winter
savory needs more room; thin
the plants to 12–20 inches (30–
50cm) apart.

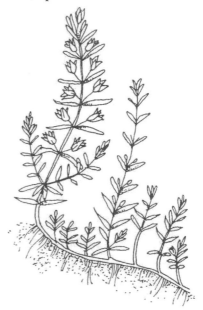

FERTILIZING AND WATERING

Do not fertilize at midseason.
Both varieties do better if kept on the dry side.

SPECIAL HANDLING

Summer savory has a tendency to get top-heavy; stake the plants if necessary.

PESTS

Savory has no serious pest problems.

DISEASES

Savory has no serious disease problems.

HARVESTING

Pick fresh leaves and stems of both summer and winter savory at any time during the growing season. In areas with a long growing season you may get two harvests. For drying, cut off the top 6–8 inches (15–20cm) of the plant as soon as it begins to flower.

STORING AND PRESERVING

Store the dried leaves in an airtight container.

SERVING SUGGESTIONS

Savory has a peppery flavor that is good with fish, poultry, and in egg dishes. Try it in vinegars, or add a little to a cheese soufflé.

Sesame

Common name: sesame

Botanic name: *Sesamum indicum*

Origin: Africa

Sesame is a hardy annual that has a unique drought-tolerant root system composed of a long tap-root and a large number of fibrous secondary roots. It's an attractive plant, with cream or pale orchid-colored flowers that grow in the angles of the leaves. Sesame used to be credited with magic powers and was associated with Hecate, queen of witches. Its uses today are less dramatic; the dried seeds are used to flavor breads, sweets and baked goods, and the oil extracted from the seed is used for cooking and in salad dressings.

PLANTING

Sesame grows well in warm, dry areas. Sow in spring.

HOW TO PLANT

Give sesame a place in the sun in well-drained, fertile soil. When preparing the soil, dig in a complete, well-balanced fertilizer at the rate of 1lb per 95sq feet (450g per 9sq m). Sow the seeds ⅛ inch (1cm) deep in rows 12–18 inches (30–45cm) apart. Thin the plants to 12–18 inches (30–45cm) apart when they are four to five weeks old.

FERTILIZING AND WATERING

Fertilize before planting and again at midseason, at the same rate as the rest of the garden.

Allow the plants to dry out between waterings.

PESTS

Sesame has no serious pest problems.

DISEASES

Sesame has no serious disease problems.

HARVESTING

Harvest about 3–4 months after planting when the mature seed pods are about the size of a peanut. Crack the pods open carefully, and remove the seeds.

STORING AND PRESERVING

Store the dried sesame seeds in an airtight container.

SERVING SUGGESTIONS

Toast sesame seeds and toss them over vegetable dishes or soups. They give an extra crunch to pan-fried fish. Or eat the roasted seeds as a snack. Sesame is used a lot in Oriental dishes and the seeds, untoasted, are added to biscuits, cakes and breads before baking.

Tarragon

Common name: tarragon

Botanic name: *Artemisia dracunulus*

Origin: Caspian Sea, Siberia

Tarragon is a half-hardy perennial that grows 24–47 inches (60–120cm) high; it has slender stems and thin narrow leaves that taste a bit like licorice, and it rarely produces flowers—they're small and whitish in color. True French tarragon is a sterile clove and cannot be grown from seed; use rooted divisions or stem cuttings. There is also a Russian variety of tarragon which has a stronger flavor and most people don't like it. Many herbs are decorative, but tarragon is not. However, its finely textured dark-green foliage makes an attractive background for small, bright flowers. The word tarragon comes from the Arabic word for dragon. The French translation, estragon (little dragon), might reflect either the way tarragon was used medicinally to fight pestilence during the Middle Ages, or the snake-like appearance of its roots.

PLANTNG

Tarragon will survive cold winters if given adequate protection. It is hardy in well-drained, sandy soils, but is less tolerant of cold in compacted or wet soil.

HOW TO PLANT

Use divisions or stem cuttings of French tarragon. Tarragon tolerates poor, rather dry soil. Fertilize the soil the first year only with a low-nitrogen (5-10-10) fertilizer; before planting, work the fertilizer well into the soil at the rate of ½lb. per 95sq feet (225g per 9sq m). Plant cuttings or divisions in spring 18–24 inches (45–60cm) apart in rows 24–35 inches (60–90cm) apart. Give

them a place in full sun; the plant will tolerate partial shade, but the flavor will be impaired.

FERTILIZING AND WATERING

Don't fertilize at midseason.

Keep tarragon on the dry side to encourage the flavor to develop.

SPECIAL HANDLING

If you live in an area where the ground freezes and thaws often in the winter, mulch after the first freeze so that a thaw will not push the plant up and out of the ground. Mulching also helps the tarragon survive the cold. Subdivide the plants every three or four years.

PESTS

Tarragon has no serious pest problems. It does well in the organic garden.

DISEASES

Tarragon has no serious disease problems.

HARVESTING

Time from planting to harvest is about 2 months and you don't need a lot of tarragon. One plant supplies the average family, so if you're growing a lot you will be able to supply the whole neighborhood. Pick the tender top leaves of tarragon as you need them. Cut back the leafy top growth several times during the season to encourage the plant to bush out.

VARIETIES

French Tarragon, Russian Tarragon. Do not bother with the Russian variety — the flavor is poor.

STORING AND PRESERVING

Tarragon is best fresh, but can be dried or frozen.

SERVING SUGGESTIONS

Put a fresh stem or two of tarragon into bottles of good cider vinegar or wine vinegar and, *voila*, tarragon vinegar; allow a couple of weeks for the flavor to develop before you use it. Since the flavor of tarragon is so distinctive, use it with a light touch. Use the leaves to decorate cold dishes glazed with aspic. Tarragon gives a kick to a good sauce tartar, and, of course, you can't have chicken tarragon without it.

Thyme

Common name: thyme

Botanic name: *Thymus vulgaris*

Origin: Mediterranean

Thyme is a fragrant, small, perennial evergreen shrub with 6–8 inches (15–20cm) stems that often spread out over the ground. It's a member of the mint family and has square stems with small opposite leaves and pale lavender mint-like flowers. Thyme is a charming, cheerful little plant and will last for years once established. It's a good plant for a border or rock garden. There are more than 200 species and many hybrids, but the common form is the one grown for flavoring. The Greeks and Romans believed that thyme gave courage and strength; their highest compliment was to tell a man that he smelled of thyme. In the Middle Ages ladies embroidered sprigs of thyme on the scarves they gave their knights. Linnaeus, the father of modern botany, recommended thyme as a hangover cure.

PLANTING

Thyme prefers a mild climate but can survive temperatures below freezing. It tolerates cold better in well-drained soil.

HOW TO PLANT

Thyme likes well-drained soil, preferably low in fertility; rich soils produce plants that are large but less fragrant. The first year, work a low-nitrogen (5-10-10) fertilizer into the soil before planting at the rate of about ½lb per 95 sq feet (225g per 9 sq m). This is generous because in adverse soil conditions thyme, like many herbs, will have better flavor. Whatever the soil's like, it's impor-

tant to give thyme a place in the sun. Sow seeds in spring, summer and early autumn ⅛ inch (0.5cm) deep in rows 16–24 inches (40–60cm) apart, and when the seedlings are 2–3 inches (5–7.5cm) tall thin them about 12 inches (30cm) apart. You can also plant thyme cuttings or root divisions. Plant them at the same time and space them 12 inches (30cm) apart.

FERTILIZING AND WATERING

Don't fertilize at midseason.

Thyme seldom needs watering; it does best on the dry side.

SPECIAL HANDLING

Some herbs, like mints, grow like weeds whatever the competition. Thyme can't handle competition, especially from grassy weeds, and needs an orderly environment; cultivate conscientiously.

Start new plants every three to four years, because thyme gets woody; reduce the clump greatly. If you've no room in the garden for extra plants, plant them in a hanging basket.

PESTS

Thyme has no serious pest problems. Like most herbs, it's ideal for the organic gardener.

DISEASES

Thyme has no serious disease problems.

HARVESTING

Pick thyme as needed. For drying, harvest when the plants begin to bloom. Cut off the tops of the branches with 4–5 inches (10–12cm) of flowering stems.

VARIETIES

Caraway Thyme, Garden Thyme, Lemon Thyme, Silver Pray Thyme, Turkey Thyme, German Thyme, French Thyme, English Thyme.

STORING AND PRESERVING

After drying, crumble the thyme and put into tightly capped jars.

SERVING SUGGESTIONS

Thyme is usually blended with other herbs and used in meat dishes, poultry, stuffings (parsley and thyme is a happy combination) and soups. It adds a nice flavor to fish chowder and is often used along with a bay leaf to give a delicate lift to a white sauce or a cheese soufflé.

Establishing a Garden

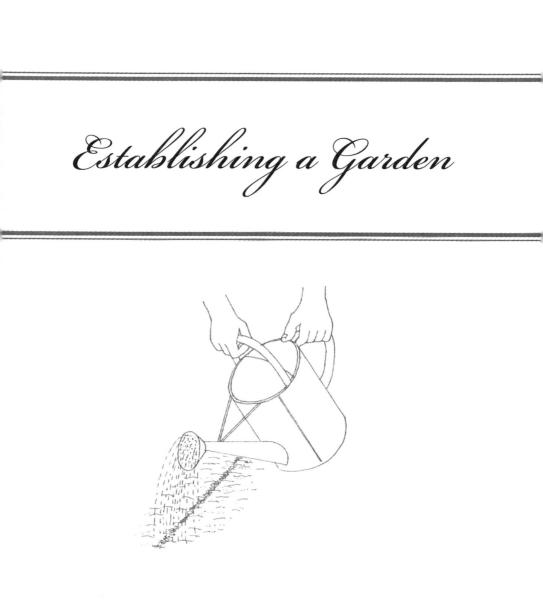

Choosing the Site

CLIMATE

Plants, like people, have definite ideas about where they like to live. Like people they flourish in congenial conditions and become weak and dispirited if life is difficult. Unlike people, however, plants can't take practical steps to improve their lot—they can't up and move, and they can't protect themselves against adverse conditions. You, the gardener, are largely responsible for how well plants do in the climatic conditions you offer them, and you'll save yourself a lot of frustration and disappointment if you have some understanding of how climate affects your garden and if you choose your crops according to the climate.

RAINFALL

The amount and timing of the rainfall in your area also affects how your vegetables grow. Too much rain at one time can wash away seeds or young seedlings and damage or even kill mature plants. Constant rain when plants are flowering can reduce the pollination of the flowers and reduce yields. This can happen to tomatoes, peppers, beans, eggplant, melons, pumpkins, and both summer and winter squash.

Constant rain can also tempt the honeybees to stay in their hives instead of pollinating the plants; again, yields will be affected.

Too little rain over a period of time can slow down plant growth and kill young seedlings or even mature plants. Limited moisture in the air can also inhibit pollination and reduce the yields of some vegetables. Too little rain can be more easily remedied than too much. You can water the garden but if it rains too much, all you can do is pray.

Rainfall is probably the easiest climatic condition to improve. Since the home garden is usually small, you can do something to regulate how much water it gets. If you don't get enough rain when you need it, you can simply water, and there are many different methods you can use. Too much rain can be more difficult to deal with, and here you need to take preventive measures.

Drainage is important; The better drained your soil is, the better it will be able to deal with too much water. When you select the site for your garden, avoid any area that is low-lying or poorly drained. If your soil is heavy clay it might be as well to take the initial trouble of laying drains. Otherwise lighten the soil by adding plenty of well-rotted compost or other organic material. The water-holding properties of light, sandy soil will be improved in the same way.

One of the most important things to remember is that even good soil will be unproductive if handled badly. Only handle soil when it is damp, never when it is wet, otherwise when it dries you are likely to find you have a crusted, caked surface, impervious to air, which will inhibit the healthy root growth of your plants.

LIGHT

The third major climatic factor is light, and it's an important factor to consider when you plan your garden. Sunlight—or some type of light—provides energy that turns water and carbon dioxide into the sugar that plants use for food. Green plants use sugar to form new cells, to thicken existing cell walls, and to develop flowers and fruit. The more intense the light, the more effective it is. Light intensity, undiminished by obstructions, is greater in summer than in winter, and greater in areas where the days are sunny and bright than in areas where it's cloudy, hazy, or foggy. As a rule, the greater the light intensity the greater the plants' production of sugar—provided, of course, that it's not too hot or too cold and the plants get the right amount of water.

If a plant is going to produce flowers and fruit, it must have a store of energy beyond what it needs just to grow stems and leaves. If the light is limited, a plant that looks green and healthy may never produce flowers or fruit. This can be a problem with tomatoes; with lettuce, where you're only interested in the leaves, it's not an issue. All the same, all vegetables need a certain amount of light in order to grow properly, and without it all the watering, weeding, and wishing in the world will not make them flourish.

How day length affects your crops. Many plants are not affected by day length—how long it stays light during the day. But for many others the length of the day plays a big part in regulating when they mature and flower. Some plants are long-day plants, which means they need 12 or more hours of sunlight daily in order to initiate flowering. Radishes and spinach are long-day plants, and this is the main reason they go to seed so fast in the middle of the summer when the day length is more than 12 hours. If you want to grow radishes or spinach in mid-summer, you have to cover them with a light-proof box at about 4 p.m. every afternoon to fool them into thinking the day's over. Other plants are short-day plants and need less than 12 hours of light to initiate flowering; corn is an example. Many varieties of short-day plants have been bred to resist the effects of long days, but most will still flower more quickly when the days are shorter.

Cold Frames

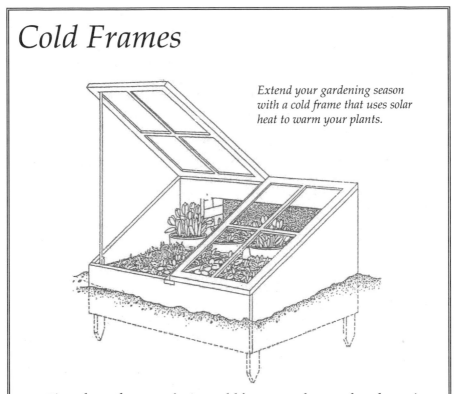

Extend your gardening season with a cold frame that uses solar heat to warm your plants.

If you have the space for it, a cold frame—a glass-enclosed growing area outside—can add an extra dimension to your garden. It's an ideal place to start seedlings or to put plants in the spring to harden them for the rigors of outdoor life. When you have started vegetables indoors, especially the cold-tolerant ones, you can move them to a cold frame and give them the benefit of much more light in a protected place.

The frame should not be too deep from front to back or you'll have trouble getting plants in and out. Cold frames capture solar heat, and can be slanted to take advantage of the greatest amount of sun.

On the days when the sun is bright you may have to provide some shade to keep the plants from sunburning, or lift the cold frame windows to keep plants from steaming. If the sun is bright enough the temperature inside a cold frame can reach 86–95°F (30–35°C) when the temperature outside is very low. But on cold nights when the temperature drops below freezing, a cold frame will need some extra protection. An old quilt or blanket under a tarp is a good cover. If you have nothing else newspapers will do, although they are a bit harder to handle.

How much sunlight is necessary? Vegetables grown for their fruits need a minimum of six to eight hours of direct light each day. Less light can mean less than a full crop. If you try to grow tomatoes, peppers, or eggplants in the shade; they'll often produce a good, green plant without giving you anything at all in the way of a vegetable. Crops grown for their roots and leaves, however, will give satisfactory results in light shade.

Root crops, such as beets, carrots, radishes, and turnips, store up energy before they flower and do rather well in partial shade, especially if you don't compare them with the same crop grown in full sun. Plants like lettuce, swiss chard, or spinach that are grown for their leaves are most tolerant of shade; in fact, where the sun is very hot and bright they may need some shade for protection. Only mushrooms and sprouts can be produced without any light at all.

Making the most of your garden light. Choose an open part of the garden which, preferably, should face north or north-east to get the best of the sun, and arrange to have the vegetable beds and the rows within the beds running north and south. If you have a sloping site, terrace the bed across the slope in step fashion, retaining the soil with wood, brick or concrete but making sure that seepage holes are left at the base of the retaining material so that water can seep away down the slope.

Don't put your vegetable garden in the shade of buildings, trees, or shrubs. Remember that as well as shading an area, trees and shrubs also have roots that may extend underground well beyond the overhead reach of their branches. These roots will compete with the vegetable plants for nutrients. Go out and stand in your garden to see just how the light falls. Walk around and find where the light fails to penetrate. This knowledge will be very useful when you come to planting time.

Providing shade from too much sun. Most vegetables need full sun for best growth, but young or newly transplanted plants may need some protection from bright, direct sunlight. It's easier for you, as a gardener, to provide shade where there's too much sun than to brighten up a shady area. You can, for instance, plant large, sturdy plants like sunflowers or Jerusalem artichokes to provide a screen, and you can design your garden so that large plants and small ones each get the light they need. You can also shade young plants with boxes or screens where necessary. However, too little sun is far more serious a problem in a garden than too much.

The Soil

It is more important for the soil to be in a good crumbly physical condition than rich in plant foods which can easily be added. If the soil packs tightly it not only prevents the easy access of water but also of oxygen from the air both of which are essential for healthy root growth. Heavy clay soils are not the only ones that pack tightly; some alluvial loams that appear gritty when dry and actually crumble up, will pack down very tightly when watered and become comparatively airless. The finer the soil particles, the closer they pack together and so the spaces between them become correspondingly smaller. It is only through these spaces between the soil particles that the movement of water and air is possible.

Even very fine sand which will never set hard can pack down so densely that it is very difficult to get water to penetrate once it becomes quite dry. The most important point when handling any soil with a clay content is to dig, weed or generally cultivate only when it is in the just damp stage. Only then is it possible to get it to crumble.

If clay soils are disturbed when they are wet and sticky they will set harder when dry. When agitated, the wet fine clay particles are forced into solution with the soil water. The result is mud, which when dry is airless and too dense to allow development of healthy plant roots.

Before disturbing clay soils after rain or watering, give them a simple test by taking a small handful of the soil and molding it together to form a ball. If in a reasonable condition to cultivate, the ball of soil should be enough to crumble on impact. If it clings together or shows signs of stickiness, then delay cultivation or planting for another day, then test again.

The only type of soil that may not react as described in the test is pure clay, which when damp will mold into a ball but is too tenacious to shatter on impact.

The soil so often recommended for vegetable growing is a "good loam." Loam is a very variable term that refers to a mixture of different soil ingredients, usually clay, sand and humus together with other organic material. Clay loams, those that remain sticky for a long period after watering and are inclined to pack very hard when dry, contain more clay than sand. Inversely sandy soils contain more sand than clay.

The ideal soil is a medium to light loam, containing sufficient clay to hold reasonable amounts

Companion Planting

One of the as yet not understood principles which govern successful gardening is that of biodynamics. Some plants grow well in the proximity of others but will fall and die if given companions of a different sort. Plants have the ability to repel or attract different insects, fungi, and soil organisms.

Vegetable	Plants that help growth	Antagonistic plants
Asparagus	Tomatoes, parsley	
Basil	Most plants	Rue
Bean	Carrots, beet, cauliflower	Onions, garlic
Beet	Dwarf beans, onions	Climbing beans, mustard
Broad bean	Potatoes	Fennel
Cabbage	Beet, dill, celery	Strawberries
Carrot	Radish, leeks	Dill
Celery	Leeks, tomatoes, beans	
Eggplant	Dwarf beans	
Kohlrabi	Beets, onions	Tomatoes
Leek	Onions, celery, carrots	
Lettuce	Carrots, strawberries	
Onion	Beets	
Pea	Carrots, cucumber, turnips	Onions, garlic
Potato	Cabbage, peas, broad beans	Dill
Pumpkin	Sweet corn	Potatoes
Radish	Lettuce, peas	Hyssop
Tomato	Parsley, asparagus, carrots	Kohlrabi, potatoes, fennel

of moisture but enough organic material and sand to allow easy crumbling and help it keep that way.

PREPARING THE BEDS

Raising the beds about 4–6 inches (10–15cm) above the surrounding soil will make certain that heavy rain will drain away more easily and that puddling will be prevented. Beds should be about 3 feet (1m) wide so that access from 10–12 inches (25–30cm) paths on either side is easy and comfortable.

Mark out the position of the beds and paths then shovel a 3-inch (8cm) depth of soil from the paths and pile it on the beds and rake smooth. On a sloping site with paths and beds running across the slope, the soil shoveled from a path will be used to build up the low side of the bed above it.

PREPARING TO PLANT

Dig in well-rotted compost and rake the soil over. Any fibrous material large enough to be picked up by the rake can be piled on one side for use as mulch later.

If preparing the ground for root vegetables, mix the decomposed material with the top layer of soil as evenly as possible and then turn it in to about fork-depth, half turning the soil several times to ensure the mixing is thorough. Do not add complete fertilizer close to planting time unless you make certain to mix it in exceptionally well.

Most vegetables like a fairly alkaline soil. An addition of half to two-thirds of a cup of garden lime or dolomite per 11 sq feet (sq m) once a year would benefit all soils that are not naturally alkaline. It is quite safe to add fertilizer at the same time. Beans, peas, onions, lettuce, cabbage and beets all appreciate lime; rhubarb, parsley, tomatoes and radishes do not. Take care with potatoes—don't use lime unless you are certain the soil is very acid.

COMPOST AND MULCH—THE DIFFERENCE IS IN THE USE

If you're an inexperienced gardener, you may be confused by the difference between composting and mulching—both processes use waste organic matter. The difference is in the use. Composted materials are dug back into the soil to enrich it and to enable the plants to use the nutrients that have been released by the decaying process. A mulch is a layer of material spread over the ground or around plants to provide protection from heat or cold, to retain soil moisture, or to maintain a certain soil temperature. Compost stays in the soil and eventually becomes part of it; a mulch can be removed when the protection it provides is no longer needed.

THE COMPOST PILE: YOUR GARDEN'S RECYCLING CENTER

Composting is essentially a way of speeding up the natural process of decomposition by which organic materials are broken down and their components returned to the soil. It's a way of converting plants and other organic wastes into a loose, peat-like humus that provides nutrients to growing plants and increases the soil's ability to control water. The decaying process happens naturally, but slowly. The proximity, moisture, and air circulation of a compost pile encourages this process.

Composting also has another advantage over leaving organic wastes to decay naturally: Organic matter has to take nitrogen from the soil in order to keep the decaying process going. Composting keeps the waste in one place where it's not depriving plants of nitrogen.

Composting can save money that you would otherwise have spent on fertilizers. It can save time, too, because it gives you a place to dispose of leaves and grass clippings.

HOW THE COMPOSTING PROCESS WORKS

Compost forms as organic wastes are broken down by microorganisms in the soil. These microorganisms don't create nutrients; they just break down complex materials into simple ones that the plant can use. Most soil organisms are inactive when soil temperatures are below 41°F (5°C); they don't begin working in earnest until the temperature goes up to about 59–64°F (15–18°C), and most of them don't work well in a very acid element. Because they are extremely small, microorganisms work faster when not overwhelmed by large chunks of material.

There are two basic kinds of microorganisms: those that need air to work (aerobic) and those that don't (anaerobic). It's possible to compost in an airtight container, thanks to the microorganisms that don't need air. A tightly covered plastic garbage bin will convert an enormous amount of organic kitchen waste into compost in the course of a winter. The classic outdoor compost pile should be turned regularly with a pitchfork to provide air for the microorganisms that need it.

HOW TO START A COMPOST PILE

If you have a fairly large garden, the best place to put your compost pile is at one end of the garden. The pile can be square, rectangular or round; 10–13 feet (3–4m) and as long as the available space. You can use fencing or concrete blocks to keep the pile under control.

If space is at a premium or if a compost pile doesn't fit in with your landscaping, start the heap behind some bushes or behind the garage. If the space available is extremely small, you can compost in a large heavy-duty plastic bag or plastic garbage bin. You can also work the material directly into the soil.

To build a compost pile, start out with 12–24 inches (30–60cm) of leaves, if you have them, or 6–12 inches (15–30cm) of more compact material, such as grass clippings or sawdust. Over this put a layer of fertilizer (manure, blood and bone, or commercial fertilizer) and some finely ground limestone (most microorganisms like their environment sweet). Then add some soil to hold water and provide a starter colony of microorganisms. Water the compost carefully. Add a second layer of leaves or other garden waste and repeat the layers. If you have enough material or enough room, put on a third layer. The pile should be kept moist like a squeezed, but not sopping, sponge. As more material becomes available, make new layers, adding more fertilizer and lime each time. Turn the pile with a pitchfork about once a month.

You can use all garden waste on your compost pile except disease- and pest-laden materials, or those that have been treated with pesticides or weed-killers—for instance, grass clippings from an area that's been treated with a herbicide. Use non-treated grass clippings, leaves, weeds and turf. You can also use kitchen leftovers like vegetable and fruit peels, vegetable tops, coffee grounds, tea leaves, and eggshells. The finer these materials are chopped and the deeper they're buried, the quicker they'll be converted and the less chance there is that they'll be dug up by inquisitive animals. You can also compost hay, straw, hulls, nutshells, and tree trimmings (not walnut). But unless they're shredded, these materials will take a long time to decompose. There are a number of ways you

can speed up the composting process. First, you can grind or shred all compost materials to give the microorganisms a head start. Second, make sure the pile doesn't dry out, and provide enough fertilizer to encourage rapid growth of the bacteria. Third, you can use a starter culture, either material from an established compost pile or a commercial starter culture.

Composting is a creative activity. There are almost as many different methods of composting as there are gardeners, and like a good stew, the proof is in the final product. And when other gardeners see your compost pile, they'll know you're taking good care of your garden and that you're not just a horticultural dabbler.

MULCHING

By keeping a mulch or organic material over the soil you automatically keep the soil in the good condition, eliminating most weed growth, the need for digging and other forms of cultivation. A mulch encourages a lively earthworm population, so you can leave these busy little creatures to carry out any aeration that is needed. Their constant tunneling from surface mulch to sub-soil does this very effectively.

The other important role of a surface mulch is to protect clayey soils from losing their good crumbly structure through the pounding of heavy rain or careless watering. In the same way a mulch prevents humus from washing out of sandy soil. It also conserves moisture and protects roots from excessive heat or cold.

WHAT TO USE AS A MULCH

Fibrous compost, spent mushroom compost and spent hops are widely used as mulches. Straw—especially straw from stables—is excellent, though the latter tends to generate heat if applied thickly, so it is just as well to moisten and heap it for a few weeks before spreading it close to plants.

Seaweed makes a valuable soil-feeding mulch. This can be salty so it is as well to hose the seaweed in a place where salt-carrying water can run off safely before spreading it on the garden.

Lawn clippings are one of the most frequently used mulches. They are also a valuable material but, like stable straw, will generate heat if spread thickly when fresh and green. I prefer to moisten and heap them for a few weeks before spreading. It is usually easy to have a few conveniently placed hideaways behind shrubbery where the clippings can be heaped prior to spreading. Alternatively, once you have a good mulch established, it

EARTHWORMS

The physical tunneling of earthworms helps to aerate the soil. They do also help to combine organic material with clay and soil particles by mixing them all thoroughly together as it passes through their bodies. Their activity also tends to deepen the top soil because as they tunnel deeper during the drier periods they take organic material down to these levels.

They also increase soil fertility. They ingest soil, pass it through their bodies, expelling it as castings that are richer in nutrients than the original soil. It has been discovered that worm castings contain 5 times more nitrogen, 7 times more available phosphorus, 11 times more potash and 40% more humus than the surrounding topsoil.

However, because of the relative fineness of their castings they can interfere with drainage so are to be discouraged for container gardening. The best way to encourage earthworms in the garden is by maintaining a surface mulch. Also be discriminate with the use artificial fertilizers.

can be maintained by adding a light sprinkling of the green clippings to it each week or so.

Most leaves, including those of deciduous trees, will make valuable mulching material. Ideal mulching material is a mixture of leaves and grass taken up by the lawnmower. It is best to moisten and heap this a few weeks before spreading.

Wood chips made from feeding prunings through a hammer mill or shredder makes a good, long-lasting mulch. Sawdust and shavings contain little or no nutriment but give insulation and protection to the soil they cover, and help to lighten clayey soils. They don't take nitrogen from the soil unless dug in or applied more than about 4 inches (10cm) deep; and in any case this can be overcome by watering them about once a month with one of the complete soluble plant foods or by sprinkling them with a little fertilizer.

Pine bark mulch also helps to keep the soil in good condition even though it has little or no nutritional value. It is more expensive than other mulches mentioned but is long lasting and more attractive for feature areas.

COMPOST AS MULCH

Compost serves to improve the soil in the ways already mentioned but it cannot be considered the perfectly balanced plant food many people assume it to be.

Compost can only return to the soil those elements contained in the plant material used in the composting. Therefore, if this plant material was grown on deficient soils, the compost will be similarly deficient. This is why some gardeners add light sprinklings or waterings with complete plant food when making a compost heap. These additions also speed decomposition.

Exponents of organic gardening prefer to use completely natural additives such as blood and bone or animal manures, but the latter, with the exception of fowl manure, may be short of the phosphorus needed in most home garden soils.

Fertilizing

Feeding with complete fertilizer prior to sowing or planting out is good practice even in fairly well-composted soil and in addition to nitrogen and potash, it supplies the phosphorus so frequently lacking locally and so essential for good germination, root growth and maturity. About one-third cup per 11 sq feet (1sqm) is enough for most crops but peas and beans can take a little more—up to half a cup.

Alternatives to complete fertilizer are complete organic plant foods (usually well balanced with phosphorus) and animal manures which are also excellent (except for carrots and parsnips, where they should not be used directly, but only "second-hand" from a previous crop). Fresh horse manure, and to some extent cow manure, have only a low percentage of phosphorus compared to nitrogen, so except for leaf crops they need balancing with superphosphate or fowl manure.

Heap fresh animal manures for a few weeks before using. The amount needed to give appreciable benefit would be 7–10½ quarts (7–10L) per 11 sq feet (1sqm) of soil and about half this amount if using fowl manure. However, reasonably well-weathered or partly decomposed horse or cow manure can be piled about 1 inch (3–4cm) thick as a surface mulch or lightly knead it into the surface.

The benefit of having a good, coarse, open-structured soil has been well stressed, but if it is too "fluffed up" there will not be sufficient contact between the new roots of seed or seedling and the moisture surrounding the soil particles. After mixing in compost and fertilizer, water the ground very gently and leave it for a week to "settle." If you are in a desperate hurry to plant, tread the soil down very lightly when it is just damp not when it is wet or even sticky, and gently rake even. That way soil and young root will be able to make contact when planting or sowing is made.

But the best way is to prepare the beds well ahead of planting time and, after watering, to leave them for a couple of weeks so that any weed seeds will germinate and show themselves. Any but the bulbous weeds can then be destroyed by scuffling the soil to cut their roots just below the surface. You can sow or plant in beds that will be weed-free for a considerable time thus avoiding much fiddly and tedious later weeding between the new little plants.

Sowing and Planting

Root vegetables, e.g. carrots and parsnips, do not transplant well and should be sown where they are to grow. Beets and onions transplant well. Peas and beans do not enjoy transplanting—sow direct. Lettuce, cabbage and cauliflower are amenable, but lettuce is less likely to run to seed during summer if spared the shock of transplanting.

GROWING FROM SEED

If seed is to germinate it needs moisture, oxygen and the correct temperature. You will find, in early spring in temperate to cool climates, that beans, cucumbers and vine crops will not germinate because although the air temperature is reasonably warm the soil is still too cool. Inversely, during summer the soil temperature may be too hot for lettuce and other seeds to germinate.

Seeds cannot germinate if they are covered too deeply. Twice their own depth is sensible. Large seeds like those of beans, pumpkin, etc. should just be pressed into the soil; peas and beans can be sown in "drills." Root crops such as carrots, parsnips, beetroot, radish, etc. should be sown in shallow depressions 1/2 inch (1cm) deep. Some people tap them from the seed packet. You can also tip seed into your left hand and then scatter it, a pinch at a time, along the furrow and press down with the back of the rake. Careful spacing at this stage will save thinning later. The ways seeds are covered is important.

Crumbly garden soil will do, but fibrous compost or spent mushroom compost is a better topping as it makes a good buffer against disturbance by heavy rain and holds needed moisture. Vermiculite, which I like to use, is even better. It is very light, holds a surprising amount of water, allows maximum air penetration to growing roots and is highly visible so that not only is it easy to tell where the seed has been sown but it helps to make identification of weeds easier. We have all known the frustration of decapitating seedlings under the mistaken impression they were weeds!

SPACED SOWING

Lettuce, cabbage, cauliflower, swiss chard, etc. can be transplanted but, if sown with an eye to spacing, can grow in situ and thereby avoid the shock of being lifted and having to re-establish themselves.

Mark out the rows and also the space within the row. You can cross each row in grid formation or stagger the plantings. At each

When to Sow

Vegetable	Temperate areas	Sub-tropical	Cool
Broad Bean	Oct–Feb	Oct–Nov	Jan & Mar
Bean (*other than above*)	Late Mar–Aug	All seasons	Apr–July
Beetroot	Feb–Oct	All seasons	Mar–Sept
Broccoli	July–Sept	July–Sept	July–Sept
Brussels Sprout	June–Sept	Not suitable	June–Aug
Cabbage	Feb–Nov	Sept–Jan	Feb–Oct
Carrot	Feb–Oct	Sept–Feb	Feb–Sept
Cauliflower	June–Sept	Aug–Sept	May–Sept
Celery	Feb–July	May–Sept	Feb–July
Chive	Sept–Jan	Sept–Nov	Fall & Spring
Cress	All seasons	All seasons	Feb–Oct
Cucumber	Mar–June	Mar–Aug	Apr–May
Dill	All seasons	All seasons	All seasons
Egg Plant	Apr–May	Mar–July	Not suitable
Endive	Feb–Oct	Sept–Feb	Feb–Sept
Herbs	Feb–Sept	All seasons	Feb–Sept
Kohlrabi	Oct–Feb	Oct–Dec	Sept & Feb
Leek	Feb– Sept	Aug–Oct	Feb–Sept
Lettuce	All seasons	All seasons	All seasons
Squash	Apr–July	Mar–Aug	Apr–May
Melon	Apr–June	Mar–Aug	Apr–May
Mustard	All seasons	All seasons	Feb–Oct
Okra	Mar–Aug	Mar–Nov	Apr–July
Onion	Sept–Jan	Sept–Nov	Fall & Spring
Parsley	Feb–Sept	July–Oct	Mar–Sept
Parsnip	Feb–Sept	Aug–Oct	Mar–Aug
Pea	Aug–May	Sept–Dec	Feb–Aug
Pepper	Apr–May	Mar–Aug	Apr
Potato	Aug & Jan	Aug–Oct	Mar–May
Pumpkin	Mar–July	Mar–Aug	Apr–May
Radish	All seasons	All seasons	Mar–Sept
Rhubarb (*seed*)	Dec–May	May–Aug	Mar–July
Rosella	Apr–May	Mar–June	Not suitable
Rutabaga	July–Oct	Sept–Nov	July–Oct
Salsify	Sept–Apr	Not suitable	All seasons
Spinach	Oct–Jan	Nov–Dec	Oct–Feb
Sweet Corn	Mar–Aug	Mar–Aug	Apr–July
Sweet Potato (*cuttings*)	Mar–June	Mar–June	Apr–May
Swiss Chard	All seasons	Sept–Feb	Feb–Sept
Tomato	Feb–June	All seasons	Mar–Apr
Turnip	Aug–Mar	Sept–Jan	Aug–Sept & Mar

marked spot sow 3 or 4 seeds, cover, and firm down the soil. If all the seeds germinate you can make a judicious thinning leaving the strongest plan to grow at the correct distance from the next.

FLUID SOWING

Apart for "sowing aids" such as vermiculite and compressed peat pots, fluid sowing is probably the most notable departure from seed-sowing tradition since man started cultivating the soil.

Seeds are presprouted by sprinkling them on wet filter paper (or some other absorbent, but not too open, material), enclosing them to maintain moisture and keeping in a warm place until germination begins.

The sprouting seed is them carefully washed in a fine sieve, tapped into a prepared fluid gel, poured into a plastic squeeze bottle with a suitably large nozzle, or into a plastic bag with one corner nicked off. And then, with slight pressure, is extruded along the rows of soil prepared for sowing like icing being piped onto a cake and it is finally lightly covered and watered.

The advantages of fluid sowing are that at indoor temperatures, germination time is halved, you know how much seed is viable and have a good idea of the germination rate before sowing—and it is much easier to control the spacing and so avoid unnecessary thinning of carrots, parsnips and onions later.

You can practice this fascinating process by purchasing a "fluid sowing kit" with its supply of gel. Some overseas experts recommend wallpaper paste for making gel but I find that most types available here contain fungicides that retard germination and growth. Try making a thin mixture with arrowroot or even corn flour but keep the gel thin or it will take too long to dissipate in the soil.

TRANSPLANTING SEEDLINGS

All plants receive some shock or setback when transplanting so it is a great advantage to transplant carefully to minimize this shock. Seedlings that have been kept in containers indoors, or even kept shaded for a few days, are likely to wilt and shrivel if planted straight out into hot sunlight. It is therefore an advantage to condition them to sunlight before planting out by giving them, say, a few hours direct sun, etc. at the same time being conscious of the fact that in this situation they will suddenly use a lot more water and dry out a lot more rapidly.

If it is essential to plant out immediately and if there is doubt about the seedlings being conditioned, the ideal time is on a dull day or late in the evening. The latter is good practice in all cases. It also helps the seedlings overcome transplanting shock if they are shaded for a few days until the disturbed or injured roots are again able to function properly. A few twigs, especially dry twigs, provide a good type of shading.

Curing very hot conditions terracotta pots large enough to comfortably cover the foliage of the seedlings are excellent, because after watering the evaporation from their porous surface cools the inside air around the seedlings. To prevent the seedlings from becoming too drawn they should only be applied during the heat of the day. Quite good sun shelters can be made by cutting plastic ice-cream containers into equal halves or quarters for larger ones, inverting the sections and pressing them into the soil on the sunny side of each seedling.

Also, it is possible to buy plastic shade cloth that can be supported on wire hoops above the seedlings or even to make a few tunnel-shaped covers of wire netting and drape the shade cloth

Planting guide: spacing

Vegetable	Approx. space between plants	Approx. space between rows	Depth of seed
Artichoke	3–4 ft. (1–1.25 m)	3 ft. (90 cm)	
Asparagus	1–1.5 ft. (30–45 cm)	2.5 ft. (75 cm)	1 in. (2–3 cm)
Beans, broad	8–10 in. (20–25 cm)	3 ft. (90 cm)	1 in. (2–3 cm)
Beans, dry	4–6 in. (10–15 cm)	1.5–2 ft. (45–60 cm)	1 in. (2–3 cm)
Beans, lima			
bush	2–3 in. (5–7 cm)	1.5–2 ft. (45–60 cm)	1 in. (2–3 cm)
pole	4–6 in. (10–15 cm)	28–30 in. (70–75 cm)	1 in. (2–3 cm)
Beans, mung	18-20 in. (45–50 cm)	1.5–2 ft. (45–60 cm)	.5 in. (1 cm)
Beans, snap or green			
bush	2–3 in. (5–7 cm)	1.5–2 ft. (45–60 cm)	1 in. (1 cm)
pole	4–6 in. (10–15 cm)	28–30 in. (70–75 cm)	1 in. (1 cm)
Beets	2–3 in. (5–7 cm)	1–1.5 ft. (30–45 cm)	1–2 in. (2–5 cm)
Broccoli	3 in. (7 cm)	2 ft.. (60 cm)	.5 in. (1 cm)
Brussels sprouts	24 in. (60 cm)	2 ft. (60 cm)	.5 in (1 cm)
Cabbage	1.5–2 ft. (45–60 cm)	2.5 ft. (75 cm)	.5 in (1 cm)
Cardoon	1.5–2 ft. (45–60 cm)	3 ft. (90 cm)	.5 in (1 cm)
Carrot	2–4 in. (5–10 cm)	1–1.5 ft. (30–45 cm)	.25 in. (.5 cm)
Cauliflower	1.5–2 ft. (45–60 cm)	2–3 ft. (60–90 cm)	.5 in. (1 cm)
Celeriac	6–8 in. (15–20 cm)	2 ft. (60 cm)	.25 in. (.5 cm)
Celery	8–10 in. (20–25 cm)	2 ft. (60 cm)	.25 in. (.5 cm)

Vegetable	Approx. space between plants	Approx. space between rows	Depth of seed
Choko	24–28 in. (60–70 cm)	5 ft. (1.5 m)	
Chick Pea	6–8 in. (15–20 cm)	1–1.5 ft. (30–45 cm)	.5 in. (1 cm)
Chicory	1–1.5 ft. (30–45 cm)	2–3 ft. (60–90 cm)	1 in. (2.5 cm)
Chinese cabbage	8–12 in. (20–30 cm)	18–26 in. (45–65 cm)	.5 in. (1 cm)
Collards	1 ft. (30 cm)	1.5–2 ft. (45–60 cm)	.5 in. (1 cm)
Corn	2–4 in. (5–10 cm)	1–1.5 ft. (30–45 cm)	1 in. (2.5–3 cm)
Cress	1–2 in. (2–5 cm)	1.5–2 ft. (45–60 cm)	.25 in. (.5 cm)
Cucumber			
*In inverted hills 3 feet apart**	1 ft. (30 cm)	1.5–6 ft.	.5 in. (1 cm)
Dandelion	6–8 in. (15–20 cm)	1–1.5 ft. (30–45 cm)	.25 in (.5 cm)
Eggplant	1.5–2 ft. (45–60 cm)	2–3 ft. (60–90 cm)	.25 in (.5 cm)
Endive	7–12 in. (22–30 cm)	1.5–2 ft. (45–60 cm)	.1 in. (.25 cm)
Fennel	12–14 in. (30–35 cm)	2–3 ft. (60–90 cm)	.25 in. (.5 cm)
Horseradish	2 ft. (60 cm)	1.5–2 ft. (45–60 cm)	.25 in. (.5 cm)
Kale	8–12 in. (20–30 cm)	1.5–2 ft. (45 –60 cm)	.5 in (1 cm)
Kohlrabi	5–6 in. (12–15 cm)	1.5–2 ft. (45–60 cm)	.25 in. (.5 cm)
Leek	6–7 in. (15–22 cm)	1–1.5 ft. (30–45 cm)	.1 in. (.25 cm)
Lentils	1–2 in. (2–5 cm)	1.5–2 ft. (45–60 cm)	.5 in. (1 cm)
Lettuce	7–12 in. (15–30 cm)	1–1.5 ft. (30–45 cm)	barely
Melon			
*In inverted hills 3 feet apart**	1.5–2 ft. (45–60 cm)	5–8 ft. (1.5–2.5 m)	1 in. (2.5 cm)
Mustard	6–12 in. (15–30 cm)	1–2 ft. (30–60 cm)	.5 in (1 cm)
Okra	6–18 in. (15–45 cm)	2–3 ft. (60–90 cm)	.5–1 in. (1–2.5 cm)
Onions			
sets	2–3 in. (5–7 cm)	1–1.5 ft. (30–45 cm)	.25 in. (.5 cm)
seeds	1–2 in. (2.5–5 cm)	1–1.5 ft. (30–45 cm)	.25 in. (.5 cm)
Parsnip	1–2 in. (2.5–5 cm)	1.5–2 ft. (45–60 cm)	.5 in (1 cm)
Pea, black-eyed	8–18 in. (20–45 cm)	1–1.5 ft. (30–45 cm)	.5 in. (1 cm)
Pea, shelling	1–2 in. (2.5–5 cm)	1.5–2 ft. (45–60 cm)	2 in. (5 cm)
Peanut	6–8 in. (15–20 cm)	1–1.5 ft. (30–45 cm)	1 in. (2.5 cm)
Pepper	1.5–2 ft. (45–60 cm)	2–3 ft. (60–90 cm)	.5 in. (1 cm)
Pumpkin			
*In inverted hills approx. 6 feet apart**	2–4 ft. (60–120 cm)	5–10 ft. (1.5–3 m)	1 in. (2.5 cm)
Radish	1–6 in. (2.5–15 cm)	1–1.5 ft. (30–45 cm)	.5 in. (1 cm)
Rhubarb	3–4 ft. (90–120 cm)	3–4 ft. (90–120 cm)	
Rutabaga	6–8 in. (15–20 cm)	1.5–2 ft. (45–60 cm)	.5 in. (1 cm)
Salsify	2–4 in. (10–15 cm)	1.5–2 ft. (45–60 cm)	.5 in. (1 cm)
Shallot	6–8 in. (15–20 cm)	1–1.5 ft. (30–45 cm)	.25 in. (.5 cm)
Sorrel	1–1.5 ft. (30–45 cm)	1.5–2 ft. (45–60 cm)	.5 in. (1 cm)

Vegetable	Approx. space between plants	Approx. space between rows	Depth of seed
Soybean	1.5–2 in. (3.75–5 cm)	2–3 ft. (60–90 cm)	.5–1 in (1–2.5 cm)
Spinach	2–4 in (5–10 cm)	1–2 ft. (30–60 cm)	.5 in. (1 cm)
Spinach, New Zealand	1 ft. (30 cm)	2–3 ft. (60–90 cm)	.5 in. (1 cm)
Squash, summer			
*In inverted hills 4.5 feet apart**	2–4 ft. (60–120 cm)	1.5–4 ft. (45–120 cm)	.25 in. (.5 cm)
Squash, winter			
*In inverted hills 6 feet apart**	2–4 ft. (60–120 cm)	5–10 ft. (1.5–3 m)	.25 in. (.5 cm)
Sweet Potato	1–1.5 ft. (30–45 cm)	3–4 ft. (90–120 cm)	3–4 in. (7.5–10 cm)
Swiss Chard	7–10 in. (22–25 cm)	1.5–2 ft. (45–60 cm)	1 in. (2.5 cm)
Tomato	1.5–3 ft. (45–90 cm)	2–4 ft. (60–120 cm)	.5 in. (1 cm)
Turnip			
greens	1–3 in. (2.5–7.5 cm)	1–2 ft. (30–60 cm)	.5 in. (1 cm)
roots	3–4 in. (7.5–10 cm)	1–2 ft. (30–60 cm)	.5 in. (1 cm)
Watermelon			
*In inverted hills 6 feet apart**	2–3 ft. (60–90 cm)	5–10 ft. (1.5-3 m)	1 in. (2.5 cm)

Herbs

	Approx. space between plants	Approx. space between rows	Depth of seed
Anise	6–12 in. (15–30 cm)	1.5–2 ft. (45–60 cm)	.25 in. (.5 cm)
Basil	5–6 in. (12–15 cm)	1.5–2 ft. (45–60 cm)	.25 in. (.5 cm)
Borage	1 ft. (30 cm)	1.5–2 ft. (45–60 cm)	.5 in. (1 cm)
Caraway	1–1.5 ft. (30–45 cm)	1.5–2 ft. (45–60 cm)	.25 in. (.5 cm)
Chervil	3–4 in. (7.5–10)	1.5–2 ft. (45–60 cm)	.5 in. (1 cm)
Chives	8–10 in. (20–25 cm)	1 ft. (30 cm)	.25 in. (.5 cm)
Coriander	1 ft. (30 cm)	1–1.5 ft. (30–45 cm)	.5 in. (1 cm)
Dill	1 ft. (30 cm)	2–3 ft. (60–90 cm)	.5 in. (1 cm)
Fennel	1 ft. (30 cm)	2–3 in. (5–7.5 cm)	.5 in. (1 cm)
Garlic sets)	3–6 in. (7.5–15 cm)	2–3 ft. (60–90 cm)	2–3 in. (5–7.5
Marjoram	6–12 in. (15–30 cm)	1–2 ft. (30–60 cm)	.5 in. (1 cm)
Mint	2–3 in. (5–7.5 cm)	1–2 ft. (30–60 cm)	.5 in. (1 cm)
Oregano	6–12 in. (15–30 cm)	1–1.5 ft. (30–45 cm)	.5 in. (1 cm)
Parsley	1–1.5 ft. (30–45 cm)	1.5–2 ft. (45–60 cm)	.5 in. (1 cm)
Rosemary	1.5 ft. (45 cm)	1.5–2 ft. (45–60 cm)	.5 in. (1 cm)
Sage	1 ft. (30 cm)	1.5–2 ft. (45–60 cm)	.5 in. (1 cm)
Savory	6–18 in. (15–45 cm)	1–1.5 ft. (30–45 cm)	.5 in. (1 cm)
Sesame	6 in. (15 cm)	1–1.5 ft. (30–45 cm)	.5 in. (1 cm)
Tarragon	1.5–2 ft. (45–60 cm)	1.5–2.5 ft. (45–75 cm)	.5 in. (1 cm)
Thyme	1 ft. (30 cm)	1.5–2 ft. (45–60 cm)	.5 in. (1 cm)

on the sunny side of the seedlings. These same wire netting shapes can double as protection from cat or bird damage.

The actual process of transplanting or introducing the seedling into its permanent position may seem rather basic but numerous trials have shown that the way this is handled can make quite a difference to the progress of the seedling. This applies particularly to lettuce and other seedlings with a fibrous root system.

The conventional practice has been to dibble a comparatively deep cone-shaped hole, suspend the seedling with the lowest leaves or crown at about ground-level, then press the soil evenly inwards from all sides to firm the seedling into position.

The objection to this rather conventional method is that it pushes all roots into a central column or close around the taproot and then the seedling makes little progress until it regains a spreading root system. Development has proved much quicker, especially with fibrous rotted plants, when a comparatively wide shallow depression is made, almost with the same action drawing up a small hump of soil in the center and spreading the roots nearly laterally over this before raking in the disturbed soil to cover them, then firming downward gently.

It is also important to have the soil just damp at transplanting time. If surface mulching is available, place it around the seedlings immediately after transplanting and before watering. This prevents the inevitable surface caking in heavy soils and in very light sandy soils keeps the shallow roots of the seedlings much cooler during summer as well as preventing the loss by washing or organic particles.

Common problems

Plants wilt	Lack of water	Water
	Too much water	Stop watering; improve drainage; pray for less rain
	Disease	Use disease-resistant varieties; keep your garden clean
Leaves and stems are spotted	Fertilizer or chemical burn	Follow instructions; read all fine print; keep fertilizer off plant unless recommended
	Disease	Use disease-resistant varieties of seed; dust or spray; remove affected plants
Plants are weak and spindly	Not enough light	Remove cause of shade or move plants
	Too much water	Improve drainage; stop watering; pray for less rain
	Plants are crowded	Thin out
	Too much nitrogen	Reduce fertilizing
Leaves curl	Wilt	Destroy affected plants; rotate crops; grow disease-resistant varieties
	Virus	Control aphids; destroy affected plants
	Moisture imbalance	Mulch
Plants are stunted and yellow	Too much water	Reduce watering
	Poor drainage	Improve drainage; add more organic matter before next planting
	Compacted soil	Cultivate soil more deeply
	Too much rubbish	Remove rubbish
	Acid soil	Test, add lime if necessary
	Not enough fertilizer	Test, add fertilizer (this should have been done before planting)
	Insects or diseases	
	Yellow or wilt disease, especially if yellowing attacks one side of the plant first	Spraying will not help; remove affected plants; plant disease resistant seed in clean soil

Seeds do not come up	Not enough time for germination	Wait
	Too cold	Wait—replant if necessary
	Too dry	Water
	Too wet, they rotted	Replant
	Birds or insects ate them	Replant
	Seed was too old	Replant with fresh seed
Young plants die	Fungus	Treat seed with fungicide or plant in sterile soil
	Rotting	Do not overwater
	Fertilizer burn	Follow recommendations for using the fertilizer more closely; be sure fertilizer is mixed thoroughly with soil
Leaves have holes	Insects, birds	Identify culprit and take appropriate measures
	Heavy winds or hail	Plan for better protection
Tortured, abnormal growth	Herbicide residue in sprayer, in grass clippings used as mulch, in drift from another location	Use separate sprayer for herbicides; spray only on still days; use another means of weed control
	Virus	Control insects that transmit disease; remove infected plants (do not put them on the compost pile)
Blossom ends of tomatoes and peppers rot	Dry weather following a wet spell	Mulch to even out soil moisture
	Not enough calcium in soil	Add lime
	Compacted soil	Cultivate
	Too-deep cultivation	Avoid cultivating too deeply
There is no fruit	Weather too cold	Watch your planting time
	Weather too hot	Same as above
	Too much nitrogen	Fertilize only as often and as heavily as needed for the variety
	No pollination	Pollinate with a brush, or by shaking plant (depending on the kind); do not kill all the insects
	Plants not mature enough	Wait

Crop Rotation

In its simplest definition crop rotation means not growing vegetables from the same family in the same place two seasons in a row. The advantages of this very basic idea are that it breaks the breeding and growth cycles of pests and diseases because the conditions change each season.

This alone is a good enough reason to practice crop rotation. But by paying a bit more attention to the needs of different vegetable families you can take advantage of each vegetable's particular habits to encourage the best possible growth and cropping.

Let's start with legumes for example. They put lots of nitrogen into the soil which benefits leaf crops, such as swiss chard, and the brassicas so it makes sense to put them in after a crop of peas or beans. Follow the leaf crops with tomatoes and other fruiting vegetables and then put in the root crops. Too much nitrogen causes leaf growth at the expense of root growth for plants such as carrot and beetroot, so putting them in a couple of seasons after the legumes gives them the best chance to develop well. Follow the root crops with a fallow season, leaving he bed, manured, composted and mulched, but empty, or grow a green manure crop. Then it's back to the legumes.

This kind of crop rotation practice might look like this. In one bed peas are planted in autumn and harvested in winter. Lettuce and Brussels sprouts are planted in winter and harvested in spring, sweet corn and zucchini are planted in spring and harvested in late summer and carrots are planted in autumn and harvested in winter. The bed stays fallow until the next spring planting of beans. If you're factoring onions into your plan, take account of their love of lime and put them in before the legumes. Follow the legumes with leaf crops, the leaf crops with root crops and the root crop with tomatoes. The soil will gradually become more acidic as the seasons pass so that by the time the acid-loving tomatoes have their turn the soil will be perfect for them.

Watering

The way you water your soil is more important than generally realized; it can make a lot of difference to you plants, your soil—and your pocket!

Some people use far more water than is needed; others water more frequently than is necessary but still leave their plants thirsty.

Then there are the "get-it-on-quickly" types who pound the soil with a hefty jet of water and turn clayey soil into mud which sets so hard it stifles plant roots and reduces the absorption rate of the soil so that much of the water they are supplying is lost in run-off.

Even if you are among the minority who water lightly and thoroughly, you could still be overdoing the water. Plant roots need air as well as water if they are to function properly.

The air on which they depend enters the soil through the spaces between the soil particles. Water is held in a thin film around these particles. As extra water is added the film becomes thicker; when too much water is added it becomes so thick that there is no room for the much-needed air.

Plants are like people; if water cuts off their air supply, they drown. It will take 4 or 5 days for the drowning to be accomplished and then the roots will rot. Sand soil absorbs water more rapidly than a clay soil can, but there are only small air spaces between fine sand particles and this hinders both water and air passage. Sand coated with decomposed organic substance can become greasy if allowed to dry out. Always water sand with a fine, mist-like spray over a long period of time. A surface mulch of coarse organic material is mandatory no matter whether your soil is light or heavy.

If you give plants a daily watering they will become dependent on this regular freshener and their roots will grow upward toward the moist surface of the soil. If there is a sudden heat-wave or you have to be away from home for a time they will suffer from the lack of moisture on which they have come to rely and will be damaged by the heat of the surface soil.

To be fair to your plants you should help them to become more self-reliant; they need a strong root system which runs deep and can tap water beneath the soil. Allow the surface of the soil to dry out the a depth of 1 inch (3cm). Do not induce the roots to grow upward. Test the dryness of the soil by troweling down, then soak the soil, gently and very thoroughly, so that the water will go down... and down...and down. If you have agricultural pipes laid for drainage, watch the outlets and if water is beginning to run you know the soil is thoroughly wet. You may need to use a sprinkler for half a day to get moisture down to where it is needed.

Newly planted seedlings and germinating seeds should be treated differently; they need a steady, reliable watering to enable them to establish their roots. Once they are established and the plant is growing well, water as prescribed.

Plants should not be left without water until their foliage hangs limp, but plants allowed to show a little stress before being given water will flower well. Until experience gives you the "feel" of the mild stress signs which say "Water!" take your guide from examination of the soil an inch (2–3cm) below the surface. Trowel up a small sample; if it is damp, leave watering for a few days. By very, very gradually extending the time between waterings, you can make your plants less and less dependent on a supplementary water supply and thereby free yourself from the chore of watering so often.

There is nothing like rain for watering soil; it falls gently, as a rule, and does not compact the soil so that plant roots are starved of oxygen. If you must water, sprinkle, and let the sprinkling be long and slow. It can take as long as 2 hours for a light spray of water to penetrate the soil to any significant depth.

If shrubs or trees need water take the nozzle off your hosepipe, lay the pipe down near the trunk and let the water run out gently and leave until the ground is soaked but not swamped. Whenever you water, do it thoroughly; give your plants enough to sustain them for a week at least. Before watering again check that the soil has dried out to at least an inch (2-3cm).

WHEN TO WATER

It has often been said that watering should never be done in the heat of the day. If you have been unwise enough to let your plants get into trouble, soak them as soon as you see their distress. If you were racked with thirst would you want to wait any longer than necessary? But make certain you give a thoroughly good soaking so that roots are not enticed to grow upward to the heat of the surface, because this would do them harm rather than good.

In summer it is wisest to water annuals and perennials with an overhead sprinkler before the sun gets hot in the morning and late in the afternoon after the heat has died down. Don't wet the plants and then leave them in the hot sun. Drops of water on leaf and blossom will be "boiled" by the fierce rays and the plant will be damaged. A hot sun will evaporate water falling in a fine spray so your plants will not get all the water for which you are paying to provide for them.

Any watering done during the hot parts of the day should be confined to soaking the ground.

In winter, watering should be kept to late morning and early afternoon. Water left on plants overnight could turn to ice or at least become cold enough to shock young growth. Lunchtime sprinkling should provide all the moisture needed as none will be lost by evaporation.

Dormant perennials and shrubs do not need much water during winter; if you give them too much they could become chilled or rotted; on the other hand the evergreens which flower in winter or spring need quite a lot—a good watering once or even twice a week could be necessary.

EQUIPMENT

The experienced gardener rarely waters the garden soil by hand— seed and seedlings growing in boxes are another matter.

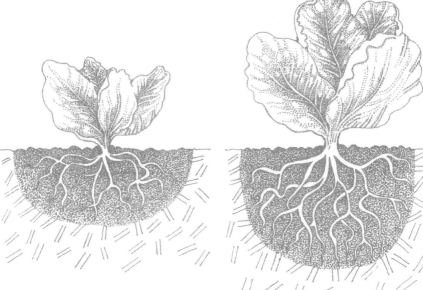

WATER CORRECTLY

The illustration at left shows what happens when a plant is given frequent, shallow waterings. Roots grow in the upper soil surface where there is water. During periods of warm, windy weather the plant is unable to absorb the water it needs. The plant at right is given deep, regular waterings. The roots penetrate deeply into the soil so they have a greater reservoir of water and nutrients to draw upon.

Every garden needs a convenient source of water—taps should be provided at strategic points so that watering is made simple and not a job to be shirked. Hosepipe and watering cans are useful but better still are the sprays and sprinklers which rotate or swing and can be easily moved from one spot to another as the ground becomes moistened to the requisite depth. When using fixed sprinklers, always place them to overlap the outer limit of their range so that all sections receive equal water. A long piece of rubber tubing with holes at regular spacing can be used too.

You can easily build up a good watering system from the many devices on offer these days. You can be as elaborate or as basic as you wish. The expense involved is one you are not likely to regret for few garden "helps" offer such a saving of labor for the gardener or better assistance to the healthy growth of the plants.